THE COMPLETE
ENCYCLOPEDIA OF
SUMMERFLOWERS

THE COMPLETE
ENCYCLOPEDIA OF
SUMMERFLOWERS

Informative text with hundreds of photographs

NICO VERMEULEN

REBO
PUBLISHERS

Explanation of the Symbols

Some of the following symbols appear at the end of each
description of a plant. This is what they mean:

[3-4]	These are the months when you may sow indoors, in this case March–April.
4-5	These are the months when you may sow outdoors, in this case April–May.
	This flower is suitable for cutting.
	This flower is suitable for drying.
	It is better to buy this plant rather than to sow it or take cuttings of it.
	This plant is suitable for flower beds.
	This plant is suitable for pots or window boxes.
	This plant does well in borders.
	This plant is fragrant.
	This plant attracts butterflies.
	This plant is sold as a cutting.
!	A plant recommended by the author.
	This plant attracts bees and other insects.
	This is a climbing plant.

© 2001 Rebo International b.v., Lisse, The Netherlands

Text and photographs: Nico Vermeulen
Editorial, production and co-ordination: TextCase, Groningen, The Netherlands
Design and inner pages layout: Signia, Winschoten, The Netherlands
Cover design: Minkowsky Graphics, Enkhuizen, The Netherlands
Pre-press services: Artedit s.r.o., Prague, The Czech Republic

Proofreading: Eva Munk

ISBN 90 366 1590 9

Contents

Introduction: sowing, taking cuttings, hanging baskets

Sowing indoors

The summer season is often too short for many of our loveliest flowering plants, which need months to grow from seed and come into flower. Since the spring is frequently too chilly to cultivate them outdoors, give them a headstart by sowing them indoors as shown below.

Use a propagator with a transparent cover and put the seed trays inside it.

There should be holes in the bottom of the trays; if there aren't any, make some. It should be possible for the soil to absorb moisture from below.

Use special seed compost or cocopeat. The sowing medium should be germ-free to prevent the rapid development of molds and algae.

Break up any lumps of compost and remove impurities. Stringy bits of peat will otherwise cause damage to roots when you are planting out.

Firm the top of the compost to provide a flat surface over which the seed can be distributed evenly.

Don't use any force when firming the soil – it should remain aerated. Oxygen is very important for plant roots.

Stand the tray in a dish or in the base of the propagator and pour water into it. The water will then be drawn up into the sowing compost.

You will know that the soil is well saturated once the surface feels moist.

While the soil is absorbing water, use the time to write the names of the species you intend to sow on labels.

Use rot-resistant labels and a pencil or waterproof felt-tip with non-fading ink.

If you have bought packets of seed, check the dates to see how long they are capable of germination. Don't use old seed.

Pour the seed into the palm of your hand. If you sow it straight from the packet, it will rarely be spread evenly in the seed tray.

Scatter the seed very evenly over the surface, or over a part of it, if you want to sow several species in the same tray.

Sowing the seeds at least $1/2$ in apart will make subsequent pricking out much easier.

Insert the appropriate label close to the seeds. This will let you tell at a glance which seeds are coming up where over the coming months.

To avoid subsequent pricking out, use a multicell tray. Sow larger seeds either on their own or with one other seed in each cell.

Insert large seeds at a depth three times their own thickness unless the instructions on the packet suggest otherwise.

Cover the seeds in the tray with a very thin layer of compost or fine grit. A colander or sieve will help to distribute it evenly.

Seeds needing light to germinate should not be covered. The relevant information is included in the alphabetical section of the book.

Seeds should be kept moist during germination. A cover or sheet of glass will ensure constant atmospheric humidity.

Seeds sown on the surface are particularly at risk of drying out and the vents of a propagator should therefore be kept closed.

Place the propagator in a light position at room temperature and protect it from harsh sunlight by placing a newspaper over it.

Once all the sown varieties are showing signs of germination, the vents may be partly opened, initially, and subsequently kept fully open.

The cover should be removed as soon as most of the seeds have germinated. Don't put the seedlings in too warm a position or their growth may be stunted.

Hardening off

Seedlings sown indoors have been nurtured in a 'protected environment'. They have not experienced any wind or torrential rain, and the differences between day and night temperatures have been slight. If plants are put out-of-doors suddenly in spring, the transition is sometimes too great and at the very least their growth stagnates. This is why they should be acclimatized gradually to outdoor conditions. Put them out-of-doors during the day and bring them indoors in the event of cold nights, heavy rain, or harsh winds. A cold frame is an ideal place for hardening off plants: they will then be out-of-doors, but protected by glass. Remove

Sunflower that was sown early and is put under a cloche if the nights are cold.

Hardening off annuals in a tunnel which is uncovered during the day.

the glass during the day and put it back at night.

Sowing out-of-doors

Seeds of hardy plants may be sown during the summer or autumn as the seedlings will withstand the winter. Half-hardy species may be sown as early as mid-April, as they will survive light frosts. Tender species will not withstand frost and should not be sown out-of-doors until mid-May. The sowing season for each species is

Lightly turn over the soil of the seedbed and rake it over until there are no more hard lumps left. (Flatten heavy clods underfoot and then rake them over again.)

If you would like the various species of annual to flower in groups, divide up the seedbed mentally into separate areas.

Scattering dry white sand is a very convenient way of marking out different areas until you are satisfied with the results.

Sowing the seeds in rows will help you to distinguish the seedlings from any weeds that may have appeared

Make very shallow drills the same distance apart at the recommended sowing distance, usually shown on packets

Drop the seeds into the drills one by one and move them yourself if they fall outside it.

Keep to the recommended sowing distance. This will require very little seed. Sowing more densely means that you will have to thin out more later on.

Cover over the drills. Most seeds germinate best if they are sown close to the surface. Thicker seeds are the only kind that need to be pushed deeper into the soil

Very fine seed and seed germinating in light should not be covered, but the seed should be pressed down to avoid drying out.

Select a watering can or hose with a very fine nozzle and lightly water the seedbed. Don't let the water gush out, otherwise the seeds will be washed away.

indicated in the alphabetical section. The following illustrations show you how to sow out-of-doors.

Thinning

The seedbed will be full of seedlings several weeks after sowing, but the seeds of weeds will have germinated as well. This is why it is sensible to sow in rows rather than at random: the plants emerging from the seeds you sowed will be easily recognizable growing in rows next to one another. This makes thinning the seedlings and weeding very easy.

Don't weed the bed until you can distinguish the rows of seedlings. Pull out any plants growing between the rows or use a hoe for the purpose.

You should also pull out all the weeds that have germinated within the drills, but take care not to pull out the plant seedlings as well.

If you have used too much seed, the seedlings will be too close together to develop properly and it will be necessary to thin them.

Pull out the unwanted seedlings or use a dibber to lift them up carefully and to avoid damaging the roots of the seedlings next to them.

The seedlings that have been removed from the bed may be planted in places where the seeds failed to come up very well, or elsewhere in the garden.

The seedlings will now be growing at a proper distance from one another. They will grow closer together in May and June, and flower profusely.

The result – flowers to pick throughout the summer.

geranium pratense, *meadow cranesbill (see separate list of captions)*

When a fruit has been inactivated (left), the springs curl open from the top. The tension is removed and the seeds remain attached at their lower end.

Harvesting seeds

Gathering seeds in your own garden gives you a wonderful sense of squirrelling away something for a rainy day. You snip, shake, peel, and gather in a magnificent harvest, because seeds, after all, are miniature plants in an outer skin. So you are really putting ripe summer into an envelope to preserve it for next year.

Most seeds are easy to harvest – you can see when they are ripe and then cut off the fruits, dry them, and remove the seeds from the outer skin. Here are some hints on how to harvest seeds of perennials and annuals that are more difficult to collect.

At the bottom of the closed fruit of a cranesbill there are five seeds which will subsequently be ejected as a result of the tension in the coiled springs.

Dry fruits with springs

Let's begin with the most difficult plants: the plants which eject their fruit. If you wait until they are ripe, it will be too late, because they will have flown away. So you will have to beat the plant to it. The following tricks will help you to gather seeds from various plants, including hardy species of *Geranium*. They are called cranesbills because the fruit terminate in a sharp point like the bill of a crane. The "bill" consists of five "springs" joined together at the top. As the fruit ripens, the tension in each spring increases until, at a given moment, it bursts open at the bottom and ejects the seed.

By cutting through the "bill" of the fruit, you inactivate the spring mechanism and the springs will no longer be able to do their work.

The shorter method

The trick shown on the left is very suitable for harvesting unripe fruit. After the bill has been cut off, the seeds will ripen normally because the flow of sap still reaches them. Wait until the fruits are nearly ripe but have not yet been ejected, then use this simple method to harvest them.

You will be too late for the fruits on the right as the seeds have already been ejected. The fruits on the left are ready for harvesting.

Use a pair of scissors to cut these ripe but still closed fruits off the plant. Leave the shortest possible amount of stem attached to them.

Toss the ripe fruit into a basket, dish, or other container. Take a tea towel or a piece of net along with you.

Cover the filled basket with the tea towel or piece of net and put it in a warm, dry place, where the fruits will burst open.

Caught between the basket and the tea towel, they can't fly away and, in two weeks, you can shake the harvest on to a newspaper.

Shake the remains of the burst fruit onto a newspaper and throw them away or scatter them in the garden.

Use a sharp knife to cut the fine remains of the fruit from the ripe seeds until you are left with a small mound of clean seeds.

Write the name of the plant on an envelope and add the year in which the seeds were harvested

You will subsequently be able to see how old the seed is and whether it is still likely to be capable of germination. Now sweep it on to a piece of folded paper.

The seed will drop into the fold in the paper. Hold the paper at an angle over the open end of the envelope and the seeds will roll into it.

Ripe green dehiscent fruits

The seeds in the fruit of busy lizzies (*Impatiens*) are not ripe until the fruits are at the point of exploding and are still green and juicy. But do not cut off the closed fruit and allow them to dry off indoors – they will not explode and the seeds inside them will go moldy. They should therefore be harvested at exactly the right moment. In the case of Impatiens glandulifera, this is unnecessary as it shoots its seeds far away and young

13

Impantiens balfouri

It is possible that the seeds will ripen just as you are going away, but you need not lose them for that reason. Cut out small pieces of gauze or net and baste them together on three sides. Don't cut the basting thread too short because you will need the ends. Slide the gauze bags over the fruit and fasten the ends of the basting thread loosely to the plant (don't pinch them).

Silene dioica, *Red campion*

Harvesting by inverting

Some plants make things a lot easier for us. The ripe seeds are loose inside the fruit. The seeds of *Silene* species, for example, are offered to us on a plate!

Wait until the fruits (those of Silene dioica in this photograph) open at the top. The ripe black seeds will be lying loose in the small hollow.

plants germinate all over the garden the following year, whether we like it

Hold the largest, oblong seeds in three fingers and squeeze them gently. If the fruit is ripe, it will burst open.

or not. In the case of the rare *Impatiens balfourii*, however, try not to lose a single seed.

To prevent the seeds going moldy, they should not be left to dry out with the succulent green remains of the fruit but must be separated from them at once.

Invert the fruit over a small bowl and the ripe seeds will roll into it. Unripe brown seeds will remain attached.

Give small spiders and other insects a chance to run out of the bowl and then pour the seed into a small bag.

Digitalis lutea, *yellow foxglove*

The long-stem trick

In the case of species with fruit ripening on tall spikes, such as *Verbascum blattaria*, *Verbascum phoeniceum* and varieties of *Digitalis*, use the long-stem trick. A bag of the type used to wrap a French loaf is required.

Wait until the plant has nearly finished flowering. The fruit will have started to ripen from the bottom of the flower spike upwards and will eventually occupy a large section of the stem.

The unripe fruit will be at the top of the plant. Cut off the top and discard it, because the seed in green fruit will not ripen and will only go moldy.

Slide a large deep bag (for example, a bag for a French loaf) over the remaining part of the stem bearing the ripe fruit.

Tie the bag at the bottom Use string or raffia and don't cut the ends too short as you will need them later.

Cut off the stem below the bag. As long as you keep it upright, most of the seeds will remain inside the ripe fruit.

Invert the bag and let the seeds fall to the bottom. Hang up the bag indoors by the ends of the string for a little longer to gather an even greater harvest.

Waiting for the falling seed

The fruits of plants such as Silene coeli-rosa 'Rose Angel' open slowly. If you have to wait until autumn, the risk of mold developing will steadily increase. It is therefore advisable to bring those slowly ripening fruits indoors at a given moment and to let them dry off there. This needs to be done very carefully and, above all, in an airy environment, because there will still be some unripe fruits remaining.

Silene coeli-rosa 'Rose Angel'

Tie up the bunch with string or raffia.

Cut off the stems below the string or raffia.

Hold the bunch upright while taking it indoors.

Suspend or hold the bunch upside down over a newspaper. The seeds will fall onto it automatically.

Harvesting other fruits

The great majority of fruits may be harvested by the following method:
* First allow the picked fruits to ripen fully in a warm and sunny location.
* Then put the harvest in a warm and airy location, but out of the sun.
* Toss the dried fruits into a pillowcase and rub or beat them until they are broken up.
* Pour everything into a shallow bowl. Blow away the chaff and the seeds will be left in the bowl.

Preserving seed

The seeds' germinative power is only in part determined by how they are harvested and dried. How you preserve them is also vitally important.
* Keep the seed dry and cool in porous packaging (envelopes).
* It is best to keep the seeds at an even temperature between 54 °F and 63 °F.
* The ideal temperature is often to be found at the back of a wardrobe. If you keep summer clothes there, you will automatically come across the seeds at the right time.
* There is another way of preserving seeds. First dry them very thoroughly and put them in a plastic bag. Keep it in the freezer compartment of your refrigerator or in a freezer.

Taking cuttings of patio plants

Many of the plants that flower in containers on the patio in summer are propagated by cuttings. There are firms whose sole business is to take cuttings so that they can put the plants on sale in full flower in the spring. You can take cuttings your-self. The best times for doing so are summer and autumn, when temperatures are still high enough to ensure rapid root-forming. To enjoy flowering plants next season, it is essential to keep the cuttings frost-free in a light location during the winter. Use the following method for taking cuttings of most species.

For taking cuttings you will need a sharp knife, small pots, cuttings compost, labels, a waterproof pen, and a propagator.

Fill the pots with cuttings compost (or ordinary potting compost mixed with a lot of sharp sand). Or you can grow cuttings in cocopeat.

Cut off a top shoot about 2–4 in long. It is better to select one that is not flowering.

Break or cut off all the leaves except for those at the top of the cutting.

Trim the stem to just below the place where the bottom pair of leaves were.

Use a pencil to make a small hole in the compost.

Insert the cutting in the hole and firm the soil around it to ensure proper contact.

Stand the pots in a bowl and pour water into it so that the cutting compost can fully absorb it.

17

Meanwhile, write the name of the plant on a label and insert it in the appropriate pot.

To limit further evaporation through the foliage, cut off a small part of the remaining leaves.

As soon as the cuttings compost in the pots has fully absorbed the water in the bowl, place the pots in the tray of a propagator.

Put the cover on the propagator and stand it in a warm, light location, but not in the sun.

After about two weeks, you should slightly skew the cover of the propagator. The cuttings will have roots by then, and will continue to grow a little during the autumn. In winter, you should put the cuttings in a light, cool place indoors, but not in the sun. Give them a little water from time to time to prevent them drying out. Repot them in good potting compost in spring, so that they can grow well and flower profusely.

Taking geranium cuttings

To prevent mildew and subsequent rotting, geranium (*Pelargonium*) cuttings should not be given a plastic cover. Put them indoors in a cool, light place in winter, but not in full sun. If you moisten the sand in the propagating tray from time to time, the cuttings will draw up some moisture from below. After they have been repotted the following spring, the geraniums will be able to grow at full speed in May.

Cut a non-flowering shoot off the plant.

Break off the bottom leaves.

Trim the stem to just below the place where the bottom leaves were.

Make a hole in the compost.

Insert the cutting and firm the compost round it.

Stand the pots in a tray filled with wet sand.

Making hanging baskets

One way of displaying your summer flowers is by growing them in hanging baskets. These have long been fashionable in England, from where the vogue has spread overseas. Hanging baskets may contain sown annuals as well as cuttings, and this is how to make them.

Hanging baskets were traditionally lined with sphagnum moss or moss raked out of the lawn.

For this basket, you need: Tillandsia moss, small scissors, a knife, the basket, potting compost, and slow-acting fertilizer.

Add a slow-acting fertilizer to the compost. Preferably choose potting compost containing clay, which will help to retain moisture over a longer period.

19

Mix the fertilizer grains thoroughly with the compost. They will gradually release their nutrients.

Line the basket with tillandsia moss (or sphagnum moss or lawn moss).

Press a sheet of plastic loosely into the hollow inside the moss.

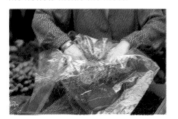

Cut off the plastic along the top of the basket. The compost will subsequently push it down.

Fill the hollow with an inch or so of potting compost and firm it forcing down the plastic.

Prick the plastic all round the basket, just above the level of the compost. Water poured into the basket will remain in the hollow.

Make crosswise cuts in the plastic a little higher up. The lower plants will be inserted through them.

Push aside the moss covering the holes to provide access for the plants.

Take a plant and insert the ball of soil surrounding the roots through a hole from the outside.

Insert the other plants in the same way until the basket has been filled evenly.

The rootballs of the plants will now lie in a circle on top of the compost.

Fill the basket with compost up to about two-thirds of its depth and firm the soil lightly.

Make a hollow in the center of the basket and put the central plant in it. Make sure that the top of the ball of soil is about ³/₄ in below the edge of the basket.

Add more compost, once again up to about ³/₄ in below the edge of the basket.

Push aside small amounts of soil to make further hollows round the center and insert the edging plants into them.

Once the entire basket has been planted, attach the chains at an equal distance from one another.

Hang in a spot sheltered from the wind outside, in the garden, or in the conservatory.

Water generously from the beginning: every other day in spring, every day in summer, and twice a day in very hot weather.

A hanging basket with coconut fiber lining

Sphagnum moss, the traditional lining for hanging baskets, comes from increasingly rare peat bogs. To protect those wetlands, it is better to use other materials for lining baskets. The tillandsias used for the production of tillandsia moss grow in abundance in tropical regions such as Central America. The most environmentally friendly solution is to use the moss that you can rake out of lawns in spring. There is another possibility: basket liners made of coconut fiber.

Sometimes the baskets are lined with a pre-formed coconut-fiber bowl, and sometimes with a separate liner.

Overlap the flaps of the separate liner and press them into the basket

21

Cut off the top edges of the liner if they stick out above the basket.

Make some transverse cuts in the edges of the liner flaps (about halfway between the saucer and the rim).

Fill the deepest part of the liner with some compost mixed with slow-release fertilizer.

Place a saucer on top. This will retain some moisture for the plants to absorb each time the basket is watered.

Now continue to fill the basket with enriched compost to just below the transverse cuts.

Press the rootballs of the plants through the slits into the basket and continue as shown for moss-lined baskets.

22

Before the plants begin to cover the sides of the basket, all that can be seen is the coconut-fiber liner – not a very attractive sight. It is easy to conceal by squeezing some moss raked off the lawn in between the liner and the basket.

Camouflaging the coconut-fiber liner

THE TRICK WITH THE ROLL

If the rootballs of the plants are too large to be inserted through the wall of the liner, you can also push the plants through from the inside. You must, of course, prevent the plants from breaking off and this may be done in the following way.

Shorten the plant (in this case a fuchsia) as much as possible. After rooting in the soil, it will rapidly sprout again, and produce more shoots than before.

Slide a lavatory paper roll over the plant and fold the top end to make a point.

Then push the roll gently through the opening in the liner from the inside.

Finally, slide the roll off the plant so that it can develop in all its glory.

23

Abelmoschus esculentus

OKRA

In Africa, Asia, and the southern states of the US, the unripe capsules of the okra are considered a delicacy. As a result of the increasing popularity of stir-fry cookery in other parts of the world, this annual plant is grown elsewhere more and more frequently. The species itself needs a long hot summer to allow it to come into flower and bear fruit. In cooler climates, it is best to cultivate it in a greenhouse; there are, however, some varieties which need less heat and may be put out-of-doors in summer. In a greenhouse, in

Abelmoschus esculentus, okra

fact, they are sensitive to temperatures above 86 °F and subject to infestation by red spider mites and whitefly. In hot, dry weather, they drop their flower buds and fruit.

It is best to sow the seed – available from specialized suppliers only – indoors in March (about $1/4$ in deep) at a soil temperature of around 68–77 °F. Grow the young plants in warm and moist conditions and don't put them out-of-doors until summer. Cultivating them in large pots filled with nutritive soil will make it possible for them to be moved indoors during long spells of cold, wet weather.

Make sure that insects can reach the flowers to pollinate them. Just over a week after they begin to set, the young fruits will be about 3 in long and ready for picking. This should not be delayed for long, as okras toughen very quickly. The hairs on the fruit may irritate the skin. Over the years, less prickly cultivars have been created, of which *Abelmoschus esculentus* 'Clemson Spineless' provides the largest crop in northern Europe. Stir-fry the fruits briefly in a wok until they are 'al dente'; the crop will usually be so small that you will need to add the okra to other stir-fried vegetables. It is,

Abutilon 'Eric Lilac,' abutilon

however, a magnificent ornamental plant, even without fruit.

[3-4] ▼

Abutilon

ABUTILON

Abutilons are grown mainly as container plants, and are taken indoors in winter and put in a frost-free place. Nowadays, however, they are also sold as bedding plants. Professional growers need just three months to grow flowering plants from seed. Other firms take cuttings of parent plants and grow them into saleable specimens in a very short time. They are on sale from mid-May and may then be planted out-of-doors in containers or flowerbeds. They continue to grow considerably during the season and continually produce flowers measuring 2 in across. In autumn there is a choice: you either let them freeze to death or you take the trouble to winterize them.

Abutilon 'Pink Niedorp,' abutilon

Abutilon 'Eric Lilac' is particularly charming, with its pinkish-red flowers standing out against a background of dark-green foliage.

Abutilon 'Pink Nierop' is another fast-growing hybrid with flowers in a soft shade of pink. The darker veins in the petals of many abutilons contrast strongly with the rest of the flower.

   ▼

Acroclinium roseum

IMMORTELLE

The immortelle, also known as strawflower, is without a doubt one of the most satisfactory flowers for drying purposes. If you intend to dry them, it is best to cut them as soon as they have come into flower. Tie them in bunches, with stems from 12–24 in long, and hang them upside in a dry spot, preferably out-of-doors under the eaves. The faster the

Acroclinium roseum 'Briljant Rose,' immortelle

Acroclinium roseum 'Pierrot,' immortelle

Acroclinium roseum 'Red Bonny,' immortelle

their approximately 16-in stems. The linear, bluish-green pruinose leaves have a rubbery texture. This enables them to hold extra moisture, like succulent plants. Australian immortelles are good at withstanding drought, but the quality of the flowers suffers in the heat. It is therefore advisable to pick them in the early morning.

Acroclineum roseum 'Pierrot' is one of the white immortelles, which are easier to combine with other plants than the numerous pink cultivars. This is certainly true of 'Pierrot' with its sparse, bluish-green foliage and slender stems, topped by delicate white flowers. The centers, almost black, are encircled by two yellow rings. The plants grow up to 16 in tall and the flowers are suitable for drying in spite of their fragile appearance.

Upright stems and an impressive height (over 20 in) make *Acroclinium roseum* 'Red Bonny' highly suitable for bouquets. The semi-double flowers are $1^1/_4$–$1^1/_2$ in wide and vary from deep to pale pink, with black centers surrounded by a narrow yellow ring. The pendent buds straighten out as they open and grow on stems with handsome bluish-green pruinose foliage.

[3–4] 4–5

flowers dry, the longer – and better – they will retain their color. They often keep their color for years, by which time the bouquet will be dusty. Then it should be replaced for that reason if for no other.

Acroclinium roseum originally came from the hot south-western regions of Australia. It does best in full sun and in poor, well-drained soil. The numerous cultivars, frequently on offer under the name of *Helipterum roseum*, are easy to grow from seed. Sow them in situ in April–May, or indoors in March–April. They will then flower from July until well into September.

The buds of *Acroclinium roseum* 'Brilliant Rose' hang their heads until the moment they open and then straighten out at the top of

Adonis aestivalis, summer adonis

Adonis aestivalis

SUMMER ADONIS

The fernlike foliage of the summer adonis forms magnificent green tufts which grow about 12–16 in tall. The crimson flowers, $^3/_4$–$1^1/_4$ in wide, appear at the end of the shoots from May until well into August. The centers are jet-black.

All parts of the plant are toxic and the substances in them have a medicinal use. Sow in a permanent position in nutrititive, preferably loamy soil in early spring. The plants like a sunny position and will languish in permanently wet earth.

[3–4]

Agastache anisata

See *Agastache rugosa*.

Agastache barberi 'Firebird'

See *Agastache* 'Firebird.'

Agastache 'Firebird'

This magnificent plant has not been on the market for long, but it faces a golden future. Everyone who sees it is enchanted. It has orange flowers, which would normally stand in the way of its popularity. This orange, however, is so soft a shade, with such a strong tinge of brick red, that the color goes particularly well with many other plants. The greyish-green foliage enhances this effect. The plant grows about 24 in tall and flowers long and very profusely from midsummer until well into October. According to some sources, 'Firebird' is a hybrid of *Agastache ruprestrus* × *Agastache coccinea*, but others regard *Agastache barberi* as its parent plant. All three species grow naturally in the dry, hot climate of northwest Mexico and the southwestern regions of the United States, and they are not reliably hardy. The cultivar is less sensitive to frost and will survive most

Agastache 'Firebird,' Mexican giant hyssop

winters. Propagation is by cuttings or division only. The plant prefers a warm and sunny position.

Agastache mexicana 'Carlile Carmine'

MEXICAN GIANT HYSSOP

The Mexican giant hyssop and its cultivars are perennials, but they are not reliably hardy in cooler climates. Not to worry – they are easy to grow from seed, so there is no need to do without their cheerful colors in late-summer and autumn gardens. 'Carlile Carmine' flowers abundantly over a long period, producing carmine-pink flowers on stems which grow about 30 in tall. The cheerful green foliage forms an attractive contrast with them. Because of the pronounced color of its flowers, 'Carlile Carmine' is difficult to combine with other plants in a border with more subdued colors. Its exotic appearance, though, makes it a most suitable container plant for

Agastache mexicana 'Carlile Carmine'

Agastache rugosa 'Blue Spike,' Mexican giant hyssop

a sunny patio. The plant forms a clump with spreading roots and will sometimes survive in dry soil provided the winter is not too severe. The seeds often germinate spontaneously in late spring. The young plants are exactly like the parent plant.

[3-4]

Agastache rugosa

Agastache rugosa is a popular perennial but, according to some, it is not reliably hardy and is therefore also sold as an annual. It is suitable for cultivation in fairly large pots and containers, but if you plant the agastache in the garden in autumn, there is a ten-to-one chance of its turning up again next season. If you sow it indoors in March, the plant will be able to start producing its spikes of blue flowers as early as July–August of the same year. The approximately 3-ft tall plant smells of liquorice; its leaves taste of aniseed and may be included in salads. It is sometimes called 'aniseed nettle'. The nomenclature of these

plants is, in fact, highly confusing and very similar plants are sold under the name of *Agastache foeniculum.*

Agastache rugosa 'Blue Spike' bears purplish-blue flowers.

Agastache rugosa 'Honey Bee Blue' is one of the new perennials cultivated as annuals. By sowing them in autumn or early spring and giving the seedlings additional light (the plant needs 14 hours of daylight to form buds), it is possible to produce flowering plants as early as spring. They will then flower until far into autumn. The two 'Honey Bee' cultivars received a Fleuroselect award. The blue one is called 'Honey Bee Blue.' It grows about 28 in tall but remains compact. The stems are well covered in leaves smelling of peppermint and aniseed. Bees, bumblebees and butterflies are attracted by the 4-in spikes of small blue flowers. The plants are completely hardy in open ground in positions that are not excessively wet. They may also seed themselves in the garden.

The white-flowered cultivar is called *Agastache rugosa* 'Honey Bee White.' It closely

Agastache rugosa 'Honey Bee Blue,' Mexican giant hyssop

Agastache rugosa 'Honey Bee White,' Mexican giant hyssop

resembles 'Honey Bee Blue' but bears white flowers.

[3–4] 4–5

Ageratum 'Dondoschnittperle'

FLOSS FLOWER

The taller cultivated forms of floss flower such as 'Dondoschnittperle' are particularly suitable for combining with other plants in a border. The flower heads of this plant of uncertain origin are produced on 28-in tall stems. They are blue, with a strong tinge of pink. They go well with blue, yellowish green, and pale yellow, and also look good when incorporated in bouquets.

Ageratums like a sunny position in light, moisture-retentive soil.

[2–4]

Ageratum 'Dondoschnittperle,' floss flower

Ageratum 'Dondoschnittperle,' floss flower

Ageratum houstonanium 'Blue Blanket,' floss flower

Ageratum houstonianum 'Wedgwood,' floss flower

Ageratum houstonianum

FLOSS FLOWER

The *Ageratums* are divided into two distinct groups, i.e. the taller upright plants suitable for incorporating in imaginative borders, and the typical low-growing plants for covering large areas and cultivating in containers. Both groups are referred to as floss flowers.

Ageratum houstonianum 'Wedgwood' is a typical example of the low-growing varieties and grows to about 6 in in height. Each small flower head is no more than $1/2$ in wide, but the flowers bloom in large quantities between July and October. Their color is described as 'blue' but there is a lot of pink mixed in. They are highly suitable for bowls, pots, and other containers. Stand them in a sunny or partially shady position and never allow the soil to dry out completely.

Ageratum houstonianum 'Blue Blanket' is a typical bedding plant on sale in large quantities in spring. Bedding plant growers sow

Ageratum houstonianum 'Blue Hawaii,' floss flower

'Blue Blanket' as early as mid-January so that they can market flowering plants by late April and early May. The small plants, 8 in high, will bear an abundance of bluish-pink flowers over a long period. As far as I know, this variety is sold as a flowering plant only. It is also suitable for pots and other containers.

The low-growing, lavender-flowered *Ageratum houstonianum* 'Blue Hawaii' once received a Fleuroselect award.

Ageratum houstonianum 'Old Grey' belongs to the taller group of floss flowers. For those who like soft color combinations, this is un-

Ageratum houstonianum 'Old Grey,' floss flower

Ageratum houstonianum 'Pink Ball,' floss flower

doubtedly the most rewarding cultivar. The soft greyish blue of the flowers blends well with numerous magnificent perennial and annual border plants. With an average height of 20 in, 'Old Grey' shows up best at the front of a border. This is also the easiest position for picking some of the slender stems for a small posy.

The flowering season depends on when the seeds were sown. If sown early (February or March), the plants may flower as early as May, but if sown directly in the garden, they will not come into flower until July and will subsequently go on flowering until the end of September.

Ageratum houstonianum 'Pink Ball' is a small plant, about 8 in high, with flowers in shades of candy-floss: white and pale pink to bright pink.

[2-3] 4-5   ▼ ♨

Ageratum mexicanum

See *Ageratum houstonianum.*

Agrostemma coeli-rosa

See *Silene coeli-rosa.*

Agrostemma githago

CORNCOCKLE

In the old days, corncockles flowered amidst the summer corn. In the course of harvesting, their seeds were mixed in with the corn and, if baked into bread, caused irritation and inflammation of the stomach lining. No wonder efforts were made to combat these problems, and the plant ultimately vanished from the fields. The splendor of the $1^3/_4$–$2^1/_2$-in wide flowers among the ears of corn disappeared as well.

It is, however, simple enough to enjoy their beauty in the garden, since corncockle is very easy to grow as an annual. Sow directly in the garden in April, preferably in a sunny position in loose, poor, dry soil. The best

Agrostemma githago, corncockle

Agrostemma githago, corncockle

results are obtained by sowing corncockle seed in a mixture including other wild flowers. The seeds will remain capable of germination for just over a year. Fresh seeds germinate after 1 or 2 weeks at a soil temperature of 54–60 °F. The plants flower from the end of June until well into August. Depending on the nutritive value of the soil, the plants will grow to between 20 in and 5 ft tall (usually between 28 in and 39 in). The magnificent pink petals with purple dotted lines leading to white centers are surrounded by a star of pointed sepals.

4-5

Alonsoa

It takes nearly four months for a small *Alonsoa* seed to grow into a flowering plant, presumably the reason why the various species are rarely seen in gardens. That is a pity, because alonsoas are colorful, decorative jewels which can be brought into flower at the odd-est of times. By sowing in summer, you can even bring them into flower in mid-winter. Professional growers sow very early in the year or in autumn to produce flowering plants in April and May. For private plant lovers, however, it is better to sow in early March, either indoors or in a heated greenhouse. Cover the seeds very lightly or not at all, because alonsoas germinate in daylight. The ideal temperature for germination is around 66 °F, at which most of the seed will come up within 2 weeks. To ensure attractive branching, it is best to pinch out the growing tips several times during the following four months. The plants are moved out-of-doors from mid-May and may then begin to flower from the end of June. The flowering season is usually long and may be extended by cutting back hard during intervals in flowering.

Alonsoas come mainly from the western mountains of South America, especially from Colombia, Peru, and Chili, where the air is cool and fresh. They like a lot of sun, but do not care for real heat. It is therefore best to grow them in pots or in the ground in a sunny but airy spot, in well-drained soil that is not excessively dry.

[2–4] 4-5 / 🌼 🌻 ▼

Alonsoa caulialata

See *Alonsoa meridionalis.*

Alonsoa grandiflora

See *Alonsoa warscewiczii.*

Alonsoa meridionalis

ALONSOA

In the course of the summer, this Peruvian species may grow quite tall, up to about 32 in in height. It produces a lot of medium-sized leaves and bears small, soft-orange to red flowers, about $^3/_4$ in wide, over a long period. The mass of foliage makes them less striking

Alonsoa meridionalis

Alonsoa meridionalis 'Fire Ball'

than many of the smaller cultivars. Even so, it is the light color of the leaves and the informal appearance that make this species so suitable for cheerful borders. The flowers are also suitable for including in informal bouquets. Picking rejuvenates the plant and makes it flower all the longer. If you think it is becoming too untidy, just cut it back hard in summer to force new growth and bring forth new flowers.

Some writers believe the species is synonymous with *Alonsoa warscewiczii*, but the plants on sale under that name have darker green foliage and more red in their stems.

From mid-April, a compact *Alonsoa* goes on sale under the name of *Alonsoa* 'Fire Ball.' The plant initially develops in a compact form, but as soon as it grows to about 8 in high, the shoots grow outwards and begin to droop. The tops produce a profusion of reddish-orange flowers. Suppliers talk about the long flowering season, supposedly lasting until the frosts but, in my experience, there are breaks in that period. If you cut back the

Alonsoa meridionalis 'Scarlet Gem'

Alonsoa 'Pink Beauty'

plant during those intervals and feed it, it may start flowering again. 'Fire Ball' is very suitable for cultivating in containers, provided the soil is not allowed to dry out. It is propagated by cuttings.

The small flowers of *Alonsoa meridionalis* 'Scarlet Gem,' ³/₄ in diameter, resemble red lead in color and, for that reason alone, mix well with red, orange and yellow flowers. The plants sometimes grow over 20 in tall and, with their loose-growing habit, look particularly well in seemingly casual borders. They also look fine in large pots.

[2–4] 4–5 ✎ ✿ ✿ ▼ ⬺

Alonsoa 'Pink Beauty'

The pale pink shade of its flowers makes this cultivar one of the best for natural-looking borders. The plants grow to about 20 in tall and, like most other alonsoas, go on flowering for months. If you sow early in March, you may rely on having flowers from July until well into October. It is also an excellent flower for cutting and the color looks very good in an earthenware pot.

[2–4] 4–5 ⬺ ✿ ▼

Alonsoa warscewiczii

MASK FLOWER

The plants on offer under the name of *warscewiczii* generally have somewhat darker foliage and more pronounced rhubarb-red stems than *Alonsoa meridionalis*. The two, however, belong to the same species, which grows naturally in the Andes mountains.

The cultivar *Alonsoa warscewiczii* 'Sutton's Scarlet,' which grows to about 12 in, is one of the shorter forms, sometimes referred to as *Alonsoa warscewiczii compacta*. The flowers are unlikely to be overlooked: they are an intensely reddish orange with contrasting yellow stamens. They look magnificent in a red border, preferably when combined with silver-leafed plants.

[2–4] 4–5 ✿ ✿ ▼ ⬺

Alonsoa warscewiczii 'Sutton's Scarlet'

Amaranthus caudatus, love-lies-bleeding

Alyssum maritima

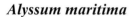

See *Lobularia maritima*.

Amaranthus

AMARANTH

Amaranths grow in the tropical regions of Asia and America and are popular there for their edible leaves and seeds. In cooler climates, these annuals are used as indoor or border plants as well as for cut flowers which can also be dried.

Amaranths do not like being transplanted and it is therefore best to sow them where they are to flower. That should not be done until after the last night frost in May, but it is also possible to sow them in a pot earlier on and then to remove them carefully from their pots in May and plant them out without disturbing their rootballs. Preferably put them in a sunny location in loose, but not excessively dry soil. In more humid, shadier loca-

tion, the leaves will not turn such beautiful colors.

[3–4] 5

Amaranthus caudatus

LOVE-LIES-BLEEDING, TASSEL FLOWER

All of the many cultivars of *amaranthus caudatus* have trailing panicles of flowers which may grow about 18 in long. They flower from June until well into October and the individual panicles remain beautiful for a remarkably long time. Those of the species itself are a shade of crimson that is difficult to combine with other border plants and is too pronounced for most bouquets. The cultivar *Amaranthus caudatus* 'Viridis' has soft-green, pendulous panicles that go particularly well with all kinds of other plants. They are very popular with flower arrangers and are also cultivated for the commercial cut-flower market. The cultivar *Amaranthus caudatus* 'Grünschwanz' has yellowish-green pendulous panicles, and those of *Amaranthus caudatus* 'Rotschwanz' are bright red. Don't plant them too close together, so that they can develop freely. For propagation, see under *Amaranthus*.

[3-4] 5 ✿ 🏺 ⚜

Amaranthus cruentus 'Oeschberg'

AMARANTH

The deep-red shade of the leaves and the red panicles make the cultivar *Amaranthus cruentus* 'Oeschberg' one of the very best for borders, bouquets, and drying purposes. The red leaves (with green shining through them) create a restful effect, particularly in borders with bright red colors. The plant will grow from 20 in–39 in tall, depending on the nutritive condition of the soil. The plant is also sold under the names of *Amaranthus paniculatus* 'Oeschberg,' *Amaranthus* × 'Oeschberg,' and *Amaranthus* × *hybridus*

Amaranthus cruentus 'Oeschberg'

Amaranthus hypochondriacus 'Green Thumb'

ssp. *paniculatus* 'Oeschberg.' See under *Amaranthus* for propagation.

[3-4] 5 ✿ 🏺 ⚜ !

Amaranthus hypochondriacus

PRINCE'S FEATHER

The apple-green shade of *Amaranthus hypochondriacus* 'Green Thumb' goes well with most other colors and is therefore a useful plant for filling in gaps in borders, as well as for bouquets. The panicles grow to about 16 in tall and, if sown early, may be admired from July onwards. They fade later on in the season and ultimately turn brown. They also make useful dried flowers, particularly when picked early in the season.

Another cultivar was presumably called *Amaranthus hypochondriacus* 'Pygmy Torch' (and not 'Pigmy Torch,' as it is featured in most catalogs) because of its small size. The deep-red panicles grow up to 16 in

Amaranthus hypochondriacus 'Pygmy Torch'

tall and fade to chestnut brown in the course of the season. The leaves, too, turn beautiful colors, especially if the plants are grown in poor soil. They look splendid in vases and as dried flowers. For propagation, see under *Amaranthus*.

[3-4] 5

Amaranthus paniculatus 'Green Thumb'

See *Amaranthus paniculatus* 'Green Thumb.'

Amaranthus paniculatus 'Pygmy Torch'

See *Amaranthus hypochondriacus* 'Pygmy Torch.'

Amethysteya caerulea 'Turquoise'

There is no point choosing this Asiatic plant for its amethyst-blue flowers – they are so small that they have very little decorative value. Subsequently, however, they form deep-blue nut fruits which are much sought-after by flower arrangers. The stems are cut off as the fruits set and are then included in bouquets. The leaves increase their decorative value. At first sight, they resemble hemp leaves, but they have delightful little blue edges.

Sow the seed directly in the border from mid-April; by continuing to sow several times until June, you will be able to pick bouquets over a long period. The seedlings dislike being transplanted. Select a sunny, open position in moist soil. Thinning the seedlings to a distance of 10 in between them will encourage strong growth. The first flowers may be picked in July, the last fruit-bearing stems in October (in the event of repeated sowing).

Amethysteya caerulea 'Turquoise'

Depending on moisture and nutrition, the plants may grow up to 32 in tall. They may also be dried.

4–6

Ammi majus

QUEEN ANNE'S LACE

The delicately branching flower heads of *ammi majus* are reminiscent of fine lace or dill, although the appearance of the latter is closer to that of *Ammi visnaga*, which is featured below. *Ammi majus* is one of the most satisfactory plants for adding volume to a bouquet, and its presence in natural borders is not to be despised.

The species originally grew in southern Europe and the neighboring areas of Asia and Africa. Its development, unfortunately, is rather slow. The plants need about 4 months to come into flower, which means that they do not usually start flowering until late July,

after which they continue until September. In the period before flowering, the plants look rather tenuous, although their feathery greyish-green foliage is quite pretty. When in flower, however, the approximately 3-ft tall plants fill out considerably and then need space to achieve their full spread.

If the seeds are sown indoors in winter or early spring, flowering may be brought forward considerably, but in that case the small plants should be transplanted with their balls of soil in May, because they dislike having their roots disturbed. Early cultivation does not affect the length of their flowering season. The plants begin to set seed several weeks after coming into flower, but their yellow-green umbels will remain in the border for weeks and new flower heads will continue to be produced for some time. Give them a sunny position and average amounts of water.

[2–3] 4–5

Ammi majus, Queen Anne's lace

Ammi visnaga

Ammi visnaga

The resemblance of the *Ammi* species to 'white' dill applies in particular to *Ammi visnaga*. In spring, the plants form compact tufts of feathery leaves that are broader than those of dill, but otherwise closely resemble them. The species originally grew in fields and rough ground in southern Europe (as far north as western France) as well as in the Middle East, where it is used for medicinal purposes. In a garden, the plants will grow to about 32 in and start producing white umbels in July. The flowers are greenish in color when they open and turn golden green as they fade. They finally close up into a nest shape. Partly because of its particularly decorative foliage, *Ammi visnaga* looks just as attractive in borders and bouquets as *Ammi majus*.

Ammi visnaga needs a little more water and a little less space to develop into a handsome plant.

[2–3] 4–5 🌱 🏺 !

Ammobium alatum

WINGED EVERLASTING

The winged stems of these everlasting flowers grow bolt upright and that is exactly as it should be, because they are grown specially for cutting purposes. This is done in July–August, as soon as the yellowy-white flowers are half open, because then they will last well as dried flowers. They are tied together in small bunches and hung upside down in an airy position to make them dry quickly and keep their attractive appearance.

Ammobium alatum is native to eastern Australia, where it grows to about 39 in in height. Cultivated varieties are usually shorter in order to keep the stems upright while they are growing. The richly flowering *Ammobium alatum* 'Grandiflorum' grows about 28 in tall. The 1996 winner of a Fleuroselect Gold Medal, *Ammobium alatum* 'Bikini,' is particularly popular among growers of flowers for drying because of the uniformity of its flowers and its sturdy stems, about 12–16 in

Ammobium alatum 'Bikini,' winged everlasting

tall. The flower heads are about $3/4$ in wide. Sow indoors in March–April, or out-of-doors in poor, well-drained soil in a sunny position in April–May.

[3–4] 4–5 🌱 🌱 🏺 🌼

Anagallis arvensis

PIMPERNEL

Some "weeds" are so pretty that we like to have them in our gardens. Pimpernels are one such example and devotees of natural gardens enjoy sowing them. The scarlet pimpernel (*Anagallis arvensis ssp. arvensis*) grows naturally in many places, particularly in soil that is not too acid or compacted. Scatter the seed in loose soil very early in spring to enable the plants to start flowering in May and to continue until well into autumn. The flowers are just over $1/4$ in wide and close up at the threat of bad weather, hence their common name "poor man's weatherglass." Their growth is straggling on bare soil; in between

Anagallis arvensis ssp. *arvensis*, scarlet pimpernel

Anagallis arvensis var. *caerulea*, blue pimpernel

other plants they grow to about 20 in tall. The blue pimpernel (*Anagallis arvensis* var. *caerulea*) closely resembles the scarlet pimpernel in almost every respect, except that its flowers are blue. That color is more popular and, for this reason, is used more often in gardens, pots, and hanging baskets.

[2-3]

Anagallis collina

See *Anagallis monelli.*

Anagallis grandiflora

See *Anagallis monelli.*

Anagallis monelli

PIMPERNEL

In south-west Europe and north Africa, there is a species of pimpernel which rarely survives winters further north, but has conspicuously larger flowers than the varieties indigenous there. It is called *Anagallis monelli* and produces flowers which can be up to 1 in wide. Numerous cultivars of this species (and of the small-leafed subspecies *Anagallis monelli* ssp. *linifolia*) are sold as annuals for rockeries, border edges, containers, and hanging baskets. They are grown from seed or cuttings and have lovely names, including *Anagallis monelli* 'Skylover,' *Anagallis monelli* 'Blue Bird,' *Anagallis monelli* ssp.

linifolia 'Gentian Blue,' and *Anagallis monelli* 'Philipii,' but the differences among the species are minimal and mostly limited to variations in the shade of the flowers.

Sow indoors during March–April, or out-of-doors from late April to early May for flowering from July, or buy glowering cuttings in mid-May. They form dense tufts of foliage about 8 in tall. The small blue flowers with red centers close up at night and in cloudy

Anagallis monelli 'Skylover'

Anagallis monelli 'Skylover'

Anchusa capensis 'Blue Angel,' bugloss

weather. New flowers are formed continually in amongst the leaves until September. The color goes very well with orange. The foliage may be scorched in hot sunlight. When growing the plant in containers, make sure the soil never dries out entirely. A dry position in the garden is not harmful.

[3–4] 4–5 🖌 € 🌼 ▼

Anchusa capensis 'Blue Angel'

BUGLOSS

With its low height of 8 in and small flowers, this South African plant is definitely not eye-catching, but anyone who appreciates delicacy will greatly enjoy it. Sow this miniature bugloss indoors early in the year and it will flower from June to September. If you sow directly in the garden in May, flowering will begin round about July.

[2–4] 5 🌼 ▼ 🐝

Anchusa capensis 'Blue Angel,' bugloss

41

Anemone coronaria

GARDEN ANEMONE

Although anemones form small tubers, they are grown nowadays as annuals for providing cut flowers. The species originated in Turkey. For a long time, small bouquets mostly came from southern Europe, where they were cultivated out-of- doors. Among the single-flowered types, *Anemone coronaria* De Caen Series was particularly well known and, among the double-flowered varieties, *Anemone coronaria* St Brigid Series was equally famous. Nowadays, species such as *Anemone coronaria* 'Mona Lisa Deep Red' are grown from seed in glass houses and you will find them at florists between September and May.

Anethum graveolens

DILL

Dill is one of the most satisfactory kitchen herbs, but its beautiful shape, color, and delicate scent ensure that it is also very popular for cutting and drying and as an annual border plant. The species originated in Asia Minor, but was brought to Europe in antiquity, where it gradually became indigenous after being cultivated in gardens. It is therefore very easy to cultivate. Sow the seeds directly in the garden

Anethum graveolens, dill

Anemone coronaria, 'Mona Lisa Deep Red,' garden anemone

between March and June. The first flowering is to be expected from June onwards. For culinary purposes, the leaves are cut off before the plant flowers, and may be used for flavoring fish dishes and as a garnish.

The foliage closely resembles that of fennel (which, in fact, may be easily crossed with dill). Dill leaves are lovely and the bluey-green foliage of *Anethum graveolens* 'Vierling' is particularly decorative. In summer, the fragrant yellow umbels of flowers enhance the effect. 'Vierling' is grown commercially for cutting purposes and may be found at florists between September and May.

Dill does not stand up well to competition from other plants and likes to grow in nutritive, well-drained but always moist soil. The plant will not recover from being allowed to become dry, however short such a period may be.

3-6

tainer plant for some time. Currently, however, suppliers also offer it for sale both as a bedding and container plant because of its profusion of flowers in summer. Flowering plants are on sale from mid-April. For that purpose, cuttings are taken by specialist firms during the previous summer. The plant is supplied as a small shrub or as a cluster of branches on a stem, in which case cultivation will take much longer.

Put the plant in a warm and sunny location in a border or in a large pot or other container. Leaving the potting compost to dry out completely will cause the buds and subsequently the leaves to wither. The plant may be kept throughout the winter in a light, frost-free, but cool position. Suppliers naturally hope that you will let it freeze to death and then buy a new one next spring!

Anisodontea capensis

Because this small South African shrub cannot tolerate frost, it was cultivated as a con-

Anisodontea capensis

Anoda cristata

Although *Anoda cristata* is native to Mexico and the dry southwest of the United States, it

Anoda cristata 'Opal Cup'

will not survive in arid soil. The plants grow along the banks of watercourses. In a garden, they like moisture-retentive but well-drained soil, which should not be too rich in nutrients as this would lead to the development of excessive foliage at the expense of flowers. The mallow-shaped flowers appear in July at the top of approximately 3-ft tall stems. They grow about 1¼–1½ in wide and have a lovely satiny sheen on the inside. The flowers of the species are white or tinged with blue. Those of the popular cultivar *Anoda cristata* 'Opal Cup' are soft pink with veins in a deeper shade. *Anoda cristata* 'Snow Cup' has snow-white flowers.

Sow the seeds directly out-of-doors in April–May, or sow them indoors in March. After mid-May, the seedlings may be planted out at a minimum distance of 10 in apart.

[3] 4–5 🌱 🏺 🐝

Anthemis arabica

See *Cladanthus arabicus.*

Antirrhinum majus

SNAPDRAGON

Snapdragons grow naturally in the warm south-west of Europe. The plant became a favorite in cottage gardens at an early date and is very easy to cultivate as an annual. The original tall cultivars were grown mainly from cuttings, because, if sown, the selected characteristics were lost. Nowadays, there are more varieties that will also produce uniform plants from seed. Apart from the tall varieties (about 39 in high) that are cultivated for cutting and as border plants, there are also intermediate-sized snapdragons (about 20 in high) as well as dwarf bedding and container ones (about 8 in high) in all kinds of colors. The two latter groups are often referred to as *Antirrhinum majus nanum.*

The flowers, particularly those of the tall and intermediate varieties, are a remarkable shape, resembling that of a dragon's jaws. If you press the sides, the "jaws" open. The flowers are pol-

Antirrhinum majus, snapdragon

linated by bumblebees, which are strong enough find to their way in through the resilient lips. In small-flowered cultivars, however, the opening is often too small, in which case the bumblebees break in by biting a hole in the side of the flower in order to suck out the nectar. Most snapdragons have a strong, sweet scent.

Antirrhinum 'Crown Light Mauve,' snapdragon

Antirrhinum 'Hobbit-mix' snapdragon

Antirrhinum majus 'Black Prince,' snapdragon

It is best to sow snapdragons indoors early in the year, or out-of-doors from April onwards. The seed requires very scant covering, as snapdragons germinate in daylight. The ideal temperature for germination is about 64 °F. After germination, it is preferable to grow them on in cooler conditions so that they develop a handsome, compact shape. Pinching out the growing tips encourages the plants to branch out. It is possible to sow in late summer but, in northwestern Europe, seedlings will need protection against severe frost just to bring them into flower a little earlier.

Keep the seeds moist at all times but, to prevent grey mold, do not let them become soaking wet. In May, forced seedlings are planted out in nutritive, moisture-retentive but well-drained soil.

Plants grown from seed begin to flower at the end of June and continue to produce flowers until well into August, particularly if the stems are cut off once the flowers are over. Flowering plants are on sale in May.

With an average height of 14 in, the snapdragons in the Crown Series are in between the dwarf and the intermediate varieties. The size is suitable for flower beds, but particularly for containers. The plants branch out nicely and flower abundantly over a long period. The time required for bringing them into flower from seed is also important for commercial cultivation and, in the case of the Crown Series, that period is shorter than it is for other varieties. It is no wonder that *Antirrhinum* 'Crown Light Mauve,' which was introduced in 1999, was awarded a Fleuroselect Quality Mark. Private individuals cannot obtain seed of the Crown Series, but pot-grown plants are on sale in spring.

The dwarf varieties have lost much of the beauty of snapdragons. Their shape in particular has deteriorated. The pointed spikes of the original species and early cultivars have been replaced by a cluster of flowers of indeterminate form. In the case of the Hobbit Series, the flowers have also lost their characteristic shape: it is no longer possible to pinch the dragon's cheeks to make it open its jaws because they are always open, in an everlasting yawn.

45

Antirrhinum majus 'Coronette Formula Mix,' snapdragon

Antirrhinum majus 'Rocket Lemon,' snapdragon

One of the advantages of these miniatures is the possibility of filling flower-beds and containers with striking colors. Those of the Hobbit Series vary from deep red to yellow and white by way of pink and orange.

Snapdragons are rarely found in the more sophisticated gardens of genuine plant lovers. The colors are usually too bright, but an exception is sometimes made for *Antirrhinum majus* 'Black Prince.' The dark green foliage of this ancient cultivar is tinged with deep red and the almost equally dark stems bear beautifully formed "dragon's heads" in deepest, velvety red. The plants can grow up to 20 in tall and are therefore very suitable for cutting and for a position in the middle of a border. Particularly in red borders, their muted colors soften the more striking shades of red and pinkish red.

By sowing in January, growers of potted plants can take their flowering Coronette snapdragons to auction by mid-April. These plants are suitable for pots and other containers, but they will flower just as profusely in beds and borders. The Coronette Series has good resistance to rust, a fungus disease that tends to mar the appearance of snapdragons by causing brown spots. The plants grow to about 20 in tall and are available in white, yellow, pale pink, deep pink, red, scarlet, coppery orange, violet, and in the mixture *Antirrhinum majus* 'Coronette Formula Mix.'

In 1998, the Rocket Series was extended to include *Antirrhinum majus* 'Rocket Lemon.' Although lemon yellow, the flower features a lot of white and this makes it look very attractive. The Rocket Series itself has long been known for supplying large quantities of excellent flowers for cutting. They are on sale at florists from mid-April until the end of August. The plants can grow to over 39 in tall and are well provided with leaves, even in old age. Other cultivars belonging to the series include *Antirrhinum majus* 'Rocket Golden' (yellow and lemon yellow), *Antirrhinum majus* 'Rocket Bronze' (salmon pink with soft orange and some yellow), *Antir-*

Antirrhinum majus 'The Rose,' snapdragon

rhinum majus 'Cherry Improved' (rose red), and *Antirrhinum majus* 'Rocket Orchid' (lavender).

Antirrhinum majus 'The Rose' is another snapdragon of which the discerning gardener need not feel ashamed. The pale pink flowers have a lovely satiny sheen and go well with other plants in a border. The handsome, classic shape of the flowers is also worth noting. The plants may grow up to 39 in tall, but are usually shorter. "Pale pink with some egg yellow round its lips" is the description provided for *Antirrhinum* Tip Top Irma,' a color combination from the Tip Top Series. Many other colors are also available in that series. The plants grow to about 32 in tall and are therefore suitable for cutting, but also merit a place in borders or flower-beds.

[3–4] 4–5

Aptenia cordifolia

Succulents like *Aptenia* are adept at surviving in arid regions. They store moisture in

Antirrhinum 'Tip Top Irma,' snapdragon

Aptenia cordifolia 'Variegata'

their foliage and stems. The South African *Aptenia cordifolia* consequently grows as a perennial in that country. It barely tolerates frost and should therefore always be over-wintered indoors in colder climates. In spring, bedding-plant growers supply plants propagated by cuttings. These mat-forming succulents spread rapidly and freely produce purplish-red flowers which open only in full sun. *Aptenia* does best in full sun and in loose, dry, poor soil. Preferably plant in a raised bed, rock garden, or a container with poor soil. Anyone able to provide the plants with a pleasantly cool but frost-free position can overwinter them (or cuttings taken in August–September).

Aptenia cordifolia 'Variegata' is the cultivar with variegated leaves that is most frequently on sale. It is a little shorter than the species and has smaller leaves.

Argemone grandiflora

PRICKLY POPPY

The 4-in wide white flowers of *Argemone grandiflora* have a lovely satiny sheen and ochre-yellow stamens with a striking, deep-red stigma disc. Their resemblance to species of *papaver* is striking except that the stems, buds, and especially the fruit of prickly poppies are provided with prickles which harden viciously as they ripen. The pointed, spiky, sea-green leaves have lighter veins and this pattern of veins differs from that of some other, closely related prickly poppies. In other respects, *Argemone platyceras*, *Argemone polyanthemos*, and *Argemeno squarrosa* closely resemble *Argemone grandiflora*. The plants grow to about 20 in tall.

They grow naturally in the hot, arid regions of Mexico and the southern states of the US. Sow indoors in March–April, but in such a way that the seedlings including their root-balls may be put out-of-doors at the end of May, because the roots must not be damaged. It may be better to sow directly in the open after mid-April.

[2–3] 4–5

Argyranthemum frutescens

MARGUERITE

This marguerite will adorn summer patios, but it does not tolerate frost. The species grows naturally in the Canary Islands where it is warm, but never burning hot, and where there is always a cool sea breeze. This should be remembered when caring for these plants. Marguerites like warmth, but not heat, and under glass they often suffer from hot sunlight. You should therefore definitely put them out-of-doors after the last night frost and make sure that the potting compost does not dry out. They flower with such overwhelming exuberance that the plants may easily exhaust their reserves. Re-pot them in nutritive soil immediately after purchase and give them liquid fertilizer several times during the summer.

In autumn, the plants will begin to wither even before the first frosts and they will also

Argemone grandiflora

Argyranthemum frutescens, marguerite

Argyranthemum frutescens 'Flamingo,' marguerite

Argyranthemum frutescens 'Sweety,' marguerite

flowers rising less far above its bluish-green foliage. The entire plant is scarcely more than 12 in high and is supplied in a small-sized pot, though the foliage is relatively spreading.

With its baby-pink flowers, *Argyranthemum frutescens* 'Flamingo,' is one of the most rewarding of all marguerites. It may grow to a maximum height of 20 in. In a border, its color goes well with sulphur yellow.

Argyranthemum frutescens 'Sweety,' a marguerite growing to about 28 in tall, is protected under plant breeders' rights and may be propagated only if the licence-holder is recompensed for investing time and money in producing the cultivar and is gradually reimbursed for it. 'Sweety' has striking green foliage and soft pink flowers with a white ring round their yellow centers.

start suffering from mildew. It is time to throw them out. In theory, enthusiasts may take cuttings in late summer and overwinter them in a light position at a minimum of 41 °F but, in practice, nearly everyone grows marguerites as annual container and bedding plants.

Cut-flower firms often treat marguerites with growth inhibitors to achieve the required compact growth. *Argyranthemum frutescens* 'Dana' is naturally compact, with its

Artemisia annua 'Spice Bush'

ANNUAL WORMWOOD

Do you ever feel you would like to see what a hedge would look like in a particular place in your garden? You might try it out with *Artemisia annua*. Sow some seed in situ in spring and six weeks later you will have plants about 5 ft tall. If they are planted side by side at intervals of about 20 in, it will look as if a hedge of conifers has grown up in less than no time. The numerous small flowers are totally inconspicuous. What is important is the light green of the widely branching

Argyranthemum frutescens 'Dana,' marguerite

Artemisia annua 'Spice Bush,' annual wormwood

Asarina erubescens, climbing gloxinia

plants. The greenery forms a splendid back-drop for summer-flowering plants.

[3–4] 4–5

Asarina erubescens

CLIMBING GLOXINIA

Fresh pink flowers, each one up to 3 in long, are formed at the tips of the climbing stems of *Asarina rubescens* throughout the summer. The Mexican climber itself will grow as tall as the support you provide for it – up to 12 ft in a single season.

Put the plant in a warm and sheltered posi-tion in nutritive soil or in a large pot and give it plenty of water, because there is consider-able evaporation from the surface of the large downy leaves. As long as the soil remains suf-ficiently damp, the climbing gloxinia may be in full sun, but if there is some shade during the hottest part of the day, the risk of the plant drying out in a pot is reduced.

In Mexico, *Asarina* is a perennial. In colder

Asarina erubescens, climbing gloxinia

climates, it may be overwintered indoors in a frost-free and light position, but annual cultivation is infinitely preferable. The plant is self-pollinating and produces spherical fruit containing winged seeds in late summer. Sow indoors as early as February–March, because the seedlings need about 4 months to come into flower. Flowering plants are on sale from May.

[2-3]

Asarina procumbens 'Sierra Nevada'

'*Procumbens*' means 'lying,' and this *Asarina* certainly grows horizontally. As soon as the sticky, hairy stems and leaves cease to find a support, they start trailing. The species grows naturally in the south-west of France and the adjoining regions of north-east Spain, but it is not fully hardy in cooler regions. In a light, airy, and dry position under glass, the

Asarina procumbens 'Sierra Nevada'

Asarina procumbens 'Sierra Nevada'

plant did, however, tolerate 14 °F during my own practical experiment.

In warm, dark positions, the species is difficult to overwinter, so cultivation as an annual is preferable. Plants propagated by cuttings are on sale in small quantities in spring. You may also sow them indoors in February–March. After germination at temperatures around 68 °F, you should put the plants in a cooler, light, and frost-free position until they can be planted out-of-doors in May. They tolerate a fair amount of shade and cool soil which, however, must be well drained. Cultivation in partial shade on a rockery, or in a hanging basket or container is ideal. The plants will come into flower about four months after sowing, and go on flowering until the frosts begin. In combination with their greyish-green foliage, the soft yellow flowers resembling those of snapdragons have an intense, modest beauty. Seeds from the spherical fruit may be harvested for cultivation next year.

[2-3] !

Asarina scandens

Asarina scandens and *Asarina barclaiana* bear a close resemblance to each other. Both species come from Mexico and need a warm position if they are to develop fully. It is best to grow *Asarina scandens* from seed. The plants do not tolerate frost and should not be put out-of-doors in a warm and sheltered position until the end of May (and preferably later). The foliage will benefit from some pro-

Asarina scandens 'Joan Loraine'

Asclepias curassavica, silk weed

tection against scorching sunshine in the hottest part of the day. The leafstalks curl around anything they can grasp and this allows the plant to grow to about 9 ft. If the seeds are sown early, flowers will appear after 4–5 months, from July onwards. Those of the species are violet pink to lavender-colored. The cultivar *Asarina scandens* 'Bride's White' bears white flowers, *Asarina scandens* 'Mystic Rose' pink ones, and *Asarina scandens* 'Joan Lorraine' has violet flowers.

[2–3]

Asclepias curassavica

SILK WEED

In Latin America, *Asclepias curassavica* grows as a short-lived perennial. In cooler regions, the plant is often grown as an annual. Taking cuttings is possible, if difficult, partly

because the sap may cause skin irritation. The plants on sale from June have usually been cultivated from seed. Sowing them yourself is quite feasible. Sow indoors in February–March (the seeds germinate at about 68 °F). Seedlings should be grown on in a light and relatively cool position to prevent straggly growth. Pinching out the growing tips makes the plants bushier. Plant them out in a warm and sheltered position in a border or a large pot after the last frost. Give them plenty of water. The plants will grow to about 39 in tall and will not come into flower until about 5 months after they were sown, but then they will go on flowering indefatigably until well into autumn. The bicolored flowers are orange and red, and attract a lot of butterflies. The pollen causes skin irritation in some people.

[2–3]

Asperula azurea

See *Asperula orientalis.*

Asperula orientalis

This low-growing species originally came from Turkey. It grows to a maximum of 12 in in height and produces whorls of narrow leaves on lax stems. The small, delightfully fragrant lavender flowers appear in May and June, attracting a large number of insects. *Asperula orientalis* is modest and refined and therefore suitable for anyone who appreciates the beauty of small plants. They do very well in partial shade and are very suitable for cultivation in pots, provided they are not placed in full sun and the soil is never allowed to dry out. Sow directly in a pot or border in April–June. Seedlings are reasonably hardy, so it is also possible to sow in autumn.

4–5 8–10

Asperula orientalis, blue bedstraw

Asperula setosa

See *Asperula orientalis.*

Atriplex hortensis

GARDEN ORACHE

Garden orache was originally grown as a vegetable. The leaves are prepared like spinach

Atriplex hortensis var. *rubra*, red orache

and, when dried, are added to tea for cleansing spring cures.

Several cultivars are popular nowadays as annual ornamental plants for colored borders or for cutting and drying. The panicles of the flowers are often the same color as the leaves: green, yellow, or reddish. They are not very striking but make good fillers for bouquets and can often be dried. The plants grow to 3–5 ft in height.

Atriplex hortensis 'Crimson Plume' has purple flowers and red foliage; *Atriplex hortensis* 'Gold Plume' is soft yellow, while *Atriplex hortensis* 'Red Plume' is deep red. With its wine-colored stems and deep red foliage, *Atriplex hortensis* var. *rubra* is a popular ornamental plant for a red border. They are sown where they are to flower from the end of March until May and look splendid right from the first.

3–5

Bacopa

See *Sutera*.

Basella alba

MALABAR SPINACH

The western species of spinach would run to seed prematurely in the tropics, but inhabitants of Africa and Asia have an alternative, Malabar spinach, named by the British after the Indian district where the vegetable is still cultivated. The plant grows there as a perennial climber, but in cooler climates it must be cultivated as an annual by sowing it indoors at about 68 °F and growing the plants on until they can be put out-of-doors at the end of May. They may be planted in a large pot to climb up a trellis or cover a pergola. It is important, though, to stand the plants in a warm place and to give them plenty of water and plant food.

Basella alba 'Rosebud,' Malabar spinach

The seeds and plants available in temperate climates are usually those with foliage and stems tinged with red, including *Basella alba* 'Rosebud,' *Basella alba* 'Rubra,' and *Basella rubra* 'Select Red.' They, too, have leaves and stems which are edible after braising or stir-frying. The plants flower unobtrusively in August–September, after which the juicy fruits holding the seeds are formed.

[2–4] 4–5

Bassia scoparia

SUMMER CYPRESS

The dense foliage of the summer cypress closely resembles that of bamboo: it is long, grasslike, and has a striking shade of pale green. In the course of the summer, the plant assumes a low, columnar shape and grows to about 24 in in height. This kind of green plant

Bassia scoparia f.*trichophylla*, red summer cypress

with a distinctive shape may provide a restful break in a border. It is also possible to plant the summer cypresses in a row to provide a low-growing, annual hedge. The plants produce small flowers, but these are totally inconspicuous.

The plant most likely to be available is *Bassia scoparia* f. *trichophylla*. It is an engrossing plant, which is just as pale a shade of green as the species in spring and summer, but changes color quite suddenly in autumn, when the leaves turn deep red. The plant is therefore now known as the red summer cypress.

Sow indoors in March–April or directly out-of-doors from mid-April. The plant has no special requirements.

[3–4] 4–5 🌱 🪴

Begonia fuchsioides

FUCHSIA BEGONIA

At first sight, the shoots, leaves, and flowers of this Venezuelan begonia resemble those of fuchsias. The small, toothed leaves, lax red stems, and racemes of pendent spherical flowers are all reminiscent of fuchsias. The plant acquires a dense shrubby shape during its rapid growth in summer. It is sometimes overwintered as a container plant, but does not tolerate temperatures below 50 °F – too cold for this begonia to be popular among gardeners. It is possible to overwinter it in a living-room, but the atmosphere is often too dry there and *Begonia fuchsioides* is therefore usually sold as an annual. Specialist firms market cuttings on a massive scale in

Begonia fuchsioides

Begonia semperflorens providing red zones in a flower-bed

Begonia semperflorens in a hanging basket

spring, and they find their way to the containers and flower-beds of those who love this bright and cheerful plant. It does not need a sunny position and, in fact, does better in a sheltered spot in partial shade.

Begonia Semperflorens Group

By nature, the 900 or so species of begonia are tropical perennials. From *Begonia semperflorens*, *Begonia schmidtiana*, and several others species, growers developed the *Semperflorens* Group, with its innumerable cultivars now on the market as indoor plants and, above all, as bedding plants. The white, pink, and red flowers were at one time particularly popular for flower-beds and public gardens. Whole sections were filled with them to form city coats of arms, dials of giant clocks, or similar imaginative patterns. Now that we are slightly tired of those colorful flower-beds, the *Semperflorens* begonias are

Begonia 'Party Dress'

Begonia 'Senator Rose'

Begonia 'Quick Rose'

playing an increasingly important part in container gardening.

The choice of cultivated varieties is huge. The color of leaves and flowers may vary, but the shapes of the various cultivars are virtually the same: slightly succulent leaves on round, succulent stems, and simple flowers, usually with two large and two smaller petals. There is also a group with double flowers.

The latter are often sterile and are therefore propagated by cuttings. The single-flowered varieties, which attract a lot of bees, are propagated mainly by seed. Professional growers scatter the dust-fine seed in greenhouses in the depth of winter so that they can market the small plants by the end of May.

Begonias are particularly sensitive to cold, especially if the soil is wet. They should not, therefore, be planted out-of-doors in flowerbeds, pots, or baskets before June. Baskets will ultimately be completely covered with their leaves and flowers.

Plant the begonias in flower-beds in full sun or partial shade in a warm and sheltered position, but avoid permanently wet soil. The plants suffer badly from wet summers and particularly from strong winds.

Allow the compost in containers to dry up before watering. In soggy, oxygen-starved soil, the threadlike roots often tend to die off and mildew may follow.

Begonia 'Party Dress' belongs to the *Semperflorens* Group and has a very special character. Its small bright-white flowers form a splendid contrast with the brown leaves. The plant may grow up to 12 in tall and will flower from May until the first frost.

Begonia 'Quick Rose' is one of those small plants traditionally used for colorful flowerbeds. Masses of them are sold in spring, often in flexible plastic pots joined together in sets of four, with a single plant, often the same color as the others, in each of them. Because of their small size – maximum height 6–8in – they are primarily intended for flower-beds. They are really too small for window boxes, hanging baskets, or pots. In addition to the

Begonia 'Super Olympia Rose'

Begonia Tuberhybrida Group, tuberous begonia

pink-flowered 'Quick Rose,' the following cultivars belonging to the same series are available: *Begonia* 'Quick Red,' *Begonia* 'Quick Pink' (pale pink), *Begonia* 'Quick White,' and *Begonia* 'Quick Bicolor' (white with a pink edge to each petal).

Within the *Semperflorens* Group, to which *Begonia* 'Senator Rose' belongs, the appearance of the plants in flower-beds is not determined by the color of the flowers alone. The color of the foliage also plays a major part in their overall effect. The varieties in the Senator Series all have dark foliage, in which dark green and deep red combine for a brownish effect. This color goes particularly well with pale flowers such as those of *Begonia* 'Senator White' and *Begonia* 'Senator Bicolor' (white with cherry-red edges). The flowers are subject to spotting in long spells of bad weather.

Begonia 'Super Olympia Rose' is a strong pale-pink cultivar belonging to the Super Olympia Series. The plants grow about 8 in tall. The available colors include the following: *Begonia* 'Super Olympia Red' (deep red), *Begonia* 'Super Olympia Deeprose,' and *Begonia* 'Super Olympia White.'

Begonia Tuberhybrida Group

TUBEROUS BEGONIA

Many begonias come from tropical regions where there is little difference between the seasons. Tuberous begonias, which withdraw underground in unfavorable months,

develop in regions where there is a significant difference between dry and rainy seasons, or cold and hot ones. They die down above ground, as do the species from the mountainous regions of Peru and Bolivia, from which the *Tuberhybrida* Group was derived. The cultivated varieties were created from numerous species that were intensively crossed, particularly since the 19th century. They include varieties with single flowers as well as those with fully double blooms, upright begonias, and trailing forms. There are

Begonia 'Nonstop Pink,' tuberous begonia

57

Begonia 'Nonstop Yellow,' tuberous begonia

Begonia 'Pin-Up Flame,' tuberous begonia

tall, with fairly robust, pointed leaves, and produce clusters of double flowers, each of which may grow to about 4 in wide. *Begonia* 'Non-stop Pink' bears pale pink flowers. The series includes many shades of reddish pink as well as white, apricot, salmon, and a lovely white flower with a red blush. *Begonia* 'Nonstop Yellow' is one of the hardiest cultivars in the Non-stop Series. Its 4-in wide double flowers scarcely raise their heads above the foliage, which often has a bronze glow.

Begonia 'Pin-Up Flame' was introduced in 1999. Its structure and round flower shape closely resemble those of *Begonia* 'Pin-Up Rose' which had been produced previously. The latter has 4-in wide white flowers with pink edges which gradually merge into the white area. It was awarded a Fleuroselect gold medal. 'Pin-Up Flame' has yellow flowers with orange-red edges. The plants grow to about 10 in tall. They are suitable for containers and flower-beds, but only in sheltered positions. The flowers dislike strong winds.

examples in every flower color except blue. The colors are usually very pronounced and should be used only to add a bright touch or as a color zone in a flower-bed.

Plants from the *Tuberhybrida* Group may be put out-of-doors in a position sheltered from the wind after mid-May. Their stems are thick, succulent, and fragile; large sections of the plant may therefore easily break off. Tuberous begonias prefer clay soil, but also do well in ordinary potting compost. They do not tolerate stagnant water. Allow the soil in containers to dry out completely between watering sessions. They may be put in full sunlight, but do better in partial shade. Tuberous begonias were formerly brought indoors in autumn and the tubers would be kept in a frost-free place. Nowadays, commercial growers cultivate them as annuals from seed on a massive scale. The following are among those that are available.

From November, growers sow seeds of Nonstop-begonias in order to market flowering plants 5 months later. They are about 8 in

Beta vulgaris ssp. *cicla* 'Vulcan,' Swiss chard

Beta vulgaris ssp. cicla

SWISS CHARD

Some vegetables are so decorative that they merit a place in a flower garden. Of course, a vegetable garden may also look lovely, hence the recent interest in ornamental 'potagers.' The colorful cultivars of Swiss chard are eminently suitable for that kind of garden. Its leaves are often puckered, green to reddish in color, and frequently have a metallic sheen. The leafstalks and veins are in strong contrast to the leaves, and may be white, yellow, pink, orange, or red. Those of the cultivar 'Vulcan' are bright red.

Varieties cultivated for ornamental purposes grow to about 12 in tall. Sow the seed directly in the garden from April, as the seedlings dislike being transplanted. The young leaves may be cut or picked just a few weeks after sowing. They are usually boiled briefly or stir-fried. The low-growing ornamental species do best in a sunny position in light, humus-rich soil. They look best in straight rows in a vegetable garden, but are also suitable for borders, flower-beds, and containers.

4-6

Bidens ferulifolia

The year 1992 saw the introduction of a new plant that looks like a trailing form of *Coreopsis.* The shoots of this Central-American plant grow somewhat untidily, usually not a good sign in the ornamental plant world, but once you have seen how this species tumbles over the edges of pots, urns, or hanging baskets, you're hooked. The plant is consequently having a stellar career and is now the most popular plant for balcony planters in southern Germany and Austria. It flowers right through the summer, with the stems producing fine, fennel-like foliage and ramifying continually. The shoots tend to grow very long, but they may be cut back hard, after which the plant will flower again 2 weeks later. The yellow flowers, about 1¼ in wide, attract bees and lots of butterflies.

Bidens ferulifolia

Bidens ferulifolia 'Goldie'

Bidens ferulifolia 'Samsara'

Sow indoors in March–April or allow the seeds to germinate outdoors in April–May. If self-sown, the plants will be in flower from the end of June until after the first night frosts, but flowering plants are also on sale from late April. They are undemanding as far as position and soil are concerned. It is best to plant them near the edge of a raised section of a border or – even better – in a trough, tub, pot, or hanging basket. If grown in a container, they should be given plenty of water and fertilizer.

Several cultivated varieties of *Bidens ferulifolia* have been developed, but they do not differ much from the species. *Bidens ferulifolia* 'Goldie' has slightly shorter leaves with broader lobes and *Bidens ferulifolia* 'Golden Goddess' has larger flowers. *Bidens ferulifolia* 'Samsara' has a more compact growth and is often marketed as a cutting in hanging baskets. In an attempt to please us, the improver of 'Samsara' surpassed himself and bred out its loose, sprawling growth. For cultivation, see the species.

[3–4] 4–5   !

Blitium virgatum

See *Chenopodium foliosum.*

Blumenbachia lateritia

See *Caiophora lateritia'*

Borago officinalis

BORAGE

There is usually no need for keen gardeners to plant borage more than once, as the plant will seed in loose soil. The seeds fall in late summer, provided they have not been extracted from the fruit by greenfinches. The seedlings will survive almost any kind of winter and then flower from May onwards. The small blue flowers are about $1/2$ in wide and attract bees and bumblebees. You may like to try them yourself – pick a few (they are quite easy to detach) and add them to a fresh green salad. Depending on the fertility of the soil, the plants will grow from 20 in to over 39 in tall. They have somewhat coarse, hairy foliage and even the buds and developing fruit are hairy and somewhat prickly. New flowers are formed continually and subsequently produce strong black seeds, often in a group of four. Flowering continues into September. If you sow in early spring, flow-

Borago officinalis, borage

ers will appear in September. If you sow again in May, the flowering season will be extended until October.

Borago officinalis 'Alba' has white flowers. It is sometimes on sale under the name of *Borago officinalis albiflora* or *Borago officinalis* f. *alba.*

Borago officinalis 'Variegata' has yellow to creamy white spots. This variegated form is

Borago officinalis 'Alba,' borage

Borago officinalis 'Variegata,' borage

Brachycome multifida, Swan River daisy

rarely on sale, but may well develop spontaneously in a garden. The variegation, however, rarely turns out to be permanent.

3–5 8–10

Brachycome multifida

SWAN RIVER DAISY

This newcomer rapidly conquered the world of containers and hanging baskets. No wonder, because it has everything going for it: beautifully divided leaves and, above them, white, yellow, or lavender-pink to blue flowers which are borne non-stop throughout the summer. The foliage tumbles over the rims of pots, containers, and hanging baskets. Because of its dense growth, it is advisable to combine this brachycome with other species in the same container. It grows trouble-free in sunlight and better still in partial shade, either in a border or in a pot. If you are growing it in a pot, make sure the soil never dries

Brachycome multifida, Swan River daisy

out completely, as the leaves will turn yellow otherwise.

Brachycome multifida comes from southeastern Australia and is grown from cuttings on a massive scale by commercial enterprises. The process of growing saleable plants from cuttings takes about eight weeks. Selections are marketed according to flower color: *Brachycome multifida* 'Blue'; *Brachycome multifida* 'Harmony,' and *Brachycome multifida* 'Royal' are called 'blue-flowered,' but you may be assured that they will include a fair amount of pink; *Brachycome multifida* 'Pink Mist' has pale-pink flowers; and those of *Brachycome multifida* 'Yellow' are pale yellow. The latter plant is less bushy.

    !

Brachycome iberidifolia

SWAN RIVER DAISY

The cultivars in the Splendour Series are delightful brachycomes to grow from seed. The blue, pink, or white daisy-like flowers are produced throughout the summer. They appear above delicate foliage, with which they form a compact plant about 14 in high. It looks best as an edging plant, but also goes well with other annuals in a cheerful, informal summer border. The small plants are also used frequently in pots and containers, but, above all, in hanging baskets, where they sway elegantly in the breeze. They are also very hardy and undemanding. The only thing that they do not tolerate is stagnating moisture.

Brachycome iberidifolia 'Blue Splendor,' Swan River daisy *Brachycome iberidifolia* 'Purple Splendor.'

The flowers are about 1¼ in wide and delightfully fragrant, thus attracting many bees. They come in white and every imaginable shade of pink and blue. *Brachycome iberidifolia* 'Blue Splendor' has violet-blue flowers, and *Brachycome iberidifolia* 'Purple Splendor' purplish pink ones.

[3-4] 5   🌱   ▼   ⚱   🐝   !

Brachyscome

The fact that Alexandre Cassini's attention strayed briefly during his Latin lesson in about 1800 has caused a lot of bickering among botanists. Cassini originally described the botanical genus as *Brachyscome* ('*brachys*' is Greek for short and '*kome*' stands for hair). According to Latin linguistic rules, the 's' should be dropped when the two words are joined. Cassini himself subsequently corrected his error and changed the name to *Brachycome*. Such a change, however, is not allowed

Brachycome iberidifolia 'Blue Splendor,' Swan River daisy

according to the strict rules for the nomenclature of plants, so the linguistically incorrect name is the acknowledged one. Since everyone should be allowed to correct their mistakes, I have opted for *Brachycome*.

Brassica oleracea

ORNAMENTAL CABBAGE

The Japanese are responsible for reviving interest in ornamental cabbages. At one time, they were used in single-colored flower-beds, but they went out of fashion. In Japan, however new cultivars have been developed, with green, pinkish red, deep red, or white leaves, which may or may not be curly. The colors are often combined, with the center having a distinctly different color from that of the encircling leaves.

Although ornamental cabbages are somewhat ungainly in appearance, they may extend the garden season for quite some time. Their colors do not develop fully until the autumn (at temperatures below 59 °F), and

Brassica oleracea, ornamental cabbage

since they tolerate a fair amount of frost, they retain their decorative appearance until March in mild winters. After that they may go on the compost heap or be fed to the rabbits, as the plants are definitely edible.

They are on sale only in autumn, but sowing them oneself is also possible. Sow in June or July and plant out in a permanent position – in a pot or a flower-bed – in July or August.

6-7

Browallia americana

The informal growth of *Browallia americana* makes the plant a favorite among gardeners. The flowering shoots tumble gracefully over the edges of pots, tubs, and hanging baskets, with their violet-blue flowers suspended like butterflies from their stems. The light spot in the center of the flowers enhances their refinement. Sow *Browallia americana* indoors in March–April at a temperature of about 68 °F. Pinch out young shoots to encourage bushiness and plant out-of-doors after the final night frost. They do

Brassica oleracea, ornamental cabbage

best in poor soil, but will also grow in richer kinds. Choose a sunny position in a border, but partial shade is better if you are growing them in pots, tubs, or hanging baskets. The plants do not need much water, but the root-

Browallia americana, bush violet

ball should not be allowed to dry out entirely, as the plants definitely do not recover from that.

Browallia viscosa is a very similar species, but has viscous stems. The plant itself makes a more compact impression and bears a profusion of small flowers that grow to about 1 in wide.

[2-3] 🌼 ▼ !

Bupleurum rotundifolium

The stems appear to pierce the cucumber-shaped leaves which are green with a blue sheen caused by the layer of protective wax. The plant grows somewhat tenuously to about 24 in tall and flowers from June to August. The small flowers are not in themselves very striking, but they grow in decorative yellowish-green umbels. The restrained colors of foliage and flowers have made *bupleurum* one of the most popular plants in the art of flower arrangement. The stems are used as fillers and form a lovely background to many other cut flowers. The same effect is created in a border including *bupleurum*. Other plants show up better alongside its blue and yellowish greenery.

Sow *bupleurum* directly out-of-doors in March–April or, alternatively, in autumn, because the plant will tolerate temperatures as low as 5 °F in dry soil. It grows best in loose soil that is not excessively wet, and amidst other plants that are able to give its thin stems some support.

3-4 9-10 🌼 🏺

Bupleurum rotundifolium

Caiophora lateritia

Calandrinia umbellata 'Amaranth,' rock purslane

Caiophora lateritia

Flowers of the palest imaginable apricot-orange are enticingly attractive, but beware – the flowers, stems, and rough leaves have very fine hairs which prick one viciously. Those on the flower heads are worst and irritate the skin. That, in fact, is precisely the intention of this Argentinian plant, which uses them to discourage grazing animals. *Caiophora* is a botanical rarity that is marketed with increasing frequency by specialist seedsmen. The plant is a climber. Its hairy stems cling to any kind of support and may reach a height of 5 ft in a single growing season. Sow the warmth-loving plant indoors early in the year and do not put it outdoors in a sheltered, sunny position until the end of May. From July onwards, it will produce flowers over $1\frac{1}{4}$ in wide in shades of apricot to brick-red, and sometimes whitish in color. Bees love them.

[3–4]

Calandrinia umbellata 'Amaranth'

ROCK PURSLANE

Calandrinia does best in a warm and dry position where it will open its wonderful magenta flowers that grow to about $^3/_4$ in wide. They open one after another over a long pe-

riod between June and September. In poor soil, the small plants remain nicely compact and grow to a height of about 4–6 in. In richer soil, their growth is thinner and the lovely greyish-green of the swollen leaves will, for the most part, change to green.

Sow indoors in March–April at a temperature of about 64 °F and do not put the plants out-of-doors until the end of May. They will flower from early July until well into September.

[3–4]

Calceolaria mexicana

SLIPPERWORT

Calceolarias are difficult to combine with other plants because of their bright colors. The pale yellow flowers of *Calceoraria mex-*

Calceolaria mexicana, slipper flower

icana appear to be no exception until you see them in a border with foliage plants, or on the rough banks of a stream. In that kind of position, the small flowers will light up like Chinese lanterns. They are only ¼ in wide and are suspended gracefully from slender red-tinged stems.

Depending on its position, the plant will grow up to 8–20 in tall and will be tallest in shady, damp, and/or nutritive places. This calceolaria is native to the forested mountain slopes of Mexico. It likes warmth, but tolerates blistering sunshine only in moist positions, where it will also seed on a massive scale.

[3] 4–5 🌱

Calendula arvensis

FIELD MARIGOLD

If you want field marigolds, you need to apply to seedsmen and growers specializing in wild flowers, the only people apparently capable of appreciating the small, ³/₄-in wide flowers. They are pale orange to ochre yellow in color. The plants grow to about 12 in

Calendula arvensis, field marigold

Calendula officinalis, pot marigold

in height and are found growing naturally on undeveloped sites and in fields in southern Europe and as far north as the warmer parts of France and Germany. Cultivation is the same as for *Calendula officinalis*.

[2–3] 4–5 🌱 ▼

Calendula officinalis

POT MARIGOLD

Pot marigolds have been popular in herb gardens and for ornamental purposes ever since the Middle Ages, when they helped to combat a large variety of disorders. Consideration is currently being given to the possibility of large-scale oil extraction from the seeds, for use as a solvent in paint and ink. This will provide an alternative to the noxious solvents causing the occupational disease *OPS* among house-painters and printers, to name but a few. For keen gardeners, marigolds are easily-cultivated ornamental plants growing a couple

Calendula officinalis, double marigold

of feet tall, seeding themselves profusely in loose soil, and germinating spontaneously in the garden in early spring.

Numerous cultivated varieties have been developed from the original wild marigold, which grows naturally in southern Europe. Their color varies from deep orange to yellow and creamy white. Double varieties have also been created. If the center of the flower is clearly visible but there are more petals (ray florets) than usual round it, the flowers are called "semi-double"; if the center has been almost entirely replaced by petals, they are "fully double."

Calendula officinalis 'Fiesta Gitana' is one of the "fully double" marigolds. The flower heads, over 2½ in wide, vary in basic color from pure orange to pale yellow, but have a dark edge at the tip of each petal (ray floret). At a height of 12 in, the plant itself is a dwarf and commercial growers keep it even more compact by growth inhibitors. It is marketed as a bedding plant on a huge scale in spring, and seeds are also available.

3–5 7–9

Callistephus chinensis

CHINA ASTER

The China or summer aster has had a long cultural history. The originally Chinese annual has been improved in China and Japan for centuries. The single flowers became semi-double and then fully double, while the original color spectrum of white to violet was extended to include all manner of bright colors. Even the petals (ray florets) underwent all kinds of changes from ray-shaped to curled and sometimes became as thin as threads.

The natural species grows to about 32 in tall, about the same height as the cultivated varieties currently grown for cutting – the principal reason for cultivating asters. Dwarf forms are also marketed nowadays: plants that grow to a maximum height of 8 in and are used mainly in colored flower-beds and tubs. The small varieties in particular are marketed on a vast scale as bedding plants in spring.

Callistephus chinensis 'Matsumoto Apricot,' China aster

Anyone with a liking for brightly colored bouquets can sow indoors in early spring. This is most successful if the seeds are barely covered and the germination temperature is

Callistephus chinensis 'Matsumoto Pink,' China aster

kept low at 59–64 °F. It is also best to grow on seedlings at low temperatures (around 59 °F). In those conditions, the plants will remain compact and are less likely to suffer from the numerous fungus diseases to which China asters are particularly susceptible. You should therefore make sure your sowing medium is disinfected (for instance, by steaming it or putting it in the oven for an hour or so – never mind the smell!).

Once the seedlings have come through their first test, they may be planted out in early May, preferably in full sun and in nutritive, loose, and relatively dry soil and in full sun. The low-growing varieties will then grow on without any problems, but the tall ones need supports or should be planted in places that are very sheltered from the wind. Never plant them in places where China asters were grown the previous year – that is just asking for the notorious wilt disease which causes stems and foliage to droop and subsequently wither.

Sowing directly outdoors after mid-April is possible, but in that case the plants will flower later. Some people sow in summer so that the plants will not come into flower in the greenhouse until the autumn or winter. Anyone still interested may choose from many hundreds of cultivars. Many new varieties are marketed every year.

Callisthephus chinensis 'Lilliput Scarlet' is grown largely for cutting. The stems, which grow to about 18 in tall, are somewhat short for that purpose. The advantage is that they are sturdy and do not need supporting. 'Lilliput Scarlet,' however, is highly susceptible to wilt.

The Matsumoto Series includes the currently most popular flowers for cutting purposes. They are grown on a commercially huge scale and cultivation techniques make early and late flowering possible. The flowering season for China asters is determined by the number of hours of daylight. The seeds are also available to private customers. Sow them directly in the garden in April–May to provide colorful bouquets of autumn flowers. If you sow indoors earlier in the year, these summer asters will flower from early August.

Callistephus chinensis 'Matsumoto Pink-tipped White,' China aster

Callistephus chinensis 'Matsumoto Salmon,' China aster

The stems grow to about 28 in and need supporting, so that they will still be upright after a thunderstorm. Like autumn asters, summer asters are sometimes cultivated in wide-mesh netting sold specially for this purpose. It is suspended over the aster bed at an appropriate height, and the plants subsequently grow up through it.

China asters, including the Matsumoto Series, are grown in a huge range of colors. There are white, deep red, blue, pale yellow varieties, as well as the following cultivars illustrated on these pages: *Callistephus chinensis* 'Matsumoto Apricot,' *Callistephus chinensis* 'Matsumoto Pink' (pale pink), *Callistephus chinensis* 'Matsumoto Pink-tipped White,' and *Callistephus chinensis* 'Matsumoto Salmon,' just a trifle darker than 'Matsumoto Pink.'

[3–4] 4-5

Campanula speculum-veneris

See *Legousia speculum-veneris.*

Cannabis sativa

HEMP

The narcotic resin marijuana or hashish is made from the tips of hemp. The plant is also important in rope production and can be used for paper-making. It forms a splendid windbreak, and female plants produce excellent birdseed. Hemp, furthermore, is a magnificent plant with decorative palmate foliage on long, sturdy stems, which may grow to a height of over 6–10 ft in the case of some varieties. The flowers are inconspicuous, but attract a lot of bees. In autumn, the female plants produce large, almost round seeds

Cannabis sativa, hemp

which are highly popular among finches, including green finches, chaffinches, and goldfinches, as well as great tits.

If you are unable to acquire seeds, pet shops selling hemp seed will provide a solution. Sow indoors in March–April or directly in the garden in April–May. The plants need nutritive soil to achieve their maximum height and most beautiful appearance.

[3–4] 4-5

Capsicum annuum

ORNAMENTAL PEPPER

Ornamental peppers make their appearance at florists in June. Most people buy these low-growing plants with their small, colorful peppers as indoor plants, but they also do well as container plants in warm and sheltered positions out-of-doors. Apart from needing a warm position, ornamental peppers make few demands. You may even sow them indoors in February–March. The ideal temperature for germination is around 70 °F. Grow the plants on at a lower temperature and put them out-of-doors in pots or other containers early in June. New little peppers are produced continually and, depending on the variety, ultimately turn red, orange, yellow, or cream.

[2–3]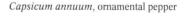

Capsicum annuum, ornamental pepper

Carthamus tinctorius

SAFFLOWER

In many regions, safflower is one of the principal crops. The plant is also known as the paint thistle because of the dyes that may be produced from it. It has been used as a medicinal herb since antiquity. Its seeds contain a useful oil and have proved to be popular among birds. In flower gardens, safflower is grown mainly for cutting and drying but, in more natural gardens, it may also brighten up a wild-flower border.

Safflowers grow about 39 in tall and have thistle-like foliage that is also somewhat prickly. Varieties for cut-flower cultivation are less prickly. The flower heads are 1 ³/₈ in wide and change from orange-yellow to orange to orange-red. They flower between June and September.

The safflower forms a taproot and likes to grow in a warm spot, preferably in full sun. It tolerates any soil provided it is not wet, but consumes a lot of nutrients and therefore prefers loose, sandy clay. Sow directly, near the surface, in April–May. Transplanting it causes growth defects.

Numerous cultivars have been developed from the original species, which grows naturally in western Asia. Special attention was devoted to the sturdiness of the plants and to eliminating the prickliness of the foliage.

Carthamus tinctorius 'Orange Grenade' has orange to reddish-orange flowers. The plant grows about 32 in tall. *Carthamus tinctorius* 'White Grenade' has the same shape, but bears pale yellow flowers with lemon-yellow streaks. Cut flowers are harvested when the first flowers open. If you want dried flowers, you should wait a little longer until flowering is at its peak but the plant still has some buds. In view of the large size of the flower heads, they should be dried quickly and airily to prevent the growth of mold.

4-5

Catharanthus roseus

ROSE PERIWINKLE

Plants that were at one time always kept indoors are increasingly seen out-of-doors nowadays. They include rose periwinkle, a warmth-loving plant from Madagascar, which is marketed on an ever-increasing scale. It has a spreading habit and may cover whole areas of flower-beds. Even so, it was the hanging basket boom that led to the popularity of the rose periwinkle. In England, it had long been used for hanging baskets, and

Carthamus tinctorius 'Orange Grenade,' safflower

Carthamus tinctorius 'White Grenade,' safflower

Catharanthus roseus, rose periwinkle

Celosia spicata, fireweed

when the fashion spread to the continent, the rose periwinkle hitched a lift along with it. In The Netherlands, however, the climate is rather less favorable, and the basket should be hung in a warm and sheltered position to achieve really good results. *Catharanthus* tolerates drought quite well, a great advantage in hanging baskets, which dry out so very quickly.

Improvers often do their best nowadays to cultivate varieties that can withstand the changeable conditions in western-European summers and the *Catharanthus roseus* Cooler Series provides a good example of their efforts.

Celosia spicata

FIREWEED

This wild plant's common name "fireweed" is highly appropriate since its seeds germinate only in places where a fire has raged. The photograph was taken in one such place in Indonesia. Its leaves are narrower than those of the more familiar *Celosia argentea*, commonly known as "cockscomb" in The Netherlands. According to some, they both belong to the same species: *argentea*. Seed merchants, however, have recently been marketing cultivars of *Celosia spicata*, and these are far more restrained than the brightly colored cockscombs.

Celosia spicata 'Flamingo Purple' closely resembles the flower in the illustration. The slender plant grows about 39 in tall, but does not flower until five months after it was sown. There are also cultivars which flower after as little as three months, such as *Celosia spicata* 'Flamingo Feather' and *Celosia spicata* 'Xantippe.' Seeds of those two are available from specialized seed merchants. The plumed flower heads are very suitable for drying.

Sow indoors in February–March and do not cover the seeds, as they need light for germination. The seeds germinate best at temperatures above 68 °F. The seedlings like moisture and warmth. They should not be put out-of-doors until the end of May, after they have been hardened off; they may begin to flower from June onwards.

[2–3]

Centaurea americana 'Aloha'

Centaurea americana 'Aloha Blanca'

Centaurea americana

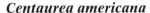

As it grows to 5 ft tall, we might call this plant a giant cornflower. It grows naturally in the southern regions of the United States, but it is fully hardy nonetheless. Even so, it does not survive the winter, simply because it is a genuine annual plant. Even if sown early, the plant will not flower until the end of July. To enable the stems to be marketed as cut flowers earlier in the year, the species is sown early at a germination temperature of about 64 °F and grown on in greenhouses.

For private gardeners, outdoor cultivation is the sole option. It is best to sow where the plant is to flower, in loose soil and a warm and sunny position. It is important to sow thinly, because the plants grow bushy as well as tall. They are ideal for background planting in a natural border or in a flower-bed where they can be picked.

Centaurea americana 'Aloha' bears violet-pink ray florets in heads that are about 6 in wide. The flowers of *Centaurea americana* 'Aloha Blanca' are white, but equally wide.

4–5

Centaurea cyanus

CORNFLOWER

It is not so long ago that fields of corn and other crops were veiled in a haze of blue, with cornflowers reflecting the light of blue skies. As a result of improved methods of seed cleaning and the use of herbicides to combat "weeds," those days are long past. There is hardly a cornflower to be seen in any of our fields these days. In the past, cornflowers grew as annuals, but usually germinated in autumn. In winter, the plants developed taproots with a compact tuft of foliage and then grew strongly the following spring.

In ornamental gardens, we might just as well sow in spring. The seeds are sown directly in the spot where they are to flower, as the seedlings soon develop taproots and dislike being transplanted. Cornflowers are without a doubt one of the easiest annuals to sow, and even germinate in hopelessly dry soil. They are quite undemanding as far as soil type is concerned, but will not do well in permanently wet earth. They like a light and preferably sunny position. It is best to provide a little support in the form of plants with

Centaurea cyanus, field of cornflowers

Centaurea cyanus, cornflower

somewhat lax growth – like a cornfield, these will keep the cornflowers upright.

The plants come into flower quite early, in mid-June, and continue well into August. They produce seed that is easy to harvest.

The single-flowered, wild species is rarely seen in gardens. It has about eight trumpet-shaped ray florets. The cultivated forms are nearly all double, and therefore have many more little trumpets reaching right into the center. They are sometimes blue, but more frequently violet, lilac, pink, red, purple, or white. Some are even bicolored. Whereas the species itself usually grows to about 24 in tall, there are now also dwarf varieties that, at a height of 12 in, fit nicely into pots and give color to entire flower-beds. *Centaurea cyanus* 'Baby Pink' is one of them and has pale pink flowers. There are also taller species which were developed specially for the cut-flower market.

Centaurea cyanus 'Black Boy' is sometimes called the black cornflower because of the deep, aubergine color of its flowers. It grows

Centaurea cyanus 'Baby Pink,' cornflower

Centaurea cyanus 'Black Boy,' black cornflower

to about 32 in tall. *Centaurea cyanus* 'Frosted Queen' is a mixture, with bicolored flowers that have a lighter edge at the tips of the florets. In addition to the purple and lavender-blue species in the phtograph, there are variations with pink, cherry red, and whitish pink basic colors. On average, the plant grows 32 in tall. *Centaurea cyanus* 'Snowman' is a pure white-flowered corn-flower that grows to about 32 in in height and

Centaurea cyanus 'Frosted Queen,' cornflower

Centaurea cyanus 'Snowman,' cornflower

is very suitable for cutting. All cornflowers, however cultivated, attract a lot of bees.

4–5 8–9

Centradenia inaequilateralis

Only the cultivar *Centradenia inaequilateralis* 'Cascade' is on sale in The Netherlands. Growers take cuttings in autumn or winter. They take root easily, but do not develop rapidly. Flowering plants appear on the market in mid-May, nearly always in hanging baskets. *Centradenia* cannot tolerate temperatures below 45 °F and therefore should

Centradenia inaequilateralis 'Cascade'

not be put out-of-doors until June. Then plant it in a sunny and sheltered position. The plant's trailing habit, rich ramification, and dense, bronze-green foliage show up particularly well in containers and hanging baskets. It is best to plant it in a clayey soil mix and add liquid fertilizer from time to time to enable the plant to go on flowering longer and more profusely.

Several flowerings succeed one another from May until well into July, and a final flowering may be expected in late summer. Cuttings may be taken in late summer and overwintered in a light, cool position – but above 45 °F. Mostly, however, people buy new plants in spring.

Cerinthe major

Cerinthe major has never become a popular garden plant although it has a lot to offer. Bluish-green leaves coated with a thin layer of wax grow on stems over 20 in tall. Handsome little tubular flowers in aubergine and pale yellow appear at the tips of stems in June and July. They grow to about 1¼ in in length and attract bees and bumblebees. Through-

out the flowering season, new bracts are added continually at the top, which bends over gracefully under their weight. Add to that the ease of cultivation and you might expect a tale of genuine success, but this failed to materialize until the blue cultivated variety appeared on the scene. *Cerinthe major* 'Purpurascens,' the blue-leafed variety, quickly became popular among trend-setting gardeners. Everyone wanted the plant with tips that looked as if they had been dipped in blue poster paint. Besides 'Purpurascens,' the cultivars *Cerinthe major* 'Atropurpurea,' and

Cerinthe major

Cerinthe major 'Purpurascens'

Chaenorhinum organifolium 'Blue Dream'

Chaenorhinum origanifolium

The compact growth and abundant flowers of this rock plant from southern Europe have now made it one of the most rewarding plants for containers and hanging baskets on balconies and patios. On closer inspection, the small violet flowers turn out to be striped and have a yellow and white spot in their throats. They are like snapdragons without lips and the plant is, in fact, closely related to the small toadflax (*Chaenorhinum minus*) that is also native to The Netherlands and southern counties of England. Its scientific name is derived from Greek: *"chaino"* means gape and *"rhis"* means "muzzle." In botanical manuals, however, the generic name is spelt variously as *Chaenorrhinum* or *Chaenarrhinum*. The seed of *Chaenorhinum origanifolium* 'Blue Dream' rarely features in any catalogue, but you might also find it under *Chaenorhinum glareosum* 'Blue Dream.' Even so, you need not do without the plant, as it is cultivated on a vast scale. Commercial growers sow it as early as January to enable them to market sturdy, flowering plants by the end of May.

Plant them in the garden in very well-drained soil and in the sunniest spot you have available. When grown in pots, they do better in partial shade so that the soil does not dry out too quickly.

Chamaemelum inodorum

See *Tripleurospermum inodorum.*

Chenopodium foliosum 'Strawberry Sticks'

Cerinthe major 'Kiwi Blue' are being introduced for comparable blue cerinthes. If compared with the species, they differ only in the color of the foliage and of the flowers, which in the case of 'Purpurascens' are not clearly bicolored, but a somewhat boring shade of purple aubergine. The value of the plant lies in the opportunity for combining it with other plants. In view of disappointing results, most growers no longer recommend it as a container plant. Wherever I saw some yellowed specimens in pots, they had always been placed in full sun. A position in the ground is right for a species which grows naturally around the Mediterranean; when they are grown in pots, they are in danger of drying out, and I suspect that the plant fails to recover if the need to water it is overlooked from time to time. It is therefore preferable not to stand a pot containing *Cerinthe* in the hot midday sun. Sow outdoors on the surface of the place where it is to flower.

4–5

Chamomilla recutita

See *Matricaria recutita*.

Cheiranthus × allionii

See *Erysimum × allionii*.

Chenopodium foliosum

RED STRAWBERRY SPINACH

The small flowers of the red *Chenopodium foliosum* or 'strawberry spinach' are packed closely in the leaf axils. After flowering, the tepals of each of the minuscule fruits swell up. Together, they form a false fruit containing numerous seeds. The false fruits are edible, but not really tasty to us. Birds eat and disseminate them.

Chenopodium foliosum originally grew in southern Europe, as well as in North Africa and adjoining parts of Asia. The plant likes warmth, calcium, and nutrients. It was not native to The Netherlands, but was planted in gardens because of its edible leaves, which are cooked like spinach. From such gardens, the plant established itself here and there in the countryside, but is found mainly in the calcareous sand dunes along the Dutch coast. The ground there warms up rapidly and the winters are less severe than they are further inland.

Chenopodium foliosum is very easy to grow as an ornamental plant. Sow directly outdoors from the end of March. It takes three to four months for the false fruits to develop, but the process can be brought forward by sowing indoors earlier in the year.

It is a suitable plant for ornamental kitchen gardens, natural borders, and containers. The plant grows about 16 in tall but may become quite bushy.

Chenopodium foliosum 'Strawberry Sticks' is the cultivar that is usually available. The species *Chenopodium capitatum* is very similar.

[2–3] 3–5 🌱 ▼

Chrysanthemum carinatum 'Cockarde,' painted daisy

Chenopodium virgantem

See *Chenopodium foliosum*.

Chrysanthemum carinatum

PAINTED DAISY

The flowers of most cultivars of *Chrysanthemum carinatum* resemble colorful parasols with exuberant stripes. You need courage to plant them in a garden, but anyone bold enough to do so will be rewarded by an old-fashioned atmosphere of unembarrassed splendour.

The species itself stems from North Africa and has white flowers with a yellow ring in the center. The cultivars come in all manner of shades of white, yellow, pink, and red in rings round the center of the flower. The plants themselves grow rapidly and without any problems. They grow about 20 in tall and may flower about ten weeks after they were sown. It makes sense to pinch out the growing tips of young plants to encourage bushier growth.

The seedlings will tolerate light frost, so they may be sown in autumn. Sowing in early spring, however, is more reliable, and the plants may still come into flower as early as June. Picking the flowers may also extend the flowering season until well into September.

Chrysanthemum carinatum 'Cockarde' creates a white impression, with red and yellow zones in the center. *Chrysanthemum carinatum* 'Court Jesters' is a cheerfully multicolored mixture, as is *Chrysanthemum carinatum* 'Rainbow Mixture.'

[2-5]

Chrysanthemum coronarium

When thinking about plants for our garden, we often concentrate too much on their flowers. *Chrysanthemum coronarium* shows that foliage is at least as important to the overall effect. This annual has beautiful feathery, divided leaves. It originally came from southern Europe, where it grows about 32 in tall. Many of the garden varieties derived from it are shorter. They are sturdy, look good even in wet summers, and flower from July to October. Sow indoors in March–April, or outdoors in April–May.

Chrysanthemum coronarium 'Golden Gem' remains compact, grows up to 20 in tall and bears semi-double, yellow-ochre flowers, 2 in wide. *Chrysanthemum coronarium* 'Primrose Gem' is the same size, but the semi-double flowers are pale yellow with deep yellow centers.

[3-4] 4-5

Chrysanthemum maritimum ssp. inodorum

See *Tripleurospermum inodorum*.

Chrysanthemum multicaule

See *Coleostephus myconis*.

Chrysanthemum paludosum

See *Leucanthemum paludosum*.

Chrysanthemum parthenium

See *Tanacetum parthenium*.

Chrysanthemum segetum

CORN MARIGOLD

At one time, when the fieds turned golden, it was not only due to the golden-yellow ears of corn, but also to the large quantities of deep yellow corn marigolds growing between them. The species originally came from southern Europe and North Africa, but for

Chrysanthemum coronarium

Chrysanthemum segetum, corn marigold

Cladanthus arabicus

Clarkia pulchella 'Snowflake'

centuries it has been an indigenous field plant in The Netherlands, where it grows in light, sandy soil with a lime deficiency but not excessively acid. It is possible that people brought the plant further north for use as a dye. Nowadays, its cultivated forms are particularly popular as easily grown garden plants. Corn marigolds grow about 20 in tall. *Chrysanthemum segetum* 'Eastern Star' bears pale yellow flowers with brown centers; *Chrysanthemum segetum* 'Eldorado' bears yellow flowers with rich-brown centers; *Chrysanthemum segetum* 'German Flag' bears red flowers with a broad yellow zone round the dark-brown centers.

3–5

Chrysanthemum tricolor

See *Chrysanthemum carinatum*.

Cineraria maritima

See *Senecio cineraria*.

Cladanthus arabicus

The large flowers – 2 in wide – and coral-like, divided foliage of *Cladanthus* always attract enquiring glances. It is one of the easiest annuals to grow, and yet is rarely seen, despite the fact that flowering continues unceasingly from early July until far into autumn. Several

new shoots develop underneath each flower, and they, in turn, bear new flowers. The species originally came from southern Europe and North Africa. It likes a warm and sunny position in loose, nutritive garden soil, but will also tolerate less favorable conditions. The plants spread nicely to form tufts of greenery about 20 in high. They impart an agreeable scent when touched. Sow indoors in March–April, or directly outdoors in April–May.

[3–4] 4–5

Clarkia pulchella

The small flowers of clarkias have a very remarkable shape which looks as if paper-cutting artists have been at work on them with a small pair of scissors. The flowers appear between July and September above bluish-green, lance-shaped leaves on plants approximately 16 in tall. The colors are often pale: white, pale pink, and lavender, but sometimes a brighter, crimson pink. *Clarkia pulchella* 'Snowflake' has white flowers.
Sow directly in a sunny spot in the garden in early spring. The seedlings dislike being transplanted. Sowing in relatively dry soil in August–September is also possible, as the species originally came from the cooler regions of the United States (including the Rocky Mountains).

3–4 8–9

Cleome hassleriana

SPIDER FLOWER

This is certainly one of the most striking of all annuals. They branch widely and, at a height of 4 ft, tower above most other annuals. The flower heads, which appear between July and October, are huge – no less than 8 in in section and longer than they are wide. They also stretch in the course of flowering. Oblong seedpods are formed at their lower end, and – curiously – grow sideways on very thin stems. The stamens protrude so far that they resemble cat's whiskers or spider's legs. Both the flowers and the foliage are intensely fragrant.

Although the stems are sturdy, they may begin to lean over under the weight of the entire plant and are sometimes given a support. If very thin bamboo canes are used for the purpose, they will be quite invisible after a while. Personally, though, I think a lop-sided spider flower looks particularly charming in a border. Palmate leaves grow on spiny leafstalks.

It is, perhaps, because of those spines that the spider flower is often called *Cleome spinosa*, which is, in fact, a very similar species from South America. This ran wild in the tropics and may have contributed to the development of the cultivated varieties. The main difference between them is the color of the flowers.

The popularity of the Queen Series is presumably due to its restrained colors, which go well with other shades, and its trouble-free growth. *Cleome hassleriana* 'Cerise Queen' bears cherry-red flowers; *Cleome hassleriana* 'Pink Queen' has pale pink ones; those of *Cleome hassleriana* 'Violet Queen' are old rose with an intense shade of crimson; and those of *Cleome hassleriana* 'White Queen' are snowy white.

It is best to sow spider flowers indoors and to plant them out at intervals of about 20 in after mid-May. They like light but nutritive and humus-rich soil. In poor soil, liquid fertilizer may be given when the flowers first appear, to stimulate a more abundant and longer-lasting

Cleome hassleriana 'Pink Queen,' spider flower

Cleome hassleriana 'Pink Queen,' spider flower

Cleome hassleriana 'Violet Queen,' spider flower

Cleome hassleriana 'White Queen,' spider flower

Cleome hassleriana 'White Queen,' spider flower

flowering season. The plants like warmth and sun and prefer to be sheltered from the wind. They are strong, though, and will also tolerate less favorable circumstances.

[3–4] 5

Clitoria ternatea

The respectable botanist Linnaeus thought the flower of this plant from south-east Asia resembled a clitoris and named the genus *Clitoria*. The photograph was taken on the island of Ternate in the Moluccas. It was there that botanists discovered the climber and named it after the island (and not after the tripartite leaves). In cooler climates, the plant is best known as a perennial climber for heated winter gardens. It cannot tolerate temperatures below 50 °F. More and more frequently, however, it is also treated as an annual and sown indoors early in the year. From June onwards, the plants may be put out-of-doors in a container or planted directly in the garden against a trellis. In autumn, they die off or are taken indoors.

The species and cultivars are rarely on sale and the seed is expensive. *Clitoria ternatea* 'Blue Sails' has double, purple flowers; those of *Clitoria ternatea* 'Ultra Marine' are blue.

[2–3] 🌱 ▼

Cobaea scandens

CUP-AND-SAUCER VINE

Although the cup-and-saucer vine appeals greatly to the imagination, it is rarely to be seen in gardens. The seeds of this perennial climber from the mountains of Mexico should be sown indoors as early as February–March. Even so, it will not start flowering until July, and the plants do not really grow much until August–September. With vines rising from the leaf base, they climb to a considerable height and bear a profusion of flowers, 2 in wide. The flowers develop from green-tinged, cream-colored buds. They are light at first and exude a somewhat musky scent. It is not until they gradually change

Clitoria ternatea

Cobaea scandens 'Blue,' cup-and-saucer vine

Cobaea scandens 'Blue,' cup-and-saucer vine

Cobaea scandens 'Blue,' cup-and-saucer vine

color and turn an increasingly deep shade of violet that the fragrance changes to that of honey.

In our part of the world, the cup-and-saucer vine is nearly always grown as an annual. Keep the seedlings moist, but not wet, while they are indoors. After the last frost, they should be planted directly in the garden next to a trellis, pergola, or other support, or in a large container with a support next to it. If planted in the ground, the plant will rarely need extra food and water (except in the poorest of well-drained soils). If the plant is grown in a pot or other container, success will depend on the provision of extra food and a lot of water during the growing period. In the absence of an upright support, the cup-and-saucer vine will cover a large area of the garden with creeping shoots. The flowers will then rise up out of that green mat.

Cobaea scandens 'Blue' is the normal, violet-flowered species; *Cobaea scandens* 'Alba' bears white bell-shaped flowers with green calyces.

[2-3] 🌼 ▼ ⚘

Coleostephus multicaulis

See *Coleostephus myconis.*

Coleostephus myconis

The compact, mat-forming habit of *Coleostephus* makes it highly suitable as an annual for rockeries, flower-beds, edges of paths and patios, and for cultivation in containers. A species from southern Europe and North Africa, it likes warmth and sunlight, and its somewhat succulent, bluish-green foliage tolerates such conditions very well.

Coleostephus myconis 'Sunlight'

Coleostephus myconis 'Gerim'

Collinsia grandiflora

Coleus Blumei-hybrids

See *Solenostemon scutellarioides.*

Collinsia grandiflora

You might feel that the name *Collinsia grandiflora* is somewhat misleading. *Grandiflora* means "with large flowers" – and that for a species with flowers ¹/₂ in wide, on stems which are only 12 in high! It is therefore a very tenuous little plant that comes into its own when grown in large drifts in a natural-looking garden. It is also a suitable container plant for anyone with a liking for sophistication.

The species grows naturally in the western regions of North America, from California in the south right up to British Columbia in Canada. It sows itself there in late summer, and the seedlings are fully hardy. In Europe, it is therefore possible to sow the seeds directly in the garden either in the autumn or in early spring. The plants like partial shade – although they can tolerate hot sunlight – and moisture-retentive, humus-rich soil. They flower from June to September, and their flowering season may be extended by repeated sowing. *Collinsia* also attracts many bees.

[3–6] 9

Commelina coelestis

See *Commelina tuberosa.*

The plants are available from May onwards. If you sow directly outdoors, you will see the first flowers by the end of June and will be able to enjoy the ³/₄-in wide flowers until far into September. They grow to about 8 in above the ground.

Coleostephus myconis 'Gerim' is very compact and therefore of particular interest to commercial growers. These plants are on sale in May and June. *Coleostephus myconis* 'Moonlight' is popular among gardeners because of its pale-yellow flowers, which go well with other colors. *Coleostephus myconis* 'Sunlight' is the egg-yellow counterpart of 'Moonlight.'

4-5

Commelina tuberosa

DAY FLOWER

Only those who are at home in the daytime can enjoy *Commelina*. The flowers, $^3/_4$ in wide, open in the course of the morning and close forever at about 4 o'clock in the afternoon. Next day, a fresh batch of buds open to display azure flowers, each with three petals. The name *tuberosa* refers to the tubers, which may be overwintered in a frost-free place. Commelina is therefore really a perennial, but commercial growers increasingly market it as an annual. Sowing them yourself is also possible. Do this early (in March–April), as the plants need about four months to come into flower. They grow to about 20 in in height and, in spite of that, are quite suitable for cultivating as container plants in large pots.

[3–4]

Commelina tuberosa

Consolida ajacis

GARDEN LARKSPUR

Larkspurs are among the easiest annuals to grow, provided you sow them directly in the garden since the seedlings cannot be transplanted. Sow early in the year and cover the seed with soil. They germinate in the dark and like cool and moist soil. The ideal germination temperature is about 50 °F. The best months for sowing are therefore September, October, March, and April. If the seeds are sown later on in the spring, the results are often disappointing. Once planted in a garden with loose soil, the plants usually return automatically year after year whenever they find an open spot in which to germinate – even if it is just a crack in between paving stones! Seedlings which germinated in autumn and survived the winter will grow into compact and sturdy plants and flower from June until well into August. Plants grown from a spring sowing of seed sown in spring will flower a little later, from July until September.

The wild larkspurs, which grow naturally in southern Europe, formed the starting-point for many different cultivars with single or double flowers in a large variety of colors. There are dwarf varieties less than 12 in tall. *Consolida ajacis* 'Dwarf Hyacinth-flowered' bears white, cherry-red, or pink to violet double flowers. *Consolida ajacis* 'Messenger White' grows up to 36 in and is cultivated specifically for snowy-white cut flowers. There are also mixtures producing plants that may grow up to 4 ft tall.

3–4 9–10

Consolida ajacis, larkspur

Consolida ajacis 'Messenger White,' larkspur

Consolida regalis 'Blue Cloud,' wild larkspur

Consolida regalis, wild larkspur

Consolida ambigua

See *Consolida ajacis.*

Consolida regalis

WILD LARKSPUR

Like the garden larkspur, the wild larkspur is sown directly in the garden in early spring or in the autumn. The seedlings can tolerate an average winter. In spring, they will grow into branching, sturdy plants and flower from June onwards. Cover the seeds with some soil as they germinate in the dark.

Wild larkspur grew naturally in The Netherlands at one time, but nowadays the plant is rarely to be found. Its principal distribution is currently in central and eastern Europe. The species was discovered long ago as a suitable garden plant and a source of cut flowers and many cultivated varieties were developed. Most of them are grown for the cut-flower

Consolida regalis 'Frosted Sky,' wild larkspur

Consolida regalis 'Qis Dark Blue,' wild larkspur

market. *Consolida regalis* 'Blue Cloud' is grown as a filler for bouquets. This is a pity, as it is one of the most rewarding larkspurs, both for natural borders and for vases. The stems, 39 in tall, branch widely so that the plant has a considerable spread and yet retains its airy appearance. It is therefore possible for it to play a leading role as a solitary cut flower – without other flowers in the vase. They are also satisfactory for drying, as the small bright-blue flowers, $3/4$ in wide, keep their color well.

Consolida regalis 'Frosted Sky' is outstanding because of its remarkable bicolored flowers with white centers that gradually blend with poster-paint-blue borders. This delightful flowering plant grows about 39 in tall, branches out gracefully, and is suitable for vases as well as for drying.

Consolida regalis 'Qis Dark Blue' and *Consolida regalis* 'Qis Rose' are meant for the commercial cut-flower market. The plants form straight, upright shoots about 36 in tall. The double flowers are dark blue and rose

Consolida regalis 'Qis Rose,' wild larkspur

pink, respectively. Other colors in this series include crimson, pale blue, pale pink, lilac, and white.

3–4 9–10

Convolvulus mauritanicus

See *Convolvulus sabatius*.

Convolvulus minor

See *Convolvulus tricolor*.

Convolvulus sabatius

Convolvulus sabatius is one of the most rewarding plants for containers and hanging baskets. Its greyish-green foliage grows on stems that are over 20 in long. They are lax, barely raise themselves up and creep across the ground. A single plant can cover over a $10^3/_4$ sq ft of soil. Where the stems fail to find a support, they will hang down, and the species has therefore become especially popular as a hanging plant, partly because the mauve flowers and greyish-green foliage have subdued colors. Other plants with blue, yellow, or orange flowers go well with them. The plants are on sale in pots or, in the case of larger plants, in hanging pots by mid-May. Once they have been transplanted into containers or hanging baskets, they may be taken out-of-doors after the last frost. They grow well in a poor or normal soil mix. Never

Convolvulus sabatius

Convolvulus tricolor, dwarf morning glory

Convolvulus tricolor 'Blue Flash,' dwarf morning glory

allow the soil to dry out entirely, because the buds will then shrivel up and part of the foliage will drop off. *Convolvulus* will, however, recover and flower right into autumn. It may be overwintered in a light and frost-free position. It is possible to grow the plant from seed (outdoors, from April), but the seed is rarely available.

Convolvulus tricolor

DWARF MORNING GLORY

Only the white-flowered convolvulus is bicolored in white and yellow. The other cultivars have three or more colors, hence the name. The center of the flower is always yellow. It is surrounded by a white zone, followed by a different color. The borders of *Convolvulus tricolor* 'White Ensign' are also white; *Convolvulus tricolor* 'Royal Ensign' has deep-blue border; *Convolvulus tricolor* 'Rose Ensign' has an outer border in two

87

shades of pink; and the border of *Convolvulus tricolor* 'Red Ensign' is a wonderful shade of crimson. *Convolvulus tricolor* 'Blue Tilt' and *Convolvulus tricolor* 'Bue Flash' scarcely differ from each other; both of them have a purplish-blue border.

Unlike many other species of convolvulus, *Convolvulus tricolor* is not a climber. The *tricolor* cultivars grow to a maximum height of about 10–16 in. New flowers are formed daily between July and September, but they open fully only when the sun is out. They are 1½ in wide and their bright colors make them particularly striking. They also attract bees, hover flies, and butterflies. Plant *Convolvulus tricolor* in a sunny position, preferably in poor soil, where leaf development is inhibited in favor of flowers.

Sow indoors in February–March, or out-of-doors between April and June. Thin the seedlings to 10 in apart.

[2–3] 4–6

Convolvulus tricolor 'Blue Tilt,' dwarf morning glory

Coreopsis grandiflora 'Early Sunrise,' tickseed

Coreopsis grandiflora

TICKSEED

Although this is actually a short-lived perennial from the southern states of the US, the species is thought of as an annual and is almost exclusively cultivated as such. Commercial growers start working on it by the end of January and extend the short daylight hours with artificial light so that they can market flowering plants by mid-May. It is better for private gardeners to wait until March before sowing indoors, or until April–May, when they can sow directly outdoors. Preferably choose a spot with loose, poor soil in full sunlight, because that is where the plants do best. Excessive amounts of fertilizer will lead to lax growth, after which the stems are inclined to bend and the plant loses its nice compact shape. If sown in April, the plants are likely to flower from July until well into October. They are much appreciated by butterflies and other insects, which are even attracted in large numbers by the semi-double cultivar *Coreopsis grandi-*

Coriandrum sativum, coriander

flora 'Early Sunrise.' That early-flowering cultivar, 24 in tall, was awarded the Fleuroselect Gold Medal in 1989.

[3] 4–5

Coreopsis ferulifolia

See *Bidens ferulifolia*

Coriandrum sativum

CORIANDER

Apart from being greatly appreciated as a culinary spice, coriander has many other uses as a medicine, an aromatic herb, and a raw material for cosmetics. The dried seeds are particularly useful. Coriander is also a magnificent garden plant, with delicate, finely divided foliage creating an aura of green. Above it, equally delicate whitish-pink umbels of flowers are borne between July and September. They exude a remarkable odor, sometimes described as a "bug smell." When the flowers are over, green and subsequently brown, almost round seeds are formed on the umbels. They may be harvested, dried, and preserved as a spice. It is also possible to cut off the flower heads while they are still green and use them as dried flowers. The species itself grows to about 20 in tall. For ornamental purposes, it is best to sow one of the cultivars such as *Coriandrum sativum* 'Bengal Giant,' which grows about 39 in tall and is more satisfactory for cutting and drying. Sow coriander directly in ordinary garden soil in a sunny or partially shaded position between March and May.

3–5

Cosmidium burridgeanum

See *Thelesperma burridgeanum.*

Cosmos atrosanguineus

CHOCOLATE COSMEA

Gardeners speak fondly of *Cosmos atrosanguineus*, now often referred to as "the black

Cosmos atrosanguineus, chocolate cosmea

cosmos." Everyone wants black cosmos in their garden, and some people display the kind of fanaticism characteristic of the bulb growers who have tried to find the black tulip for centuries. What is fortunately also true of black cosmos is the fact that it is not black at all. The flowers, over 1½ in wide, are the deepest possible shade of red, and smell – that is really true – of chocolate. They tower above the foliage on their long stems. The foliage is somewhat ordinary, and unevenly divided into leaflets, rather like those of elderberry.

Cosmos atrosanguineus originally came from Mexico and is not fully hardy in cooler climates. If grown as a potted plant, it may be overwintered indoors. The plants on sale here were propagated by cuttings or by division of the radical tubers. As soon as firms specializing in cuttings discover this "black gold," it will, without a doubt, be marketed on a massive scale.

Cosmos bipinnatus 'Dazzler,' cosmea

Cosmos bipinnatus

COSMEA

Cosmos is simply one of the most useful annuals for large borders. Some perfectionists think the colors are rather bright and the flowers too big, but since cosmeas with smaller flowers and more subdued colors have now appeared on the scene, it should be possible, even for these gardeners, to find suitable cultivars. People who like an exuberant profusion of flowers discovered them long ago: bright and cheerful colors above a sturdy tuft of finely divided, and therefore graceful foliage. The taller cosmeas grow to between 32 in and over 5 ft tall depending on circumstances, but they will be tallest in nutritive, moist soil in partial shade. They are eminently suitable for planting at the back of borders. The plants create an informal impression, produce splendid feathery foliage with very narrow leaflets, and allow the flowers to bend over gracefully from the background.

Cosmos bipinnatus 'Dazzler,' cosmea

Cosmos bipinnatus 'Purity,' cosmea

Cosmos bipinnatus 'Radiance,' cosmea

Cosmos bipinnatus 'Dazzler' bears flowers which are bright red when they open but fade to crimson after a few days. It is a magnificent plant.

Cosmos bipinnatus 'Purity' has pure white flowers and gracefully lax growth.

The flowers of *Cosmos bipinnatus* 'Radiance' has firmly overlapping petals (ray florets) so that the flower forms almost a perfect circle. The area round the yellow center is deep pink, with an encircling band of paler pink. The tall cosmeas are particularly suitable for vases.

Nowadays, there are also relatively low-growing cosmeas on the market. They grow about 20 in tall and are therefore also suitable for flower-beds. The low-growing cosmeas are available at garden centers in spring. The first cultivar to make an impression was *Cosmos bipinnatus* 'Sonata,' a white-flowered plant for flower-beds. It was awarded a gold medal by Fleuroselect in 1991. 'Sonata' was subsequently elevated to a series, and other colors are now available as well. The white-flow-

Cosmos bipinnatus 'Sonata Pink,' cosmea

Cosmos bipinnatus 'Sonata White,' cosmea

ered 'Sonata' is now called *Cosmos bipinnatus* 'Sonata White.' Other major compact cosmeas in this series include *Cosmos bipinnatus* 'Sonata Carmine' (bright crimson), *Cosmos bipinnatus* 'Sonata Pink,' and *Cosmos bipinnatus* 'Sonata Pink Blush' (pink with a rose-red ring surrounding the center). All compact cosmeas are suitable for large pots.

It is best to sow cosmeas indoors in March–April and to move the seedlings out-of-doors after the last frost. Alternatively, scatter the seed directly in the garden from the end of April. The plants do best in loose soil in a sunny position.

[3–4] 5

Cosmos sulphureus

YELLOW COSMEA

Yellow cosmeas originally came from slightly more southern regions of Latin America, not only from Mexico, where *Cosmos bipinnatus* grows naturally, but also from the warmer regions of Central America and the north of South America. It is consequently even more sensitive to cold and suffers more from cool, wet summers. Its cultivation is otherwise the same as that of the ordinary cosmea, certainly now that recent decades have seen the development of lovely cultivars which are better at withstanding cooler climates.

It is best to sow the seed indoors in March–April and not to put the plants out-of-doors in pots, containers, or directly in the ground until the end of May. They will then

Cosmos sulphureus, yellow cosmea

begin to flower by mid-July, but if you sow out-of-doors in May, the flowers will not appear until August.

The cultivars often grow up to 39 in tall, but dwarf varieties which grow no taller than about 10 in are also available. *Cosmos sulphureus* 'Bilbo' is one of those small ones and bears semi-double orange flowers. It is on sale as a flowering plant as early as mid-May.

The name "yellow cosmea" is misleading because most of the cultivars bear orange to reddish-orange flowers. They are about 1½ in wide. They naturally have about eight or nine petals, but there are also many semi-double cultivars on the market; *Cosmos sulphureus* 'Klondyke Sunny Red' is a good example. The variations in the color of yellow cosmeas shows up clearly: it varies from yellowish to reddish orange. The flowers of *Cosmos sulphureus* 'Diablo' are deep, flaming red.

Still, there are also truly "yellow" cosmeas. *Cosmos sulphureus* 'Crest Lemon' is a real

Cosmos sulphureus c.v., yellow cosmea

Cosmos sulphureus 'Crest Lemon,' yellow cosmea

beauty because of the magnificent lemon-yellow shade of the single flowers towering above the foliage. The plant does not grow more than 20 in tall; in spite of this, it provides magnificent cut flowers for vases. Unfortunately, 'Crest Lemon' is available only in small quantities.

[3-4] 5

Craspedia globosa

The spherical flowers of craspedias will enrich any bouquet, either fresh or dried. They appear at the top of 20–39-in tall stems which have a few leaves at the base only. Below them, there is a rosette of oblong leaves forming hairy channels. Drops or water roll across those hairs to the center of the plant. In the mountains of Australia, where these perennials grow naturally, they can do with some extra water at the roots. In cooler climates, however, the combination of moisture and wintry cold will

Cosmos sulphureus 'Klondyke Sunny Red,' yellow cosmea

Craspedia globosa 'Billy Buttons'

deliver a final blow to craspedias. They do not survive such winters, and are consequently cultivated as annuals.

It is essential to sow craspedias indoors early in the year, as it takes them almost six months to come into flower. Sow indoors in February–March, and then the first spherical flower heads will be ripe for picking by the end of July. Sowing later for a later harvest is also possible. The flower heads are about 1¼–1½ in in diameter. Put the plants out-of-doors in a warm, sunny position and in well-drained but moisture-retentive, and humus-rich soil from the end of May.

The principal cultivars hardly differ from one another. *Craspedia globosa* 'Billy Buttons' has one of the most popular English names for the species. *Craspedia gloriosa* 'Drumstick' is the cultivar that is most frequently available.

[2-3] 4

tubular flowers. They are red with a strongly contrasting white spot at the aubergine-colored mouth. The plant also shows up well in a large pot or other container on a patio. Don't put it out-of-doors until the end of May, as the cigar plant likes warmth. It also needs a lot of water – particularly in a sunny position – to compensate for the considerable amount of evaporation from the foliage. Although it is possible to take cuttings of the cigar plant in late summer, and to overwinter it indoors, it is definitely easier to grow it as an annual.

Sow indoors in March–April. The plants will be in flower after about three months, and flowering plants are also on sale by May. Don't put them out-of-doors until the end of May. It is also possible to sow directly in the garden by May, so that the plant will flower from August onwards. *Cuphea ignea* 'Coan' is a mixture of plants bearing brick-red and creamy white flowers. *Cuphea ignea* 'Dynamite' flowers early, bearing brick-red flowers. The plants are compact, growing up to 12 in tall.

[3–4]

Cuphea ignea 'Coan,' mixed

Cuphea lanceolata 'Firefly'

See *Cuphea × purpurea* 'Firefly.'

Cuphea lanceolata 'Purpurea'

This is a plant from another world. where anything is possible. Long, sticky stems up to 32 in tall produce reasonably normal foliage, but the strangest flowers imaginable are borne at the tips. Their basic color is crimson. Two petals point upwards, each one with a large spot in deepest purple. Only the veins are a little lighter. The plant flowers most profusely in a warm and sheltered position, but one that is not too sunny. Its mysterious nature shows up fully in partial shade, and its slender, vertical growth reinforces the atmosphere of science fiction.

[3–4] 4–5

Cuphea llavea var. *miniata* 'Firefly'

See *Cuphea × purpurea* 'Firefly.'

Cuphea miniata 'Firefly'

See *Cuphea × purpurea* 'Firefly.'

Cuphea pallida

The nomenclature of cupheas is a jungle, in which it is easy for an afficionado to get lost. There are not many groups of plants for which there are so many synonyms, and incorrect names abound. My own favorite is a plant that is not to be found in standard botanical works and for which not even primary suppliers can give an explanation. That does not make the plant any less beautiful, though. The stems grow in all directions and form an attractive bushy plant with innumerable small, wine-red flowers. They look lovely in a pot or hanging basket. Cuttings are taken as early as September to make it possible for flowering plants to be on sale in June. Once they are in flower, they will continue to bear more blooms, even after the first night frosts, finally dropping off to sleep only when the frosts become more severe.

Cuphea platycentra

See *Cuphea ignea.*

Cuphea pallida

Cuphea pallida

Cuphea lanceolata 'Purpurea'

Cuphea lanceolata 'Purpurea'

Cuphea pallida

Cuphea procumbens

Cuphea procumbens

Strangely enough, this species can be admired only in botanical gardens. Seed merchants will obviously not risk including this warmth-loving species in the selections marketed by them. Still, it is no more difficult to cultivate than other cupheas.

Sow indoors in March–April or outdoors in May. The plants develop rapidly and, if sown early, may start bearing their violet-pink flowers by June. They will go on flowering until October, so that can't be the reason for their exclusion either.

[3–4] 5

Cuphea × purpurea

The parent plants of this hybrid are *Cuphea lavea* and *Cuphea procumbens*. The most popular cultivar developed from the hybrid by improvers is *Cuphea × purpurea* 'Firefly,' an appropriate name for a plant with such bright-red flowers that, like fireflies, they light up a border from afar. Even in a pot, 'Firefly' will steal the show. The drawback to the bright color is the fact that they can be combined only with deep-red flowers. The cultivar grows to a maximum height of 12 in and may therefore also be used as a colored zone in a flower-bed.

[3–4] 4–5

Cynoglossum amabile

HOUND'S TONGUE

The small flowers are no more than $1/4$ in wide, and yet they manage to cover an entire section of a garden in an unforgettable blue haze. The color resembles that of forget-me-nots. As evening falls, the blue lights up as in a fairy-tale, causing the spectator to marvel and reflect. The species originally came from China, and is sometimes called a Chinese forget-me-not.

Several lovely cultivars have been developed from the species: *Cynoglossum amabile* 'Firmament' bears small sky-blue flowers and grows to about 16 in in height. *Cynoglossum amabile* 'Blue Shower' is of particular interest to flower arrangers. Its stems grow to over 24 in long with a mass of flowers in a slightly darker shade.

Cynoglossum will tolerate some frost and may therefore be sown out-of-doors from May onwards. The flowering season is relatively short, and it is therefore advisable to repeat sowing until well into June. The plants will flower from late June.

Cynoglossum amabile, hound's tongue

Cuphea ×*purpurea* 'Firefly'

Cynoglossum amabile 'Blue Shower,' hound's tongue

Cynoglossum amabile 'Firmament,' hound's tongue

Dahlia

DAHLIA

Many people will remember dahlias as long tubers that were kept in the cellar in a bed of peat dust waiting for spring. They were then planted out to provide colorful flowers in late summer. Fortunately, there are still devotees of this romantic way of enjoying dahlias, but there is no need for anyone to do without them if they no longer have a cellar or any-where else in the house where it is cool enough to prevent the tubers from drying out. The plants may also be grown from seeds or cuttings and commercial growers produce huge quantities of plants for flower-beds and containers by these methods.

Dahlia plants grown from seed will have de-veloped some tubers by the end of the season, and this also applies to some dahlias grown from cuttings. Some of the specialist firms, however, strike the cuttings in such a way that the plants will produce hardly any viable tubers, thus ensuring that you will be obliged to buy more dahlias next year.

Low-growing dahlias for pots and flower-beds are the principal kinds grown from seed or cuttings. Their ancestors include *Dahlia merckii* from the warm regions of Mexico. It never freezes there, so the plants – and this applies to all dahlias – do not tolerate a sin-gle degree of frost. The very first autumn night

Dahlia 'Bambi Red Orange,' dahlia

Dahlia 'Bambi White,' dahlia

frost causes the leaves and stems to turn black and die off immediately. It will then be time to remove the tubers of all tuberous plants from the soil. They will be protected briefly by the cushioning warmth of the soil, but will not tolerate any further frost.

None of this is of any concern to us in the case of dahlias grown as annuals: the plants turn mushy in autumn, safe in the knowledge that there will be fresh plants in spring. Do not plant them out-of-doors in a flower-bed until the risk of a night frost has been reduced to a minimum, say, by the end of May. You may chance it a little earlier if they are in contain-ers, in which case you can always bring them indoors again if there is any threat of a frost.

It is quite possible to sow dahlias yourself, and packets of seed are on sale at most garden cen-

Dahlia 'Dahlietta Emily,' dahlia

Dahlia 'Dahlietta Linda,' dahlia

Dahlia 'Bambi Light Pink,' dahlia

Dahlia 'Dahlstar Amazone,' dahlia

ters. It is best to sow them indoors at room temperature in March. Cover the seeds with a thin layer of sand or fine grit so that they make proper contact with the soil and do not dry up. The seedlings should be pricked out early on to allow their roots to develop freely. You should give them some space as soon as the second pair of leaves has developed. The pricked-out seedlings should be in a light position – for instance, on a windowsill – but it should be airy (to prevent mildew) and not too warm, in order to prevent etiolation. A greenhouse or frame at a temperature of 50–59 °F is ideal, as it will provide the young dahlias with the large amount of light that they need. Opening the windows increasingly wide in May will make it easy to harden them off. The soil should never be allowed to dry out. Commercial growers sow by the end of January to enable them to market flowering plants

Dahlia 'Dahlstar Maroon,' dahlia

Dahlia 'Dahlstar Scarlet,' dahlia

Dahlia 'Dahlietta Emily' belongs to the old Dahlietta Series, with flowers that are strikingly large for small bedding plants. They are propagated by cuttings. The series is available in many colors, including wine red, orange, yellow, and white. 'Emily' has pale pink flowers; and those of *Dahlia* 'Dahlietta Linda' are apricot-colored. *Dahlia* 'Amazone' is also included in the Dahlstar Series, but differs so much from it that it was proposed as a new introduction, outside the series, for 1999. The flowers of this 12 in tall plant are semi-double. The advantage is that it is possible to admire the yellow center surrounded by a crimson ring which, in turn, has a pale pink outer ring round it. This plant, too, is propagated by cuttings.

The genuine Dahlstar Series includes *Dahlia* 'Dahlstar Maroon,' with deep wine-red flowers; *Dahlia* 'Dahlstar Scarlet,' with orange-red and orange flowers; and *Dahlia* 'Dahlstar White,' which features a pretty white center amidst the white petals. White-flowered vari-

Dahlia 'Dalina Light Violet,' dahlia

by mid-May. If you sow in March, the plants may be in flower by the end of June. The number of dahlia varieties is huge and there are associations of devotees of this group of plants, who swop plants and news. Commercial cultivation of seeds, seedlings, and cuttings is concentrated mainly on the low-growing varieties for mass-planting in flower-beds and containers.

Dahlia 'Bambi Red-Orange' has semi-double flowers in a subdued shade of orange red. Commercial growers are particularly pleased with the compact growth of the plants in the Bambi Series, as they need relatively little cultivation space for transporting them. Their spherical growth also makes the 12-in tall plants suitable for mass-planting in flower-beds; if grown in containers, they just look boring. Dahlias belonging to this series are propagated by cuttings. The series includes yellow-flowered and purple-flowered plants, as well *Dahlia* 'Bambi White' (with double flowers), and *Dahlia* 'Bambi Light Pink' (pink and white, semi-double, less formal flowers).

eties are often less sturdy, but that is definitely not so in the case of 'Dahlstar White.' Contrary to what the name *Dahlia* 'Dalina Light Violet' suggests, the plant's flowers are distinctly pink. It is propagated by cuttings.

[3-4]

Datura metel

ANGELS' TRUMPETS

The white-flowered variety of *Datura metel* is particularly beautiful. The flowers grow up to 8 in long and are pertly upright. There are other colors as well, even among those growing wild, including purple, violet, and yellow. *Datura metel* 'Flore Pleno' has purple double flowers tinged with white. The species itself stems from Asia, but is to be found both as a garden plant and a weed in many subtropical regions nowadays. The entire plant is highly toxic. Although the stems with their soft, downy leaves can grow to 5 ft tall, the plant usually remains much in cooler climates, particularly when grown in a container.

Datura metel, angels' trumpets

Sow the seeds of this annual indoors in March–April or in a sunny position outdoors in May. The plants have no further requirements, apart from having a distinct liking for loose, nutritive soil. They will flower about three months after they were sown.

[3-4] 5

Dahlia 'Dahlstar White,' dahlia

Datura stramontium, angels' trumpets

Datura stramontium var. *tatula*, angels' trumpets

Datura stramonium

ANGELS' TRUMPETS

The reason the Dutch nickname for this plant is 'thorny apple' is easy to guess when you see its spherical fruits which are densely covered in spikes. In their American homelands, their purpose was probably to fend off grazing animals in search of an evening meal. The animals concerned must have had special stomachs, because the plants are exceedingly toxic. The poison anaesthetizes and was at one time used for that purpose during surgery. The 'thorny apple' presumably arrived at some time as a medicinal plant in a herb garden – the first botanical gardens. From there it escaped, and the plant now grows wild in open, nutritive soil such as rubbish tips. This indicates where it feels most at home in a garden: near a sunny manure or compost heap. Make sure there is loose, nutritive soil in a border and the species will sow itself freely there as well. It will sometimes even germinate in autumn and survive a mild winter. After a severe winter, a second

crop will germinate in March–April. It is best to do your own sowing in April–May. The flowers will then appear from July until well into September. They are usually white and jut out sideways.

The common datura has several divergent varieties and forms. *Datura stramonium* var. *tatula* has lilac-blue flowers and is very beautiful. *Datura stramonium* f. *inermis* is highly sought-after, and its fruits do not have any spines ('*inermis*' means 'unarmed').

3-5

Delphinium ajacis

See *Consolida ajacis*.

Delphinium 'Centurion Sky Blue'

DELPHINIUM

The only reason why this perennial plant is mentioned here is the fact that it is also grown as an annual for providing cut flowers. The

Delphinium 'Centurium Sky Blue,' delphinium

seed is sown in greenhouses in November in order to supply the cut flowers that turn our summery flower arrangements into romantic masterpieces. 'Centurion Sky Blue' has lovely sky-blue flowers with white centers.

Delphinium chinense

See *Delphinium grandiflorum*.

Delphinium consolida

See *Consolida regalis*.

Delphinium Clear Springs Series

DELPHINIUM

The Clear Springs Series is derived from the popular *Delphinium* Pacific Giant Series but, at a height of 30–44 inches, it is considerably

Delphinium 'Clear Springs Lavender,' delphinium

Delphinium 'Clear Springs White,' delphinium

shorter. This is why they are sometimes referred to as *Delphinium* Dwarf Pacific varieties. These perennial delphiniums are cultivated as annual flowers for cutting. Seeds are planted – in greenhouses – between March and June. The seedlings are subsequently kept in the greenhouse or planted outdoors. The first flowers may be expected by mid-May. You could try it out for yourself. Sow the seeds near the surface and stand the propagator in a dark place during germination. Shelter the plants from the wind if you put them out-of-doors. *Delphinium* 'Clear Springs Lavender' bears lavender-blue flowers. The double, bright-white flowers of *Delphinium* 'Clear Springs White' are closely packed along the stems, which are often flattened at their tips. Because the stems remain shorter than those of larkspurs and are also very sturdy, the delphiniums in the 'Clear Springs Series' do not need supports in places sheltered from the wind.

[3–4]

Delphinium grandiflorum 'Blue Pygmy,' delphinium

Dianthus chinensis 'color Magician,' Indian (Chinese) pink

Dianthus chinensis 'Ideal Rose,' Indian (Chinese) pink

Delphinium grandiflorum 'Blauer Zwerg'

See *Delphinium grandiflorum* 'Blue Pygmy.'

Delphinium grandiflorum

DELPHINIUM

Of all the perennial delphiniums, this is the one most likely to be grown as an annual. Many gardeners have difficulty in keeping other delphiniums alive anyway . They often disappear for the most inexplicable of reasons. The cultivars of this species are particularly short-lived and are grown as annuals for that reason.

A first flowering may be expected from June to August. The plants grow to a maximum height of 20 in and branch out strongly, so that they provide beautiful bright-blue cut flowers, particularly for posies of wild flowers. By sowing at intervals, you will be able to cut them over a longer period.

Delphinium grandiflorum 'Blue Pygmy' has bright-blue flowers; those of *Delphinium grandiflorum* 'Blue Butterfly' are ultramarine; and those of *Delphinium grandiflorum* 'Gentian Blue' are deep blue.

[3] 2–6

Dianthus chinensis

INDIAN PINK, CHINESE PINK

Most of the 300 species of carnations are perennials. This is also true of *Dianthus chinensis*, which does indeed come from China. It has been popular there for centuries and was crossed and selected, so that many cultivars were created. Modern seed improvers have added hundreds more. In The Netherlands, Indian pinks are always grown as annuals.

From April, they are marketed on a vast scale for filling flower-beds and containers. Seed companies make every effort to produce increasingly compact varieties, sometimes only 6 in high. It is good for growers who can sell a lot of plants to cover a small area, but sad for plant lovers.

Indian pinks like a partially shady or sunny position and normally moist soil, preferably containing lime. They tolerate a little frost and may therefore be planted out-of-doors as early as April. Many varieties do not flower for long, although there may be a second flowering if they are looked after properly.

You can also sow Indian pinks yourself. They will need two to three months to come into flower. Sow indoors for early flowering, or outdoors from April onwards.

Dianthus chinensis 'Color Magician' has flowers in a special mixture of white and colors varying between pink and bright rose red. The plants grow to about 12 in in height.

Dianthus chinensis 'Ideal Rose' grows to about 8 in high and is a compact plant which bears violet-pink flowers and goes on flowering for a reasonably long time.

Dianthus chinensis 'Parfait Strawberry' is another compact plant from the Aristo Series

Dianthus chinensis 'Parfait Strawberry,' Indian (Chinese) pink

Dianthus chinensis 'Telstar Purple Picotee,' Indian (Chinese) pink

and grows to 6–10 in in height. It has attractive greyish-green foliage. The flowers have red centers surrounded by white tinged with red to a greater or lesser extent.

Dianthus chinensis 'Telstar Purple Picotee' is still a dwarf, although it grows to 10 in tall. Things went slightly wrong when this variety was named: the term "picotee" is used to denote flowers with petals edged in a distinctly contrasting color, but this is not at all true of 'Purple Picotee' with its rose-red centers which gradually change to white. The Telstar Series is well known for its relatively large flowers. Flowering starts early and continues for some time, although there are considerable differences between the various cultivars in this respect.

[2–3] 3–5

Dianthus Marquis Series

PINK

These strong, sweet-scented cultivars were produced from a cross between Indian pinks (see above) and Sweet Williams (*Dianthus barbatus*). The latter biennial – sometimes grown as an annual – is famous for its delightfully sweet-scented flowers. Its growth is far less compact than that of Indian pinks. The Marquis Series, with plants 8 in tall, produced more dwarfs, but they have the more upright growth of Sweet Williams and the foliage is less attractive. But what a fragrance! Plants belonging to the Marquis Series are supplied, in flower, in early spring. Seed is not (yet) available to private gardeners.

Dianthus 'Marquis Cherry Picotee,' Indian (Chinese) pink

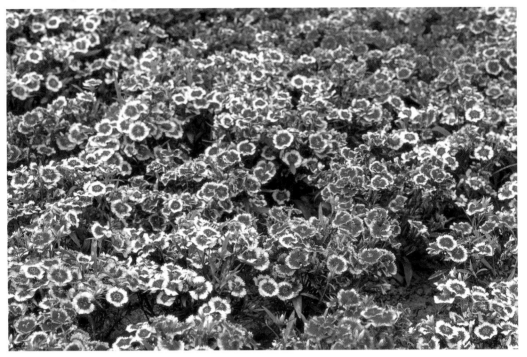

Dianthus 'Marquis Violet Picotee,' Indian (Chinese) pink

Dianthus 'Marquis Cherry Picotee' has cherry-red centers in flowers which nearly always have white – but occasionally pink – edges to their petals. *Dianthus* 'Marquis Violet Picotee' resembles the above to some extent, but the spot in the center is larger, more regular, and crimson-colored; the surrounding edge is white.

Diascia

Diascias grow naturally in South Africa: the annual species in the low-lying, dry regions, and the perennials in the mountains, particularly the Drakensbergen, where they flower on rocky ledges or along the banks of brooks. The perennial species from the mountains are the types cultivated in our part of the world. They rarely survive northern winters, however, and stem cuttings are therefore taken in late summer, and root cuttings in autumn (these are kept frost-free). Alternatively, they are propagated by seed in early spring. If sown early, nearly all species and all cultivars will flower by mid-summer of the same year. The only seed on sale is that of *Diascia barberae*.

Sow indoors in February–March. The seeds will germinate within two weeks at the fairly cool temperature of 60–64°F. Grow the seedlings on at a cool temperature 54–60 °F. Pinch out the growing tips several time to encourage branching, and take the seedlings out into the fresh air as soon as possible. They will tolerate several degrees of frost.

Flowering will then begin in July and continue until well into September. You may, if you like, sow directly out of doors in April–May, but then the plants will not flower until August.

Flowering plants are on sale from April–May, nearly all of them grown from cuttings. Look out for them at nurseries specializing in patio plants. Only purchased plants will show you how inexhaustibly diascias can flower from the day you bought them until early autumn. The plants should be cut back rigorously during intervals between flowering. They will soon sprout again and come into flower a few weeks later. This will prevent the plants from becoming increasingly untidy. They like a sunny position and flower best there, especially in hot summers, but diascias may also be grown in partial shade if need be. Shade and excessive feeding will benefit leaf growth and curb flowering.

In the garden, diascias like loose soil that is not excessively nutritive. The likelihood of the plants surviving the winter will be greatly

Diascia barberae 'Pink Queen,' diascia

Diascia barberae 'Pink Queen,' diascia

Diascia barberae 'Ruby Field,' diascia

increased by planting them in very well-drained soil, preferably under the eaves, and at the foot of a south-facing wall. In summer, the plants like moist soil. Diascias are very suitable for planting out in containers. They flower most profusely in poor soil, but only if it is never allowed to dry out entirely.

Diascia barberae

This perennial is so short-lived that some people regard it as an annual. It is also transitional between annuals and perennials in the way that it is treated, because *barberae* is far less fond of moisture than the other species. This is what makes it so suitable for cultivation in containers, where the soil is nearly always drier and better aerated than in the garden itself.

Diascia barberae grows to about 12 in in height. As the stems – with the plant's characteristic pointed leaves – grow longer, they can no longer support their weight and begin to trail. Pink flowers grace their tips between July and October. Those of the cultivar *Diascia barberae* 'Pink Queen' are pale pink with a milky bloom, those of *Diascia barberae* 'Salmon Queen' are salmon pink, and those of *Diascia barberae* 'Apricot Queen' are apricot colored. All the flowers have a small yellow spot in their centers.

Diascia barberae 'Ruby Field' has deep-pink flowers which are borne in profusion over a long period. The dark-green foliage forms a low clump with the flower stems rising above it. The plant is highly suitable for bor-

Diascia 'Blackthorn Apricot,' diascia

Diascia 'Elegans,' diascia

der edging or for growing along paths and pa-tios. It is also an excellent plant for contain-ers and hanging baskets. It is propagated on a vast scale by cuttings, but also from seed. After germination (at about 66°F), the seedlings are grown on at a cool temperature 54–59 °F. They come into flower from 3–4 months after the seeds were sown.

[1–3] 4-5

Diascia 'Blackthorn Apricot'

With a touch of salmon pink and more than a hint of apricot, the pale flowers of 'Black-thorn Apricot' look lovely in an earthenware pot. Their relatively thick stems are fairly lax and start bending over at a height of 8 in. This gives the pot a fabulous appearance and, in a border, the stems become interwoven with other delicate flowering plants.

At 1 7/8 in long and 1 in wide, the flowers are remarkably big, and the honey spurs – over $1/2$ in long – at the back of the flowers are very striking. The exact ancestry of 'Blackthorn Apricot' is not quite certain, but the plant is presumably descended from *Diascia bar-berae*.

Diascia 'Elegans'

There is a lot of confusion about the origins of this plant. According to the manuals, it is regarded as synonymous with *Diascia vig-ilis*, but that is an entirely different species

with dark green, shiny leaves and pale pink flowers. The difference between the plants on sale as 'Elegans' and *Diascia fetcaniensis*, on the other hand, appears to be minimal: they have the same light green, downy foliage and even downier stems, as well as pink flow-ers with darker centers.

Be that as it may, 'Elegans' is is one of the hardiest diascias – a vigorous, rewarding plant with dense foliage. Even so, plants

Diascia fetcaniensis, diascia

propagated from cuttings are marketed every May as excellent plants for hanging baskets, pots, and other containers, or for a sunny open spot in a border.

Diascia felthamii

See *Diascia fetcaniensis.*

Diascia fetcaniensis

The honey spurs at the back of the small flowers of *Diascia fetcaniensis* curl back remarkably in the direction of the flowers, which are $^3/_4$ in wide and a deep shade of pink with dark red markings. The plant flowers profusely over a long period and grows to about 10 in in height.

The leaves are relatively large, round, green, and covered in fine hairs, which make the plant look dense even without flowers – not

Diascia 'Lilac Belle,' diascia

a frequent occurrence, as new flower shoots are formed continually.

Diascia 'Jack Elliot'

This striking cultivar of unknown parentage is big in every way. It may grow to 16 in in height and is well supplied with lush green fo-

Diascia 'Jack Elliot,' diascia

Diascia 'Jack Elliot,' diascia

Diascia 'Lilac Belle,' diascia

Diascia rigescens, diascia

liage. The flowers are at least 1 in wide and long. They are pink with shades of deep pink, cherry-red, and aubergine in their throats. The throats also have a large yellow blotch, which is particularly striking because the flower is relatively shallow. This is a very suitable plant to grow in containers and is therefore regularly on sale at specialists in "patio" gardening.

Diascia 'Lilac Belle'

Firms specializing in cuttings propagate this *Diascia* on a vast scale. At least ten weeks are needed to grow on rooted cuttings until they come into flower. The flowering plants appear on the market early in May, often without a name, or under the name of 'Lilac Bell' or 'Lilac Bells.' The lilac flowers are only 5/8 in wide, but there is an abundance of them. Each small flower is slightly

pinched lengthways, so that the yellow spots are often invisible. The leaves are about 1¹/₂ in long, and the plant grows to about 12 in tall. It is very suitable for containers or for weaving in amongst plants with straggly growth.

Diascia rigescens

In southern and western England, *rigescens* is cultivated as a perennial for it is one of the hardiest species. However, it fails to survive most winters in a country like The Netherlands, though it is still marketed there by optimistic suppliers of perennials. Those wishing to try it out as a perennial, should plant it against a southeast-facing wall, preferably somewhere under the eaves or a gutter, so that the soil will remain dry during the winter. Otherwise, you could overwinter it in a greenhouse. It takes quite a long time to

Didiscus caeruleus, blue lace flower

Dimorphotheca sinuata (mix), Cape marigold

grow plants capable of flowering from cuttings, so specialist firms prefer to concentrate on other species. Once you have a flowering plant, however, it will turn out to be amazingly beautiful. Its pink flowers, $^3/_4$ in wide, are packed tightly on 20-in stems, which branch out frequently from the base and produce a wealth of leaves. These turn reddish brown in autumn.

Didiscus caeruleus

BLUE LACE FLOWER

The pale lavender blue of the blue lace flower may be easily combined with other plants. It goes very well with all shades of blue and green, will adorn a grey-and-white border, and, in an impressionistic one, may create brilliant color combinations with lemon yellow, apricot, salmon pink, and even orange, which is so often a problem. The plants with their pale green leaves take up hardly any room, and the long stems bearing the 2-in wide flower heads may need some support. It is best to use bushy plants for the purpose. They should not be more than 20 in tall, and

the blue lace flowers will then appear just above them.

Find the most sheltered and warmest possible place for the plant, because it grows naturally in western Australia. It prefers loose, fairly dry soil, which may well be nutritive – to enable it to flower even more exuberantly.

Sow the annual indoors in March–April, or outdoors in April–May. The strikingly beautiful flower heads – eminently suitable for vases – develop between July and October.

[3–4] 4–5

Dimorphotheca aurantiaca

See *Dimorphotheca sinuata.*

Dimorphoteca calendulacea

See *Dimorphoteca sinuata.*

Dimorphoteca sinuata

CAPE MARIGOLD

"Sophisticated marigolds" – that may be the

113

most succinct way of describing *Dimorphoteca sinuata.* This South African species bears orange-yellow flowers, but has a far more expensive aura than the "cheap and cheerful" marigolds. Perhaps that is because of its stylish shape and its contrasting center. Or is it due to the satiny sheen on its petals? Whatever the reason, Cape marigolds add distinction and beauty to flower-beds and, above all, to containers adorning a smart patio or balcony.

The plants, about 12 in tall, like airy warmth, with their foliage and flowers enjoying a refreshing wind, and their roots preferring loose, warm soil. The plants are on sale at container plant specialists from May onwards. You will have a choice of soft shades ranging from orange to white by way of yellow, often with a contrasting ring round the center. In less favorable climates, the plants open only to their fullest extent in full sun. They close up again at night.

It is quite feasible to grow Cape marigolds from seed yourself: start under glass in March–April if you want them in flower by the end of June. Sowing outdoors in April–May will ensure flowers between July and September.

The seed is often sold as a mixture. The almost white flowers of *Dimorphoteca sinuata*

Dimorphotheca sinuata 'Salmon,' Cape marigold

'Salmon' have an added tinge of salmon pink and an aubergine-colored ring round the center. For more plants closely resembling *Dimorphoteca sinuata* see *Osteospermum.*

[3–4] 4–5 🌿 ▼

Diplacus glutinosus

See *Mimulus aurantiacus.*

Dolichos lablab

See *Lablab purpureus.*

Dorotheanthus bellidiformis

ICE PLANT

Ice plants flower best in the driest, poorest, and hottest places that no normal plant would tolerate. They come from arid regions in South Africa. After a shower of rain, the leaves fill with water and swell. The moisture is also contained in small blisters on the surface of the leaves. They sparkle like ice crystals in sunlight, hence their name. The plant is also known as the Livingstone daisy, and belongs to the Aizoaceae family. In this family, flowers do not open until the afternoon, and then only in fine weather. They are closed in the morning and when it rains. That is when the 'crystals' are most evident.

Sow outdoors in April or May. Because of the weak transition between roots and stem, the plants dislike being transplanted. Ice

Dorotheanthus bellidiformis, ice plant

plants are carpet-forming and flower most profusely in June and July, though they continue to bear flowers until well into September. They are usually on sale in a mixture of colors. The flowers, $1^1/_2$ in wide, bear flowers in all kinds of bright colors: yellow, red, white, orange, and, above all, pink.

Dorotheanthus bellidiformis 'Gelato Dark Pink' bears flowers with bicolored petals: white in the center, with crimson borders.

4-5

Dorotheanthus bellidiformis 'Gelato Dark Pink'

Dracocephalum moldavica 'Blue Dragon,' dragon's head

Dracocephalum moldavica 'Blue Dragon,' dragon's head

Dracocephalum moldavica

DRAGON'S HEAD

From July, dragon's head bears lovely lilac-blue flowers which resemble dragon's heads. Bees, particularly, are attracted to them. The square stems grow up to 12–24 in tall. They have beautifully serrated leaves and a lemon fragrance. In a large pot, they make an unforgettable sight.

If sown in March or April, it will bloom from July until late summer.

Sow indoors in March, or outdoors from April, and put the plants in a sunny, preferably in poor soil.

Dracocephalum moldavica 'Blue Dragon' bears violet-blue flowers, and *Dracocephalum moldavica* 'Album' pure white ones.

[3] 4-5

Dyssoida tenuiloba

See *Thymophylla tenuiloba*.

Ecballium elaterium

SQUIRTING CUCUMBER

Although squirting cucumber seed is rarely on sale, the plant is far too amusing to ignore. Seed merchants, take note! Otherwise, you will have to collect it yourself if holidaying in a hot area, where squirting cucumbers grow like weeds in sunny, open spots and on dung-heaps. Make sure you are wearing old clothes and sunglasses – contact lenses are unsuitable – before you begin to collect them. Approach the plant cautiously and look out for one of the gherkin-like fruits with a yellowed stalk. Hold a small bag next to the stalk, with its open end facing the fruit. Use your other hand to push the fruit upwards. It will break off the stalk and squirt a jet of yellow fluid – containing the fruit – into the bag. Dry the seed and sow it directly in the garden the following spring. The low-growing plants need a warm position. The female flowers produce fruit about 1½ in long. As soon as they are ripe, you can play a sticky trick on someone – mind people's eyes, though.

3–4

Ecballium elaterium, squirting cucumber

Eccremocarpus scaber

CHILEAN GLORY FLOWER, GLORY VINE

The glory vine develops from seed to a climber growing up to 10 ft tall. In its natural environment in Chile, it behaves like a perennial climber and forms a fat radical tuber in the soil to survive the dry season. In warmer climates than The Netherlands, the tuber may remain in the soil – covered if need be. In these circumstances, however, cultivation as an annual is infinitely preferable. The fragile seedlings grow rapidly and you will therefore need a large greenhouse, or you will be obliged to start later, in March. Wait until May before moving the plants out-of-doors to a warm and preferably sunny position in well-drained but nutritive soil. It is quite feasible to grow the plant in a large container, but in that case you should give it fertilizer regularly to maintain the speed of its growth. The climber will obviously need supports for the tendrils to entwine.

Eccremocarpus scaber, Chilean glory flower, glory vine

Eccremocarpus scaber, Chilean glory flower, glory vine

The plants produce dense foliage, from which stems bearing rose-red, bright red, orange, or yellow flowers emerge at intervals from July to October.

Eccremocarpus scaber 'Tresco Gold' bears golden yellow flowers; those of *Eccremocarpus scaber* 'Tresco Rose' are cherry pink with orange mouths; and *Eccremocarpus scaber* 'Tresco Scarlet' has orange and scarlet flowers with ochre-yellow mouths.

[3]

Echium lycopsis

See *Echium plantagineum.*

Echium plantagineum

VIPER'S BUGLOSS

Officially, the name viper's bugloss is reserved for the native plant *Echium vulgare,* which tends to grow in places like the sand dunes along the Dutch coast. In gardening circles, however, it is also used for this slightly divergent species from southern Eu-rope, which is also found in poor soil along the coasts of France and southwest England. If grown in richer soil, its foliage develops vigorously at the expense of flowers, and plants are also more likely to be blown over.

Plant breeders have made an effort to produce compact cultivars which also do well in ordinary garden soil. They grow about 12 in tall and are great assets in blue and pink borders, to the satisfaction of butterflies and bees, and bumblebees in particular.

Sow directly out-of-doors between March and May and prick out superfluous seedlings rigorously, so that the plants are at least 18 in apart. Only then will they have enough space to spread satisfactorily.

Echium plantagineum 'Bedder Mixture' is multicolored, but includes white flowers as well as those in shades of mauve, blue, and pink. *Echium plantagineum* 'Blue Bedder' has bright-blue flowers. In fact, the buds of blue-flowering echiums are pink at first, and the faded flowers turn crimson. *Echium*

Echium plantagineum, annual borage, viper's bugloss

Echium plantagineum 'Bedder Mixture,' annual borage, viper's bugloss

Echium plantagineum 'Blue Bedder,' annual borage, viper's bugloss

plantagineum 'Light Blue Bedder' bears pale sky-blue flowers and goes well with the pop- ular shades of pale yellow, salmon pink, and apricot in borders.

3–5   **!**

Echium plantagineum 'Light Blue Bedder,' annual borage, viper's bugloss

Echium plantagineum 'White Bedder,' annual borage, viper's bugloss

Eleusine coracana 'Green Cat'

Erigeron karvinskianus, Spanish daisy

Erigeron karvinskianus, Spanish daisy

Eleusine coracana

The flower spikes of this tropical miniature grass are a very special shape – in fact, they are split. At the top of the stem, between one and eleven spikelets jut out in all directions. In most grasses, there are three or four of them.
The grass grows to no more than 12 in in height, but continually produces new shoots from its creeping roots. Frost is guaranteed to put an end to that, and the plant will not, therefore, grow rampant.
Sow directly in the garden in April–May, or in a field intended for cut flowers, because *Eleusines* are very suitable for that purpose. The flower spikes are also used in dried flower arrangements.
Eleusine coracana 'Green Cat' is named after the green flower spikes which, when ripe, curve towards one another like cat's claws. By the time they are ripe – in August – they will have grown to almost 20 in in height. Apparently, the seed may be used as a cereal.

4–5

Erigeron karvinskianus

SPANISH DAISY

This small perennial from Central America is one of the greatest discoveries of recent years, though it had, in fact, long been growing wild in southern Europe, where it often appears in the joints of walls. With the boom in patio cultivation, firms supplying flowering plants for containers and hanging baskets in May can no longer even think of doing without fleabane. Rightly so, since keen gardeners are unlikely to come across a more rewarding plant.
Its growth is compact and yet it looks attractively casual in a hanging basket. New daisy-like flower heads are borne on thin stems throughout the summer. They are pink when they open, then rapidly turn white, and finally, as they grow older, change back to rose-red again. This makes the plant always look two-tone. Don't be misled by the cultivars marketed by the plant trade. I, for one, cannot see any difference between them and the wild species.

This delightful plant will tolerate about 5 degrees of frost and cannot therefore be over-wintered outdoors in colder climates. Fortunately, it may be brought into flower within 3–4 months of being sown. Sometimes the seed will germinate in the garden, especially in open, sandy spots, or in between steps, paving stones, or joints of walls. Those are places where the seeds have been wafted on their "parachutes."

Sow this small jewel indoors between March and April or outdoors in April–May. In the first case, the plant will come into flower by the end of June. It is possible to cut back the plant in autumn and overwinter it at a minimum temperature of 23 °F.

[3–4] 4–5 ⬠ 🌼 🪴 **!**

Erigeron mucronatus

See *Erigeron karvinskianus.*

Erysimum × allionii

A close relative of wallflowers, *Erysimum perofskianum* grows wild in the mountains of Afghanistan and Pakistan. This biennial plant was the principal ancestor of the hybrid *Erysimum × allionii,* from which quite a number of lovely cultivars have been developed. Basically biennials, they are grown mainly as annuals and then marketed, in flower and without a name, in April–May. The one frequently available is *Erysimum × allionii* 'Gold Shot', which has golden yellow flowers. Specialist seed merchants stock seeds of more sophisticated plants for people to sow themselves. They include *Erysimum × allonii* 'Lemon Delight,' with lemon-yellow flowers; *Erysimum × allonii* 'Apricot Delight,' with apricot-colored flowers; and *Erysimum × allionii* 'Orange Monarch,' with flowers in a warm shade of orange. The plants grow to about 14 in high. The stems rise above a rosette of greyish-green foliage, and bear fragrant flowers from April onwards, provided the seed was sown in June or July of the previous summer. The seedlings will tol-

Erysimum × allioni 'Gold Shot'

erate a fair amount of frost but, in very cold areas, it is better to overwinter them in an un-heated greenhouse and plant them out in early spring. If you sow in early spring, you will be able to enjoy flowering plants in the autumn of the same year. Flowering plants are on sale in spring.

[2–4] 6–7 ⬠ 💮 🌼 🪴

Eschscholzia californica
CALIFORNIAN POPPY

Eschscholzias are without a doubt among the most rewarding of all annuals, as well as being some of the easiest to grow. Their beautiful greyish-green leaves, often with a tinge of blue, are finely divided and form dense and yet loose tufts in a border. The first flowers may be expected in June, followed by increasing numbers every day. Before they open, they are covered by a membrane closely resembling a nightcap, hence the Dutch common name "slaapmutsje." On the day that the flower opens, it pushes the "cap" from the stem, so you can then pull it off and, as it were, awaken the flower. Children, of course, love doing this.

Although eschscholzias grow naturally along the west coast of the United States, they tolerate a fair amount of frost. Some people even sow the seed in late summer and autumn, hoping that the seedlings will survive the winter, grow sturdier, and come into flower earlier. That is how the plant seeds naturally, especially in gardens with sandy soil. The seedlings will not, however, survive severe, wet winters. In that case, sow again in early spring – March–April. The seeds may be sown indoors earlier in the year, but because of the weak transition between root and stem, they do not like being transplanted. It is better to sow directly in the garden. Eschscholzias thrive in almost any kind of soil, but they will remain more compact in poor, sandy soil and the color of their leaves will also be more beautiful there. In richer soil, longer and more lax stems will grow up to 24 in tall.

Eschscholzia californica 'Ballerina Mix,' Californian poppy

The flowers of the species have four petals and are usually orange. Plant breeders have managed to exploit natural variation and cultivate eschscholzias with single or double flowers in every shade between creamy white, yellow, orange, orange-red, and pink. The single flowers attract a lot of insects.

Eschscholzia californica, Californian poppy

Eschscholzia californica 'Apricot Chiffon,' Californian poppy

Eschscholzia californica 'Esonson,' Californian poppy

Eschscholzia californica 'Purple Gleam'

Eschscholzia californica 'Fire Bush,' Californian poppy

Eschscholzia californica 'Purple Gleam'

Eschscholzia californica 'Milky White,' Californian poppy

Eschscholzia californica 'Apricot Chiffon' is one of the new cultivars, with beautiful sea-green foliage. The double flowers are striking not only because of the variations in their color, but also because of their frilled petals. The different ways that the light can fall on the ripples make the flowers look even more colorful: they are mainly cream and yellow, but have soft tinges of apricot and salmon pink. Here again, of course, every advantage has a disadvantage – the flowers of this culti-var have become slightly too heavy for their slender stems, and have a tendency to droop. *Eschscholzia californica* 'Rose Chiffon' is in every way similar to 'Apricot Chiffon,' except that the flowers are distinctly pink on the outside. *Eschscholzia californica* 'Fire Bush' bears double flowers, almost as red as poppies, with yellow centers. Their petals are frilled and the heavy flowers break off easily. *Eschscholzia californica* 'Rose Bush' is a comparable cultivar, but has crimson flowers. *Eschscholzia californica* 'Ballerina Mix' has its name against it. The term "mix" automat-ically makes me think "nothing of anything." In this case, though, there is a lot of every-thing: double flowers with frilled petals and all manner of bright colors – orange, pink, or yellow with lighter centers. They are ex-tremely difficult to combine with other flow-ers, but fine for a colorful flower-bed.

Eschescholzia californica 'Esonson' is an il-lustration of transience. Ten years ago, this small group was growing in the test beds of a renowned nursery. The flowers were

Euphrasia stricta, eyebright

Euryops pectinatus

creamy white, with touches of pink to intense cherry red on the outside. In spite of all that, nothing more was ever heard of this particular cultivar.

Eschscholzia californica 'Milky White' does not have any pink or red on the outside and, for that very reason, goes well with other annuals as well as perennials, and is a real treasure for planting round the base of roses. The plant bears creamy white single flowers. A cultivar with double flowers, intensely cream-colored, was introduced recently as *Eschscholzia californica* 'Buttermilk.'

Eschscholzia californica 'Purple Gleam' combines subtlety and distinctive color. The eye-catching crimson of its flowers merges with softer shades of pink and yellow.

8-9 3-5

Euphrasia stricta

EYEBRIGHT

In an ordinary garden, you need not waste time on sowing eyebright, because the soil is too rich there. In Northern Europe, the small plant, 4–12 in high, grows naturally in poor grassland. The species, however, is deterio-

rating all the time, and nature lovers are therefore trying to preserve the small plant in botanical gardens and nature reserves. It is quite feasible to create a reserve for rare native plants in almost any garden. It is worthwhile sowing eyebright in poor, preferably rather acid, loamy, or sandy soil, where there are low-growing plants. The seed is marketed by specialists in native plants and may also be available through natural history associations. The reward in the form of small flowers in late summer seems small, but there is great satisfaction in having such a rare little plant in one's own garden. Sow this frost-sensitive little species directly in the garden, not too early, and perhaps cover it with a very thin layer of soil. It needs light to germinate.

4-5

Euryops pectinatus

Euryops is rarely absent from the May flower markets. A green-leafed cultivar, *Euryops* 'Sonnenschein,' also known as *Euryops* 'Sunshine,' is usually available. The grey-leafed *Euryops pectinatus*, unfortunately, is

not on sale quite so often. Its leaves are covered in white, feltlike hairs, which will remain particularly beautiful if the plant is cultivated in full sunlight. It will, however, need a lot of water in such a position. The risk of drying up is particularly great if the plant is cultivated in a pot. Both plants are sometimes labelled incorrectly as marguerites.

Euryops plants are propagated by cuttings. Specialist firms take cuttings in winter so that they can supply flowering plants in May. In winter, you can leave the plants outdoors, where they will freeze, or overwinter them indoors at a minimum temperature of 41 °F. You can also take cuttings yourself and overwinter them at a minimum temperature of 41 °F.

Eustoma grandiflorum

PRAIRIE GENTIAN

It is not so long ago that prairie gentians had sunk into oblivion, but then Japanese companies began to take a fresh interest in these formerly well-known plants. They developed long-stemmed flowers for cutting and low-growing potted plants. The variations in their natural flower colors (blue, pink, red, and white) were increased, and now they are also available in pale yellow, apricot, and lilac, often bicolored and sometimes "picotee" (with a narrow border).

You will not be able to get hold of the seed. It goes to commercial growers, who, in theory, can grow 15,000 plants from $^1/_{10}$ oz of seed. Cultivation takes about three months and, by using a lot of heating and extra lighting, growers can market the plants at almost any time of the year. If you prefer low-energy cultivation, buy them from July onwards for flowering in late summer. At that time of the year, the warmth-loving plants may be placed out-of-doors in flower-beds or containers. The low-growing varieties are on sale as indoor plants for the rest of the year.

Eustoma grandiflorum belongs to the gentian family, and originally came from the arid prairies of the southern states of the US and northern Mexico.

Eustoma russellianum

See *Eustoma grandiflorum.*

Exacum affine

PERSIAN VIOLET

The Yemenite island of Socotra lies in the Indian Ocean. A warm and dry place, the island is a paradise for plants, including species that are not to be found anywhere else in the world. The Persian violet is one of them, although the plant is now on display in countless living-rooms. Danish companies are par-

Exacum affine, Persian violet

Exacum affine, Persian violet

Exacum affine, Persian violet

ticularly active in marketing it on a vast scale. You will find Persian violets with their purplish-blue or white flowers at garden centers and florists between April and November. They are then about five months old.

Persian violets are compact and make no special demands as far as their care is concerned. If they are given average amounts of water, preferably a lot of plant food, and plenty of light, but not excessively strong sunlight, the plants will flower over a long period and its slightly succulent leaves will remain in good condition. The only thing the Persian violet really cannot tolerate is cold, and it is sold as an indoor plant for that reason. From June onwards, it is warm enough for the plants to be put out-of-doors. They may be planted in a flower-bed or else in a trough (traditionally in a row of alternatively white and blue flowers). Try the plant on its own in a zinc pot (with drainage holes) or in a hanging basket.

Fagopyrum esculentum, buckwheat

Fagopyrum esculentum

BUCKWHEAT

Although buckwheat has much to offer, it is used very little. The plants from the moderate regions of Asia grow about 20 in tall, with a fairly loose type of growth. Clusters of delightfully fragrant, white to pale pink flowers appear from July onwards, and attract many bees. Buckwheat honey is very popular. The flowers are followed in September to October by small triangular fruits, which provide buckwheat flour and are also used as a medicine. Even the husks of the seeds are used, either for stuffing cushions or for those suffering from insomnia. If you don't want to harvest the seed yourself, you will be able to watch the birds enjoying them in the autumn. It is therefore an ideal plant for flower-filled fields and natural gardens. Wait until May, after the last frost, before sowing the seed in broken-up soil in a sunny, or partially shaded position. There is nothing else you need do apart from enjoying the generous gifts of buckwheat.

5

Felicia amelloides

BLUE MARGUERITE

It is best to treat *Felicia amelloides,* a small shrub from South Africa, as an annual in our part of the world. There are firms which strike large quantities of cuttings every year to meet the demand for flowering plants. These are on sale from the end of April, but it is best to buy the blue marguerite at the end of May, so that it can be put out-of-doors right away. The plant likes a lot of fresh air but cannot tolerate wet roots, especially if combined with cold weather conditions. You should therefore make sure you have a well-drained soil mixture in a container with sufficient drainage holes. Stand the container in a warm position, but preferably not in hot midday sunlight. The buds will shrivel up if the containers are left to dry up temporarily, and in the event of extended drought, part of the foliage will drop off.

If cared for properly, the plant will flower

Felicia amelloides, blue marguerite, kingfisher daisy

abundantly over a long period. Fresh flowers appear continually and, if flowering decreases, use liquid fertilizer to encourage them again. Remove dead flower heads. By cutting back hard, you will not be troubled by disfiguring brown flower stems. As no seed is being formed, the plant will flower longer.

Felicia amelloides 'Aurea' is a variegated form. Its leaves have broad or narrow yellow edges, and some leaves are entirely yellow.

Blue marguerites may be overwintered by putting them in a light and frost-free (but cool and airy) position in the winter. First cut back the plants hard, so that they will keep their compact form.

Fuchsia

Fuchsias are well known as container plants, and the small woody shrubs are overwintered indoors. Enthusiasts, as well as commercial growers, strike cuttings in early spring. They take root easily and come into flower soon afterwards. The mass-produced plants find their way to the containers and hanging baskets of consumers who normally allow the plants to freeze to death in autumn.

There are also fuchsias that are grown from seed early in the year. *Fuchsia procumbens* is a characteristic example. This New Zealand species has thin trailing stems with

delicate leaves and small erect flowers in the most improbable colors for a fuchsia: deep egg yellow, aubergine, and olive green with rose-red stamens and old rose anthers. You will need to look closely, because the flowers are only about $3/4$ in long. After the plant has flowered, reddish berries appear. These con-

Fuchsia 'Fuseedia Rose-Blue,' fuchsia

tain the seeds, which germinate easily, but briefly. Do not stand the plant in full sunlight and give it plenty of water.

In addition to the genuine species suitable for sowing, there are also cultivated forms that are propagated by seed. They include the Fuseedia series (from "fuchsia" and "seed"). *Fuchsia* 'Fuseedia Rose-Blue' has a rose-red calyx and shades of violet in its corolla. *Fuchsia* 'Fuseedia White-Blue' has an almost white calyx (tinged with pale pink). The violet-blue corolla with conspicuous, protruding red stamens is suspended below it. At a height of 8–10 in, both plants remain very short and are intended mainly for planting out in flower-beds, although the latter plant also looks good in a pot or other container.

Fuchsias like warmth, but dislike drought, sun, and wind, which affect the thin leaves. It is therefore best to hang or place them in partial shade and to give them plenty of water and food.

Fumaria officinalis, common fumitory

Fumaria officinalis

COMMON FUMITORY

Fumitory appears like a jack-in-the-box, and you suddenly find it flowering away in odd places: in between paving stones alongside the house, in a vegetable garden, or on a forgotten heap of sand. But once you have taken a good look at it, you don't want to get rid of it again. This is not as simple as it may seem, because small changes in conditions are enough to drive it away. Try planting this indigenous annual in loose, sandy, but moist and fairly nutritive soil in early spring. It will then be able to flower from June until well into autumn on stems which are 4–20 in long and that like leaning up against one another or other plants. You will need to buy the seed from specialists who include wild flowers in their assortment.

3–4

Gaillardia pulchella

BLANKET FLOWER

Although many perennial gaillardias are also grown as annuals, this plant is a genuine one. It comes from Texas and adjoining states, where it covers the prairies in shades of red and yellow. Gaillardias, however, have been doctored so much that it is often difficult to recognize them as such. Double flowers are now quite common, and the petals are often bicolored and have sometimes become tubular in shape.

This applies to, for example, *Gaillardia pulchella* 'Red Plume' with its deep red flowers, and to *Gaillardia pulchella* 'Yellow Plume,' which bears flowers in a strong shade of lemon yellow. At a height of 16 in, both are on the short side and therefore well able to withstand wind. Flowering plants are on sale in May and may then be planted out-of-doors immediately, either in a flower-bed, or in containers. Growers start sowing as early as January–February.

It is better for private gardeners to put off sowing until March or, better still, until April–May. It will then be possible to sow directly outdoors, where they will come into flower between the end of June and October. It is important to plant them in a sunny spot.

[3] 4-5

Gaillardia pulchella 'Red Plume,' blanket flower

Gaillardia pulchella Yellow Plume,' blanket flower

Galeopsis speciosa

LARGE-FLOWERED HEMP-NETTLE

Galeopsis speciosa is undoubtedly the most beautiful of all our native hemp-nettles. The pale yellow, lipped flowers have an eye-catching purple spot. They appear on stems which may grow up to 39 in tall, especially if sheltered by wooded banks or the fringes of a wood, places where they like to grow. They also like acid, nutritive soil and, as a result of current agricultural methods, there is plenty of that about. Even so, the plant is only sporadically found to be growing wild.

Although the hemp-nettle is a genuine annual, its seed is sown in autumn, preferably in partial shade in moist, humus-rich soil. The

Galeopsis speciosa, large-flowered hemp-nettle

seed is available from specialist suppliers only, as this is a wild flower which is not yet cultivated often enough.

8–10

Gaura lindheimeri

These flowers, $3/4$ in wide, are balanced like white butterflies at the top of their tall thin stems, which grow up to 39 in in height. The perennial originally came from the south of the United States and became a popular plant for borders in England. On the continent of Europe, however, it cannot survive most win-

Gaura lindheimeri

ters. It is therefore better to grow the plant there as an annual, either by taking cuttings in summer, or by sowing indoors early in the year. In that case, the plants will bear flowers from July of the same year until far into September.

The cultivar most frequently on sale is *Gaura lindheimeri* 'Whirling Butterflies,' a strong grower bearing pure white flowers. *Gaura lindheimeri* 'Corrie's Gold' has gold-variegated leaves.

[2–4]

Gazania pinnata

The fact that this characteristically mat-forming gazania grows only 6 in high makes it particularly suitable as a summer-flowering plant for containers and hanging baskets. The stems will ultimately trail over the rims. The plant has a layer of felty white hairs to shield it from the glaring South African sunlight, but that is really not required in northwest Europe; the layer of felt retards the plant's growth, which makes it less interesting for commercial growers. They cultivate it by cuttings and supply flowering plants in May. Flowers are carried over a long period, well into September, though not in profusion. Make sure you put the plant in a sunny and relatively dry position.

Gazania pinnata

Gazania rigens

Gazanias have a trailing habit and look up at the sky with their great eyes – flowers that sometimes grow to about 3¼ in wide. Those of the species are orange, with a curious blackish-green ring round the center. Small white dots frequently light up from within that ring. The leaves are green on top, but white and feltlike underneath.

Gazania rigens is the ancestor of quite a number of cultivars which were developed by selection and hybridization with other species. The plants in the Daybreak Series are currently the best-known examples. *Gazania rigens* 'Daybreak Garden Sun' has a ring round its center in a shade of green that I can describe only by likening it to the sunlit back of a plover. The petals change from orange in the center to yellow round the edges. *Gazania rigens* 'Daybreak Red Stripe' has that same gleaming shade of deep green round its center. The flowers are orange yellow with a brownish-red stripe down the cen-

Gazania rigens 'Daybreak Red Stripe'

Gazania rigens

ter of each petal. Both cultivars have received Fleuroselect awards: 'Red Stripe' was awarded one of the gold medals in 1998. Both of them are now cultivated on a vast scale as bedding plants.

Apart from being used as bedding plants, gazanias are also suitable for edging purposes and for growing in containers. Put them in a sunny spot in well-drained soil. You can sow them yourself. If you want flowers by

Gazania rigens 'Daybreak Garden Sun'

Godetia bottiae 'Lilac Blossom'

Godetia hybrids

Selective breeders have developed many different varieties from various species: tall ones for the market in cut flowers, and short ones for bedding purposes. The photograph shows one of the experimental F1-hybrids in a test plot. It closely resembles plants belonging to the well-known *Godetia* Satin Series. These grow to about 10 in in height and are marketed in flower in May. Transfer them to a flower-bed or container without disturbing the rootball. They will flower profusely for about a month. Cutting back the stems when the flowers are over may encourage a moderate second flush.

Put them in a position which is sunny, but not scorching hot, and do not let the soil in pots dry out.

Gomphrena dispersa

GLOBE AMARANTH

Whereas the normal globe amaranth, *Gomphrena globosa*, sometimes grows to a height of 20 in, and is popular for cutting and drying purposes, *Gomphrena dispersa* has a trailing habit. From a single point, the cylindrical shoots spread in every direction and eventually cover a square meter $10^3/_4$ sq ft of ground. From June, the cultivar *Gomprena dispersa* 'Pink Pinheads' bears $^1/_2$-in wide flower heads in which the bracts provide the color. If you want to dry the flowers, they should be picked as soon as they are almost fully developed.

As soon as the plant fails to find any further support, it will begin to trail. It is therefore an excellent plant for hanging baskets. Make sure it is in a warm position, as globe amaranths come from tropical regions of the American continent and have a strong dislike of the cold, especially damp cold. Sow in March–April and wait until May before planting out the seedlings in a warm and sheltered place. You may also sow them directly in the garden from May.

[3–4] 5

Gypsophila muralis

BABY'S BREATH

You do not need not look far to find something beautiful. This gypsophila, which obviously grows on walls, is a wild annual from central and eastern Europe, among other places. It is therefore fully hardy. Its gossamer-thin stems are reasonably tensile, but are bent down by the weight of the tiny flowers which, however, are borne in such quantities that the plant is covered with them. Strangely enough, it is almost impossible to buy seeds of this rewarding little plant. It forms a neat, loose tuft of delicate greenery and looks just right for hanging baskets.

Plants are available from firms specializing in plants for patios and balconies, but why are there not more of them? It can't be the growers' fault. They market several cultivars, in-

cluding *Gypsophila muralis* 'Gypsy.' Some flowers are double. *Gypsophila muralis* 'Garden Bride' is an old favorite with single flowers. *Gypsophila muralis* 'Tweeny' closely resembles the above cultivar, but is even more compact.

Sow it indoors in March. It needs light to germinate and should not be covered. Keep properly moist during germination.

Grow the seedlings on at 50–15 °F. They may

be moved out-of-doors early in May, and will then come into flower in June and go on flowering right through the summer. If they are sown directly in the garden from early May, they will come into flower by the end of July. Find a partially shaded spot and do not let the rootball dry out.

[3–4] 5   !

Gomphrena dispersa 'Pink Pinheads,' globe amaranth

Gypsophila muralis 'Gypsy,' baby's breath

H

Hebenstretia dentata

This is a plant for those who enjoy small things, because the flowers are minute but amazingly beautiful. They are only a few fractions of inches wide, and appear to be white, but a close look will reveal flecks of orange below the three-pointed white "quiff." They are tightly packed along the stem. As the stem grows, the flowering zone, about $3^1/4$ in long, will move upwards, and the seed will develop below it. All this will continue until the stem is about 20 in long and flowering has ceased. That is the moment to cut off those stems, leaving a hand's length above the ground. New shoots will develop and the plant will therefore flower from the end of June until well into September.

Hebenstretia dentata 'Attraction'

Helianthus annuus, sunflower

Hebenstretia (also called *Hebenstreitia*) is an easily cultivated annual from South Africa. Sow indoors in March–April, or outdoors from the end of April. Pinch out the growing tips of seedlings to encourage branching. They may be planted out in a sunny position at the end of May. They are highly suitable for a white border, but will also give the overall design a look of airiness elsewhere. The small flowers become fragrant towards evening and attract a lot of bees in daytime.

Seed merchants usually supply the cultivar *Hebenstretia dentata* 'Attraction.'

[3–4] 5   **!**

Helianthus annuus

SUNFLOWER

This is the king of the annuals, growing several yards tall, with a thick stem as hard as a broomstick and almost as strong. The leaves feel slightly rough. From the beginning of summer, sunny flower heads, 10 inches or more wide, develop at the top of the plant. Within the ring of petals, there are hundreds of tubular florets, each one of which may produce a single sunflower seed. The tubular florets are arranged in perfect harmony, forming patterns in relation to one another, criss-crossing spirals in a ratio that accords with the golden section, the ideal proportion, as propounded by

the artists of the Renaissance. They, of course, copied this natural measurement from plants and not the other way round.

Bees visit these spirals of tubular florets for the pollen and nectar that they find there, and golden yellow sunflower honey is to be seen on many a breakfast table. As the tubular flowers fall out of the disc, the fat seeds appear, within the same pattern of spirals. If you want to harvest them, you must be quick at this stage and cut off the flower and dry it in as warm and airy a place as possible. This is because the great tits, as soon as they discover the seeds, will be clinging to the drooping flower heads to peck the seeds out of them. In short, sunflowers provide a feast for both people and birds. To achieve the optimum effect, it is best to sow common sunflowers and not bother about cultivars developed especially for the cut-flower trade. Of course, the "yellow snow" of the pollen falling out of the flowers does annoy some people, which is why "improvers" have de-

Helianthus annuus 'Prado Gold,' sunflower

Helianthus annuus, sunflower

Helianthus annuus 'Prado Red,' sunflower

veloped varieties without pollen – but has no-one thought of the bees?

Sow sunflower seed directly in the garden from April. The seedlings tolerate light frost. Most annuals will not benefit much from being sown early, but sunflowers will definitely be at an advantage, and will grow taller in the course of the summer. They stop growing as soon as the flowers develop. Even plants sown early in the year do not come into flower until July–August, because the budding process is determined by the number of hours of daylight. Here again, of course, there are always those who cheat: in this case, the improvers who cultivate varieties for the cut-flower market. They have developed varieties that are less sensitive to the amount of daylight.

Sunflowers have shallow roots and are sometimes blown over. A support inserted deep into the earth will keep them upright. The plants absorb a lot of water from the soil and grow considerably taller in fertilized soil. This applies not only to the plants, but also to the flowers which may grow up to 12 in wide.

Helianthus annuus 'Sunrich Orange,' sunflower

Sunflowers come in all sizes and colors. The flowers are single, semi-double (with more petals round the edge), or fully double, in which (many of) the tubular florets have been turned into sterile ray flowers.

Helianthus annuus 'Italian White' – see *Helianthus debilis* 'Italian White.'

Growers of flowers for cutting purposes pinch out the growing tips of *Helianthus annuus* 'Prado Gold', which then ramifies and bears about five flowers, each one about 6 in wide. They are deep yellow, with dark centers. The plants grow to about 3 ft tall.

Helianthus annuus 'Prado Red' has the same characteristics as 'Prado Gold,' except that the color of the flowers varies from orange to brownish red. They produce hardly any pollen.

Helianthus annuus 'Sunrich Orange' is quite a different kind of flower grown for cutting. Each plant bears just one flower on a stem as tall as a man. A ring of yellow petals encircles

Helianthus annuus 'Velvet Queen,' sunflower

Helianthus debilis 'Italian White,' sunflower

a black disc of tubular florets that produce hardly any pollen.

The color of *Helianthus annuus* 'Velvet Queen' resembles that of 'Prado Queen,' except that, at a height of about 5 ft, 'Velvet Queen' looks more natural and also branches out well. The color of the flowers fades from wine red to a lovely velvety orange brown.

[3] 4–5

Helianthus curcumerifolius

See *Helianthus debilis.*

Helianthus debilis 'Italian White'

SUNFLOWER

The common sunflower is somewhat crude for a sophisticated garden, where the cultivated varieties of *Helianthus debilis* are more appropriate. The plants rarely grow taller than 5 ft and branch out well without having their tops cut off. The triangular leaves have a slight satiny sheen.

Helianthus debilis 'Italian White' bears magnificent flowers. Its petals are shaded from creamy white at the tips to soft yellow at their dark center. For cultivation, see *Helianthus annuus.*

[3] 4–5

Helichrysum bracteatum

STRAWFLOWER

The rustling dried flower heads of strawflowers are often included in dried flower bouquets. Their sunny colors are welcoming: deep red, pink, orange, yellow, white, and all manner of shades in between. They have a lovely sheen while they are still young, but become dull and dusty later on. The brightly colored strawflowers keep their colors longer than any other dried flowers.

The plants producing the dried flowers have little ornamental value of their own. They grow rather tall and straggly up to about 28 in in height, and have somewhat uninteresting leaves. It is therefore best to plant them in rows next to beetroots or other vegetables in a kitchen garden, or in a separate section for growing flowers for cutting or drying. Pick them just before the flowers are fully open and hang them upside down in an airy, dry, and preferably warm place in the shade. They will dry best out-of-doors under the eaves.

Helichrysum bracteatum, strawflower

139

Helichrysum bracteatum 'Chico Orange,' strawflower

Helichrysum bracteatum 'Chico White,' strawflower

Potted plants grown specifically for containers and flower-beds are on sale in spring and summer. The prize-winning Chico Series consists of plants between 12 in and 16 in tall in dazzling colors. Commercial growers sow them as early as March and give them extra lighting to keep them short. They are supplied as flowering potted plants from May onwards. They go on flowering for six to eight weeks, and will then be ready for the compost heap. The flowers of *Helichrysum bracteatum* 'Chico Orange' are a warm shade of orange; *Helichrysum bracteatum* 'Chico Pink' has bright pink flowers; and those of *Helichrysum bracteatum* 'Chico White' are pure white, which makes their golden yellow centers show up beautifully.

Helichrysum bracteatum 'Chico Pink,' strawflower

Sow the tall varieties indoors yourself in March–April, or directly in the garden from mid-April, for them to flower in August–September. Strawflowers like a sunny, warm position and loose, well-drained soil.

[3–4] 4–5

Helichrysum lanatum HORT

See *Helichrysum petiolare.*

Helichrysum microphyllum

See *Plectostachys serphyllifolia.*

Helichrysum petiolare

Helichrysum petiolare

Somewhere, a sorcerer's apprentice is inventing names for the deviant forms of one of the most rewarding patio plants – *Helichrysum petiolare*. The green foliage and stems of this South African plant are covered in grey hair. Within such a species, there have of course always been mutants, plants with totally different characteristics. Some, for instance, are

Helichrysum petiolare 'Limelight'

strikingly hairy, whereas others are almost bare. The color of the leaves may be variable, and yellow-leafed or variegated forms may also occur. The variant forms are much in demand. And, like the species itself, they are propagated by cuttings on a vast scale to adorn containers and hanging baskets. The plants scarcely tolerate frost and are therefore propagated by cuttings year after year.

Their care presents few problems. As long as you don't let the potting compost dry out entirely, the plants will send forth their spreading shoots in every direction, several tens of centimetres (a couple of feet) upwards, but, above all, horizontally, which means that they will start trailing as soon as there is nothing left to support them. In short, it is an ideal plant for containers and hanging baskets, where they form a quiet background to flowering plants.

Helichrysum can, of course, flower too, producing long stems with clusters of straw-colored flowers at their tips. Many keen gardeners cut them off prematurely, because, to them, the foliage is all-important. Do wait until the small flowers open before cutting off the stems. If you dry them, you will be able to enjoy their delightful honeyed fragrance for a long time to come.

Helichrysum petiolare 'Limelight' has lemon-yellow to light golden-yellow foliage. The very same cultivar is sold under, inter alia, the following names: *Helichrysum petiolare* 'Aurea'; *Helichrysum petiolare* 'Gold' (there is also

Helichrysum petiolare 'Limelight'

a variegated form with this name); and *Helichrysum petiolare* 'Yellow.'

Helichrysum petiolare 'Silver' is very hairy and this, combined with the relatively large bluish-green leaves, strengthens its silvery effect.

Helichrysum petiolare 'Variegatum' has green foliage with irregular buttery yellow patches along the leaf margins. The leaves are slightly curved and hairy, making this a really striking and beautiful cultivar.

One final tip: try growing *helichrysum* at the foot of a warm wall in full sun. The plant will branch out and climb up against the wall to at least the height of 39 in.

     !

Helichrysum petiolatum

See *Helichrysum petiolare.*

Heliotropium arborescens

HELIOTROPE

Heliotropes were among the familiar bedding plants in large-scale displays in the gardens of palaces and country houses. The deep colors of foliage and flowers contrasted strongly with the lighter shades of other plants, and complex patterns were created with them. It is still possible to see that kind of summery flower-bed here and there, but they are long past their heyday. Heliotrope is now used for a new craze – that of patio gardening. The

Helichrysum petiolare 'Silver'

Helichrysum petiolare 'Variegatum'

plant is, in fact, highly satisfactory as a container plant.

Sow indoors in early spring at about 68 °F. The seed requires light to germinate and so should not be covered with compost. It should also remain wet during germination, so cover the propagator with plastic or glass to create a warm and humid atmosphere. In spite of all that cosseting, the seed will germinate irregularly. Don't put the plants out-of-doors until the end of May, and find a warm and sunny position in nutritive soil for them. Be careful about watering them with cold water.

Plants grown from seed or cuttings by professional nurserymen are also available on sale in spring.

Heliotropium arborescens 'Early Violet' flowers particularly early. The plant grows about 18 in tall and yet bears flower heads that, at 4–12 in, are remarkably wide. They are also delightfully fragrant.

Heliotropium arborescens 'Early Violet,' heliotrope

Heliotropium arborescens, heliotrope in a flower-bed with *Begonia semperflorens*

Heliotropium arborescens 'Marine' has a compact habit with leaves in the deepest shade of reddish green. The fragrant violet flower heads are about 6 in wide. There is an even more compact form on the market – its name is *Heliotropium arborescens* 'Mini Marine.'

[2–4]

Heliotropium peruvianum

See *Heliotropium arborescens.*

Heliotropium arborescens 'Marine,' heliotrope

Heliotropium manglesii

See *Rhodanthe manglesii.*

Heliotropium roseum

See *Acroclinium roseum.*

Heliotropium arborescens, heliotrope

Hibiscus trionum, flower-of-the-hour

Hibiscus trionum, flower-of-the-hour

Heterocentron 'Cascade'

See *Centradenia inaequilateralis* 'Cascade.'

Hibiscus esculentus

See *Abelmoschus esculentus.*

Hibiscus trionum

FLOWER-OF-THE-HOUR

The flower-of-the-hour owes its name to its

brief appearance. It flowers for a few hours in the morning and then closes for good early in the afternoon, but a fresh bud will soon appear in the axil of every newly formed leaf. There will be no need for you to be without hibiscus flowers for a single day. They are about $1\frac{1}{2}$ in wide, creamy on the outside, and with a center that at first sight looks white, but turns out to be deepest purple. When the flower is over, the calyx swells up to form a striking pouch holding the seeds. In warm regions, it sows itself freely, and the plant has become a weed in many (sub)tropical countries. The stems with inflated calyces look splendid in a bouquet of dried flowers.

The plants themselves are not very decorative – they grow about 20 in tall with lanky stems and green foliage that may vary considerably in shape. Seed merchants frequently market cultivars. Sow flower-by-the-hour indoors in March, or outdoors from mid-April. It is best to put the plants in loose, well-drained but nutritive soil.

3 [4–5]

Hibiscus trionum 'Sunny Day,' flower-of-the-hour

Hyoscyamus niger, henbane

Hyoscyamus niger, henbane

Hymenostemma paludosum

See *Leucanthemum paludosum*.

Hyoscyamus niger

HENBANE

The fact that witches could fly off on their broomsticks was due to henbane, or so it was thought at one time. This indigenous plant certainly contains hallucinogenic substances, which, furthermore, are extremely toxic. That may explain why it is rarely seen in flower gardens today.

It is a pity, because henbane has a very special aura and is highly suitable for a natural garden. Sow the seed in nutritive soil in an open spot in early spring and, if you are lucky, you will be able to enjoy looking at the remarkable flowers in late summer. If not, they will flower from June onwards the following summer. The flowers are about 1¼ in wide and are a pale, indeterminate color, criss-crossed with a network of deep-purple veins. They flower right through the summer until well into autumn, by which time the plants will have grown to about 32 in in height.

By then, swollen fruits will be attached in a row to the stems and, in a strong wind, they will burst open to disperse the seed. You can pick the stems before the storm and dry them so that you will be able to enjoy looking at the fruits of the mysterious plant throughout the winter.

3–4

Iberis amara

WILD CANDYTUFT

Iberis amara, a small annual with a honey-sweet fragrance, grows in loose, calcareous soil in Europe. Its flowers are sometimes pale lilac or soft pink in color, but usually white. The stems grow to about 12 in high. The wild species, a familiar weed, particularly in the fields of southern Euope, was improved until it became a garden plant. It now wafts its fragrance along garden paths and across flower-beds and patio containers. There are several lovely cultivars, including the well-known *Iberis amara* 'Iceberg' with its pyramidal white flowers, which are called "hyacinth-flowered" because of their height. *Iberis* 'Snowbird' is a cross between *Iberis amara* and an unknown species. It has

Iberis umbellata, candytuft

a spreading habit and bears flattish heads of small white florets in July–August. Cutting off flower stems (for vases) or stems that have finished flowering will prolong the flowering season.

Iberis 'Snowbird'

Iberis umbellata, candytuft

Iberis umbellata 'Rose Flash', candytuft

Impatiens balfourii, balsam

Sow the seed of *Iberis* thinly in situ in late summer or early spring.

8-9 3-4

white, and crimson may be discerned in addition to shades of pink.

8-9 3-4

Iberis umbellata

CANDYTUFT

This is the more familiar candytuft, with larger florets in each flower head, but without the delightful fragrance of *Iberis amara*. The color of the flowers varies from white to pink to purplish and crimson, although the last color is rare, and the red-flowered varieties do not self-seed so well. Sowing candytuft is, in fact, very easy, and it is quite a good idea to let children experiment with this "fast flower." They will be in full flower ten weeks after they were sown. They also sow themselves and often germinate in the cracks between paving stones. Sow directly in the garden in late summer or early spring, in loose soil and preferably in a sunny spot. It is also true that picking helps to prolong the flowering season of this species.

Iberis umbellata 'Rose Flash' bears deep-pink flowers. It is one of the color choices in the *Iberis* 'Flash-mix' mixture, in which lilac,

Impatiens balfourii

BALSAM

In the villages on the Spanish side of the Pyrenees, old olive tins, buckets, and all kinds of other containers are full of the extremely graceful flowering balsam. They are so happy there that they also germinate spontaneously between the paving stones. In containers, they grow about 39 in tall and the splendidly colored flowers are also smaller than those of the familiar giant balsam. They attract just as many insects, although the openings are too small for larger bumblebees.

This magnificent species originally came from the warmer regions of the Himalayas, and the plant certainly likes warmth, but also adequate amounts of moisture. It is no wonder that they germinate between stones, which warm up quickly, while the roots find sufficient moisture underneath them.

Until a short time ago, the species was not

Impatiens balfourii, balsam

on sale anywhere, but in recent years the seed has become available sporadically, and proud specialists sell plants from time to time. Sow this balsam indoors in a pot with a very sandy soil mixture, or sow it outdoors in moist, sandy soil. For inexplicable reasons, the seeds sometimes germinate poorly or fail to do so at all. Once they are in flower, the plants produce fruits that burst when they have ripened. The seeds often germinate spontaneously in the garden the following spring.

[3-4] 5   !

Impatiens balsamina

BALSAM

The flowers of balsam plants are borne along the upright stems, which are also covered in dense foliage. In combination with the green, oval leaves, this creates a compact type of inflorescence. The entire plant usually grows to a height of 20–32 in, but there are also dwarf cultivars that are about 8 in high. The color of the flowers varies considerably. It is often white, creamy yellow, or pink, but shades of red and violet occur as well, and multi-colored flowers have also been created, often single, but sometimes semi-double or fully double. Balsam plants are sold in spring as indoor or bedding plants. They dislike the cold, and should not be put out in the garden before June, when they may be planted in partial shade. For the method of sowing, see *Impatiens walleriana*.

[2-4]

Impatiens glandulifera

GIANT BALSAM

The giant balsam – also known as touch-me-not – is a plant to enjoy over a long period. Its seeds germinate in the garden on a massive scale every spring. Some people consequently regard this plant – which grows up to 6 ft tall – as a weed. I always leave a few plants so that I can enjoy the sound of bumblebees around the large flowers from July onwards. They crawl right inside the flowers as they buzz, taking care of pollination, and thus ensure the excitement that follows. The small

Impatiens balsamina, balsam

Impatiens glandulifera, giant balsam

Impatiens hawkeri New-Guinea hybrid

fruits of balsams gradually come under pressure and then burst open suddenly to eject the seeds. The giant balsam's fruits are largest and therefore the most entertaining. Try holding one when it is nearly ripe – it will burst open in your hand. After that, you will find it hard to resist touching more of the fruit, whether they are ripe and explode immediately or not yet ready to do so.

The large seeds germinate easily. Sow them in any soil that is not excessively poor in April–May.

4-5

Impatiens hawkeri New-Guinea hybrid

Impatiens hawkeri

BALSAM

Flowering plants labelled *Impatiens* 'New Guinea Hybrids' appear on the market round about Mothering Sunday. They are derived from, among other plants, *Impatiens hawkeri*, a perennial from the Indonesian Archipelago. In The Netherlands, 'New Guinea Hybrids' are grown from seeds as annuals, and nurserymen start sowing as early as January or February so that they can market flowering plants by mid-May. The seedlings need a lot of light and warmth but, to avoid the risk of fungus disease, should not be cultivated in excessively wet conditions.

The plants develop a compact shape, often with very dark foliage, and bear a profusion of colorful, sometimes double, flowers which may be as much as $2^3/_4$ in wide.

Stand the plants in a light place on a windowsill, or plant them out-of-doors in a flower-bed or container sheltered from the wind and fierce sunlight from mid-June. Water them regularly, but never allow the soil to become saturated.

Impatiens holstii

See *Impatiens walleriana*.

Impatiens niamniamensis

Impatiens niamniamensis has succulent stems which may grow up to 39 in long.

149

Impatiens niamniamensis

Impatiens walleriana, busy lizzie, as a hedge, 39 in high, in Madeira

Branching off them are not only the oblong leaves, but also thin stalks bearing pendulous flowers at their tips – like parrots on perches. The greenish to whitish petals are quite inconspicuous. Their task is taken over by the enlarged sepal, which forms a kind of horn and ends in a reflexed spur. This is either red, rose-red, or red and yellow. The final color combination is apparently the most popular one, and has led to cultivars being named *Impatiens niamniamensis* 'Arared' and *Impatiens niamniamensis* 'Congo Cockatoo.'

Impatiens niamniamensis comes from tropical East Africa and likes a very warm position out of the wind and sheltered from fierce midday sun. It is often marketed as a container or indoor plant, but may be put out-of-doors from mid-June. Basically, it is a perennial that is actually marketed as an annual and it soon dies if left out-of-doors in the autumn. It is possible, however, to overwinter the plant in your living-room.

Impatiens niamniamensis

Impatiens roylei

See *Impatiens glandulifera*.

Impatiens walleriana

BUSY LIZZIE

In regions where there are no frosts, busy lizzies grow into shrubs about 3 ft.4 in tall.

Impatiens walleriana 'Accent Lavender Blue,' busy lizzie

Impatiens walleriana 'Explore Blue Satin,' busy lizzie

Impatiens walleriana Explore Series, busy lizzie

Impatiens walleriana 'Evening Blush,' busy lizzie

A row of these plants forms a long and richly flowering hedge, thus creating a very festive appearance. Why, then, do those engaged in improving cultivated varieties always go to such pains to select the very smallest plants? In bad weather, the rain splashes the soil up against the underside of leaves and flowers and, if they remain wet for more than a few hours, glassy spots will appear on them and subsequently become slimy.

No wonder that busy lizzies are most popular as indoor plants. They grow taller indoors and, provided the plant-lover waters the soil and not the leaves, the foliage will look good for a long time. On a light windowsill, they will go on flowering over a long period. Still, busy lizzies may also flower well in a garden. They are very suitable for containers and hanging baskets, and will also thrive in flower-beds in dry summers. Lengthy wet spells are the greatest problem, so you should always put them in a place where a gentle breeze will dry them off again. Sunlight is not required at all and, in fact, the plants do well in a light position in the shade. The color of the flowers also remains better in those conditions, whereas they would fade in bright sunlight.

The stems and foliage are very lax and watery, and break off easily in strong wind or driving rain. Although drying winds will do the plants good out-of-doors, they suffer badly on windy balconies and other draughty places.

Most keen gardeners buy busy lizzies and then leave them to the mercy of the elements in autumn. After the first frost, they will have disappeared. It is possible to sow them yourself, but not easy. The seed requires light, and therefore needs very little cover, if any. It is also very sensitive to drying out. So always cover the propagator with glass or plastic and stand it in a light position, but not in full sunlight. The seeds germinate best at temperatures between 68 °F and 77 °F. That, though, means fairly warm conditions which also encourage fungi, and the danger of grey mold is therefore very real. One of the effects of this disease is that seedlings dissolve at the base and topple over. There are two important steps you can take to reduce the danger of grey mould: always use new or clean pots and trays and fill them with special seed compost or other soil that has been sterilized. Secondly, once the seed has germinated, the humidity should be reduced. Allow fresh air in as soon as possible and increase the size of the opening during the next few days until the cover can be left off altogether. Reduce the temperature to 59–64 °F. As soon as the seedlings are over $\frac{1}{2}$ in high, they may be pricked out and grown on at moderate temperatures. The critical phase is now past. Put the plants out-of-doors during the daytime from early May to harden them off, and bring them indoors again in the evening. They may be planted out-of-doors by the end of May. The various seed merchants for commercial growers have developed their own series, the main difference between them being the relative ease

Impatiens walleriana 'Novette Rose Star,' busy lizzie

Impatiens walleriana 'Pride Pink,' busy lizzie

of cultivation. As a consumer, you are unlikely to notice much difference, except in the color of the flowers. The plants on sale are nearly always miniatures because of selection on the basis of dwarf characteristics and the use of growth inhibitors during cultivation.

Impatiens walleriana 'Accent Lavender Blue' is one of a series of spreading miniatures 6–8 in high. They spread even farther in the shade. The name 'Lavender Blue,' however, is somewhat misleading for this pink cultivar with a touch of lavender.

The *Impatiens walleriana* 'Explore Series' is currently one of the most important series. It was developed from the Accent, Expo, and Tempo series. The improvers were trying to produce larger flowers at an earlier date. Unfortunately, both flowers and foliage are easily affected by wet weather.

Impatiens walleriana 'Explore Blue Satin' is a soft shade of pale pink with a bluish glow and a salmon-pink center.

Impatiens walleriana 'Evening Blush' is one of the fully double cultivars. It has soft pink flowers and, at a height of 12 in, it is no longer a dwarf and is therefore more convenient for planting in containers. Double-flowered busy lizzies are sometimes grown from seed, but the results are unreliable and many of the plants will have single flowers. Double-flowered busy lizzies are therefore often propagated by cuttings.

Impatiens walleriana 'Novette Rose Star' has clearly bicolored flowers in crimson pink with a white star.

Impatiens walleriana 'Super Elfin Rose,' busy lizzie

Impatiens walleriana 'Victorian Rose,' busy lizzie

Impatiens walleriana 'Pride Pink' will fill an area in a flower-bed with soft pink.

Impatiens walleriana 'Super Elfin Rose' comes from one of the superior series of plants that are more likely to tolerate a wet summer. It includes some lovely pastel colors. 'Super Elfin Rose' is one of the deeper shades, but this goes well with its dark foliage.

Impatiens walleriana 'Victorian Rose' was awarded a Fleuroselect gold medal in 1998. The variety must owe the award to the consistency of the product and the short time required for growing it from seed, because its resistance to poor weather, the other quality attributed to it, was not at all apparent from the trial arrangement of this rose-red, double-flowered plant. In my opinion, it is a disappointing product for the consumer.

[2–4]   ▼

Incarvillea sinensis

This is a species cultivated over a vast area from Manchuria in the northeast to Tibet in the extreme southwest. No wonder that the species is somewhat variable, with differences in both shape and color. In some regions, the plants grow as perennials; in others, as annuals. The creamy yellow flowers of the cultivar called 'Cheron' most probably belong to *incarvillea sinensis* ssp. *variabilis* f. *przewalskii*, a natural form from the western area of distribution. 'Cheron' grows about 12 in high. Its creamy white flowers appear above feathery, fernlike foliage. The plants come into flower about ten weeks after they were sown and, because new stems are formed continually, flowering continues over a long period.

[3] 4–5 ❀ ▼

Ipomoea lobata

Although this species is peerless, it has many different names, including *Mina lobata* and *Quamoclit lobata*. Whatever its name, it is always the same magnificent Mexican climber that displays its beauty best in southern countries. In cooler climates, it needs a warm and sunny position, but even then it will not flower until the second half of the summer. Sowing indoors early in the year will

Incarvillea sinensis 'Cheron'

Ipomoea lobata

Ipomoea lobata

encourage it to come into flower slightly sooner.

After mid-May, you can plant the *ipomoea* in open ground up against a pergola or, even better, in a pot or other container, as the soil will then warm up faster. The claret-colored stems wind their way upwards on tall supports and produce elegant trilobate leaves. The flowers follow from July onwards on separate stems, which may be picked for displaying in vases. While still in bud, the flowers are red but, as they develop, they become lighter and lighter until they are almost white. At this point, they open and release their stamens and pistil. The plant may ultimately grow several yards tall tall, but, in a pot, its growth is splendidly modest.

[2–4]

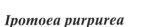

Ipomoea purpurea

COMMON MORNING GLORY

A wall of blue flowers – this seems an impossible achievement for an ordinary keen gardener. Yet the common morning glory makes it all so simple! Choose a fence or wall, preferably facing east, or south if need be. Fix vertical strings at a distance of about 6 in from one another. Provide nutritive soil at the foot of the wall or fence. Soak the large black seeds in tepid water for 24 hours. Then sow them directly in the garden, or in a large pot or other container. The seeds may be covered by over $1/2$ in of soil. The seedlings cannot tolerate frost and snails love them. If you have succeeded in averting those two threats, guide a plant towards each of the vertical strings and pull out the remaining plants (or give them away). They do not mind being transplanted. This also makes it possible to sow them indoors earlier in the year and then plant them out later on, which also reduces the risk of fatal damage being caused by snails or frost.

Once they have started up the rigging, the plants will continue to climb aloft at top speed and then come into flower by the end June. New flowers, $1^1/4$–2 in wide, in shades of blue, purple, pink, white, or combinations of those colors, will open daily. The flowers'

throats are always white – a characteristic difference between this plant and the very similar *Ipomoea tricolor*, which always has a yellowish throat. The flowers often open in the evening, but otherwise do so at night or in the early morning. They fade in the afternoon of the same day, and around midday in hot weather. As long as you keep the plants growing by ensuring that they have enough water and nourishment, there will be many new flowers every morning. The leaves, too, are highly decorative. They are heart-shaped, pointed, and often three-lobed.

[3–4] 5 ✿ ▼ ! ⚘

Ipomoea quamoclit

CYPRESS VINE

The winding shoots of this *Ipomoea* grow slowly but steadily up strings or twigs, which makes this species very suitable for pots or other containers. Its magnificent, deeply divided leaves and relatively small but subtle red flowers grow on the winding stems. The Cypress vine will bear flowers every day from July until the end of September, though not as many as *Ipomoea purpurea*. The species is sown indoors and may be taken out-of-doors to the warmest and sunniest spot you can find by the end of May. It is also possible to buy the plant, though it is not widely available.

[3–4] € ✿ ▼ ! ⚘

Ipomoea rubro-caerulea

See *Ipomoea tricolor*.

Ipomoea tricolor

This tricolored *ipomoea* closely resembles the common morning glory. Even so, according to some botanists, the differences between them are so great that the two species belong to quite different genera of plants. In a garden, however, they are both equally rewarding, as well as being suitable for the same purpose of covering a wall with a mass of flowers. To find out what to do, see *Ipomoea purpurea*.

Ipomoea tricolor, this is how the tricolored *ipomoea* climbs

Ipomoea tricolor 'Heavenly Blue'

There are several cultivars with different kinds of flower on the market. Those of *Ipomoea tricolor* 'Early Call Mixture' are almost 4 in wide, but their size is all that can be said in their favor. The flowers are misshapen and have white margins to basic colors such lavender blue and pink. One to avoid, I think. But then there is the unsurpassed *Ipomoea tricolor* 'Heavenly Blue,' a real treasure with sky-blue flowers, sometimes tending towards mauve. They can grow up to 4 in wide, and their throats are yellow and white. *Ipomoea tricolor* 'Pearly Gates' also has a yellow

throat but, apart from that, is pure white. The basic color of *Ipomoea tricolor* 'Flying Saucers' is sky-blue, but it also has irregular white streaks leading from the center to the margin of the flowers.

[3-4] 5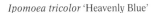

Ipomoea violacea

See *Ipomoea tricolor*.

Ipomoea tricolor 'Early Call Mixture'

Ipomoea tricolor 'Heavenly Blue'

Ipomopsis elegans

See *Ipomopsis rubra*.

Ipomopsis rubra

With its scarlet flowers and fine needle-shaped foliage on stems about 39 in long, *Ipomopsis rubra* would be one of the most popular of patio plants, were it not that it flowers so late in the season. It takes at least four months from the date of sowing for the plant to come into flower. It is, in fact, a biennial or perennial from the south of the United States, but it is cultivated as an annual in The Netherlands. Sow indoors in March–April to be able to enjoy the spectacle of its flowers in August and September.

The *Ipomopsis rubra* Arrow Series enables you to choose from several lovely flower colors: yellow, apricot, salmon pink to red. *Ipomopsis rubra* 'Red Arrow' bears flowers which are scarlet on the outside and creamy yellow specked with scarlet on the inside.

[3–4] 5

Ipomopsis rubra 'Red Arrow'

Iresine

BLOOD LEAF

The *Iresine* species were at one time popular as foliage plants for the flower-beds of large parks and country estates, where they were also planted in handsome urns. Fashions changed, and people lost interest in the species of *Iresine*. These plants are now beginning to return to red borders and as 'old-fashioned' plants in the gardens of historic country houses. In the old days, they were propagated almost exclusively by cuttings. Nowadays, plants grown from seed are also available. It does not look as if there will ever be a craze for them because, irrespective of whether they were grown from seed or cuttings, these typically tropical plants will not tolerate a single degree of frost and must not be put out-of-doors until the end of May. They are also disappointing in cold, wet summers.

Plant them in zones in flower-beds, or put them in pots or hanging baskets to serve as a background to other plants, as their small flowers are not at all decorative. They need well-drained soil which should never be let to dry out entirely, as that is something the plants

Iresine acuminata, blood leaf

Iresine herbstii 'Brilliantissima,' beefsteak plant

Iresine lindenii, blood leaf

herbstii has greenish-red foliage with blunt tips and light red veins. The leaf color of the cultivar 'Brilliantissima' is far more pronounced, a purplish red with striking rose-red veins. The leaves curl slightly inwards and are clearly pointed. Pinch out growing tips several times in spring to encourage bushy growth. The plants are eminently suitable for filling sections in flower-beds or for edging purposes, but they need a warm summer if they are to develop fully.

cannot tolerate. Find a sunny position to enable their intense leaf color to develop fully.

Iresine acuminata

BLOOD LEAF

Plants with the pointed leaves referred to by their scientific name and grown from seed are marketed under this name. The leaves of *Iresine lindenii*, however, may be even more pointed. The plants hardly differ from *Iresine herbstii* 'Brilliantissima' and may be used in the same way.

Iresine herbstii '**Brilliantissima**'

BEEFSTEAK PLANT

This is by far the best-known *Iresine. Iresine*

Iresine lindenii

BLOOD LEAF

This blood leaf is, if possible, even more sensitive to cold than the other species. This plant from Colombia has pointed leaves, but is about the same color as the above iresines – deep purple and rose-red.

Iresine reticulata

See *Iresine herbstii*.

Iresine axillaris

See *Laurentia axillaris*.

Isotoma fluviatilis

See *Laurentia fluviatilis*.

158

K, L

Kochia scoparia

See *Bassia scoparia.*

Lablab purpureus

AUSTRALIAN PEA, HYACINTH BEAN

In tropical and subtropical regions, the Australian pea is a familiar vegetable and its large purple pods are processed into food for both humans and animals. We can grow the climbing bean as an ornamental plant because of its relatively small, but very lovely, purple or white flowers, and because its foliage is so beautiful. That of the cultivar *Lablab purpureus* 'Ruby Moon' is pale greyish green when it comes out, but turns deep purple as it ages. Sow the

Lablab purpureus 'Ruby Moon,' Australian pea, hyacinth bean

lablab indoors in March–April, or directly outdoors from mid-April. Find the warmest and sunniest spot possible for it and give it plenty of water, whether it is in a pot of nutritive soil or planted in the garden.

[3–4] 4–5

Lantana camara

YELLOW SAGE

The florets making up the flower heads of *lantana* change color when they are out: orange turns deep red, yellow turns pink. The plant originally grew as a shrub in South America, but became naturalized in many tropical and subtropical countries, and is sometimes a real nuisance there. In The Netherlands, however, the shrub is guaranteed to freeze to death in winter.

Lovers of conservatory plants put the *lantana* in a light position at a minimum temperature of 50 °F in winter, so that it does not drop its leaves and soon starts to sprout again in spring. Once it has started, the plant grows rapidly, and nurserymen make good use of that. They propagate the shrub in winter, mainly by cuttings, but occasionally by seed, and are therefore in a position to market flowering plants in spring. These have a herbaceous appearance, and their spread is often greater than that of the woody conservatory plants.

Lantana camara, yellow sage

Lantana camara 'Aloha'

Lantana montevidensis

All you need to do is put them in pots or in a border, where they soon grow into small shrubs with a height and spread of about 20 in. Their non-stop flowering has a magnetic effect on butterflies. The plants will remain in flower until the first frosts of autumn. You can, of course, take cuttings, provided you are in a position to shepherd them through the winter correctly. Most people, however, will buy new plants every year.

Lantana camara 'Aloha' is rightly becoming popular. It has a spreading habit, which makes the plant particularly suitable for containers and hanging baskets. It is also useful in a border, where it might be combined with grey-leafed plants or, alternatively, with shades of blue. Its pale yellow flowers appear above variegated foliage with greyish-yellow edges. *Lantana camara* 'Goldsonne' also has a spreading and herbaceous growth, and bears lemon-yellow flowers.

Lantana montevidensis

Besides the familiar *Lantana camara*, you will occasionally find *Lantana montevidensis*. More suitable for containers and hanging baskets, its stems are so lax that they become pendulous almost immediately. The flower heads, usually a couple of inches in diameter, are mostly lilac pink to violet in color, but there are also white and yellow-flowered cultivars. The plants like to grow in a warm and sunny position, but have no other special requirements.

Lantana camara 'Aloha'

Lantana camara 'Goldsonne'

Lathyrus odoratus, sweet pea

Lathyrus odoratus, sweet pea

Lathyrus odoratus

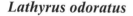

SWEET PEA

Sweet peas have lovely flowers and a delightful fragrance, hence their name. The fact that they really are peas is something you notice as soon as the spherical seeds roll out of the packet. Sow them directly in the garden in mid-April. Plant the seeds at the depth of about half a little finger. Be sure to enrich the spot where they are to flower with stable manure or other plant food, because sweet peas love that. As they climb, most sweet peas use their tendrils to hold on to any support they can find. They usually grow over 6 ft tall and may completely cover a wire-netting fence with flowers. Fix threads for them to climb up against wooden fences and walls. There are also low-growing cultivars which creep along the ground, or remain short, and do not need any support.

Plants sown outdoors in April will flower from the end of April and, in ideal circumstances, will go on flowering until September. in poor, dry soil or shady conditions, they will not flower for so long and may also fall victim to mildew. Picking the flowers will extend their flowering season. The stems are only about 8 in long, so that they make small bouquets. But oh, that scent! Sweet peas are among the loveliest bouquets you can give anyone.

The seed is usually provided in colorful mixtures, including that of *Lathyrus odoratus* 'Bouquet,' which grows to hip level without any support. It is similar in type to the Spencer Series and very suitable for cutting. Anyone gardening according to color will be interested in selected varieties with a clearly defined color. It remains to be seen, though, whether the plants will actually bear flowers in the color shown on the packet. Seed that you have harvested yourself is reasonably germinative, but the results are even less predictable. Bees and bumblebees are greatly attracted to the flowers and ensure cross-pollination.

Lathyrus odoratus 'Bouquet,' sweet pea

Lathyrus odoratus, sweet pea

Lathyrus odoratus 'Matucana' is a genuinely antique variety, and was cultivated in Italy before 1700. The blue and purple flowers are relatively small but their scent is wonderful! *Lathyrus odoratus* 'Spencer Lilac' belongs to the famous Spencer Series that was developed around 1900 and still stands out because of its large flowers, soft colors, and vigorous growth.

4-5

Lathyrus odoratus 'Matucana,' sweet pea

Lathyrus odoratus, sweet pea

Lathyrus odoratus 'Spencer Lilac,' sweet pea

Laurentia axillaris

This perennial from Australia creates a so-phisticated effect on our patios. Its star-shaped flowers grow to about 1½ in wide. They show up perkily above the compact plant, which may grow to between 4 in and 12 in high. The plant is, in fact, a genuine new acquisition which has only been culti-vated on a major scale for a few years, and is still available only from a few specialized sup-pliers of patio plants. Firms dealing in cut-tings provide flowering plants in spring. The same effect may be achieved by sowing in late summer the previous year. If sown in early spring, the plants will come into flower after about 4 months.

Sow the seed between August and October. Cover the seedlings carefully in severe winter weather, or sow in bowls which may be brought indoors temporarily. Overwintering them in an unheated greenhouse or cold frame is ideal. Commercial growers sow be-

tween December and March, but it is better for private gardeners to wait until March.

Put the plants out-of-doors in a sunny posi-tion and well-drained soil. Giving them plenty of water will not harm them, but the moisture must be able to drain away freely.

The color of the flowers varies between blue and pink. The differences are apparent from the names of the selections: *Laurentia axil-laris* 'Blue Stars' is supposed to have sky-blue flowers. Those of *Laurentia axillaris* 'Star-light Pink' are more or less pink. There is also a white-flowered cultivar, *Laurentia axillaris* 'White Star,' with slightly more vigorous growth.

[3] 8-10

Laurentia fluviatilis

As they are just over ½ in wide, you really need a magnifying glass to appreciate the beauty of these small flowers. They are borne

Laurentia axillaris

Laurentia axillaris 'Starlight Pink'

Laurentia axillaris 'Blue Stars'

Laurentia axillaris 'White Star'

Laurentia fluviatilis

Lavatera trimestris 'Pink Beauty', tree mallow

Laurentia fluviatilis 'County Park'

on a creeping plant that forms a small mat of minuscule, bright green leaves. The plant is actually a perennial that will tolerate about 12 degrees of frost in well-drained soil. There is, however, a problem in that, in Australia, it grows in very damp places and, in the Netherlands, likes moisture-retentive soil. It is therefore best to grow it in a patio container in partial shade. The plant is divided and on sale every spring.

Laurentia fluviatilis 'County Park' bears lavender-blue flowers about 5/8 in wide.

Lavatera trimestris

TREE MALLOW

With its colorful flowers, about 4 in wide, tree mallows certainly catch the eye in a border of annuals. The plants grow between 20 in and 20 in–5 ft tall, depending on the cultivar and the soil. The plants do best in loose, poor soil, where they grow less tall and flower even more profusely.

Sow directly in the garden in April–May to provide flowers from July. The flowering season lasts for a long time, and new flowers attracting all kinds of insects appear continually until October. You can pick lovely bouquets, after which the plants will branch out and flower again.

Lavatera trimestris 'Pink Beauty' is a very fresh-looking cultivar with a basic color that is palest pink (almost white) and purple veins ending in a purple throat. The plants grow to an average height of 24 in.

Lavatera trimestris 'Silver Cup' has brightly colored pink flowers with deep pink veins running through them. Their height depends on their position, but averages 28 in.

[4] 4–5 🌱 🏺 🐝

Legousia speculum-veneris

VENUS'S LOOKING-GLASS

The name Venus's-looking-glass is fully justified. The small violet-blue flowers are no more than $^3/_4$ in wide but have an unearthly beauty and look up to the skies like miniature radio telescopes. They are carried on spreading, bushy plants about 8 in high. Venus's looking-glass is a native plant in many parts of Europe, including Britain and The Netherlands, where it is now rare. It grows mainly on arable land in loose, moisture-retentive, and nutritive soil. All we need do is scatter its seed in ordinary garden soil from April onwards and enjoy the small flowers from June. They do not flower for very long, so it is advisable to sow repeatedly.

As a result of an error by one of the largest seed merchants, the plant is marketed on a large scale under the name of a different botanical genus, *Downingia*.

4-6

Leonotis leonurus

Lavatera trimestris 'Silver Cup,' tree mallow

Lavatera trimestris 'Silver Cup,' tree mallow

Legousia speculum-veneris, Venus's looking-glass

LION'S EAR

This South African plant starts flowering about three to four months after it was sown. It is better known as a container plant and may be kept in a cool and, if need be, dark place in winter to allow it to sprout again in spring after hard pruning. Firms specializing in plants propagated by seed or cuttings, market flowering plants intended for cultivation as annuals as early as June. Put the plant in a large pot on your patio and you will spend months imagining you are in the tropics. Provide *leonotis* with a sheltered, warm, and sunny position, and give it plenty of water and fertilizer to keep it flowering. The orange whorls of flowers develop from the bottom upwards on flower stems which may ultimately grow to 6 ft.

Leptosiphon grandiflorus

See *Linanthus grandiflorus*.

Leptosiphon 'Stardust'

The assertion that there is strength in numbers is proved by the miniature flowers of 'Stardust', which appear in such large numbers that they completely cover the 4-in high plants with their colors. The foliage is delicate, hairy, and needle-shaped, and, on poor soil, it forms a dense mat of greyish greenery. In richer soil, the stems grow longer, greener, and more untidily at the expense of the com-

Leonotis leonurus, lion's ear

Leptosiphon 'Stardust'

pact appearance of this carpeting plant. Comparable plants are to be found under the names of *Linanthus* ssp. *leptosiphon* 'Confetti Mixture,' *Gilia* × *hybrida,* and *Linanthus* × *hybridus* 'French Hybrids.' Sow them all directly in the garden in April–May, and find a sunny position for them – for instance, on a rockery or along the patio. The plants flower profusely from the end of June, reaching a peak in July and continuing with a modest second flowering in August and September. The flowering season may be extended by repeated sowing.

4-6

Leucanthemum paludosum

This is a miniature marguerite from the south of Spain and Portugal. It grows to no more than 6–8 in tall and its flowers are $^3/_4$–$1^1/_4$ in in diameter. The plant provides ideal groundcover in flower-beds and along the edges of

Leucanthemum paludosum

167

Limonium perezii, sea lavender

Limonium sinuatum 'Forever Gold,' sea lavender

a patio. It is also suitable for pots and other containers. Sow the seed directly in the garden in loose soil and preferably a sunny position in April–May.

4-5

Limonium perezii

SEA LAVENDER

In the Canary Islands, this species of sea lavender grows wild, but also in gardens amongst the petunias, as shown in this photograph. The species carries impressive flower heads, and this gave nurseries specializing in cut flowers the idea of growing the plants from seed in greenhouses, and adding the flowers to summery bouquets. The stems grow up to about 24 in long. It takes about 4 months to grow flowers for the cut-flower market from seed.

The seed is rarely on offer to private gardeners. If you manage to acquire some, let it soak in tepid water for 24 hours, and then sow it indoors in March–April. The plants like warmth and should not be planted out-of-doors until mid-summer.

[3–4]

Limonium sinuatum

SEA LAVENDER

When it comes to the properties of flowers suitable for cutting and drying, those of sea lavender are unsurpassed. Its sturdy, winged stems branch out widely. The actual flowers are minute and usually white. They are surrounded by sepals fused into tubes and providing color. They continue to color the stems, even after the petals have fallen. The species originally had blue sepals but there are currently cultivars in all kinds of shades, mostly blue, but also pink, yellow, red and white. They are not picked and dried until they are fully colored. They retain their color remarkably well and are therefore very popular among dried-flower enthusiasts. They are also sold in large quantities as cut flowers, although a summery bouquet of sea lavender could hardly be called subtle. Fortunately, more subdued colors such as pale yellow and lavender blue are also available.

The original species is about 16 in tall, but that size is rare nowadays. The flowers for cutting and drying are taller – up to 32 in – and potted plants are also available. They grow about 12 in high and are meant for flower-beds and containers.

Limonium sinuatum 'Forever Gold' is typical of the plants cultivated for the markets in

Limonium sinuatum 'Fortress Dark Blue,' sea lavender

Limonium sinuatum 'Fortress Heavenly Blue,' sea lavender

Limonium sinuatum 'Fortress Yellow,' sea lavender

cut or dried flowers. Its stems are relatively thin and, in greenhouses, are supported by chrysanthemum mesh, which would hardly be suitable for flower-beds.

Limonium sinuatum 'Fortress Dark Blue' belongs to the popular 'Fortress Series,' which also does well out-of-doors. At a length of 28 in, the stems are on the short side, thin and yet sturdy. The same series includes, inter alia, *Limonium sinuatum* 'Fortress Heavenly Blue,' with lavender-blue flowers, and *Limonium sinuatum* 'Fortress Yellow,' with soft yellow flowers.

The new Qis Series covers about the same color spectrum. The plants have stiffly upright, sturdy stems about 32 in tall. They are intended mainly for the cut-flower market. *Limonium sinuatum* 'Qis Dark Blue,' with purplish-blue flowers, and *Limonium sinuatum* 'Qis Heavenly Blue,' with lavender-blue flowers, were new introductions in 2000. *Limonium sinuatum* 'Qis Rose' has been on the market for longer and has flowers in a soft shade of pink.

Limonium sinuatum 'Turbo White' has white flowers with a tinge of yellow.

If you want to sow sea lavender yourself, it is best to scatter the seed directly in the garden in April–May. You may then expect to have flowers in the months of August and September. It is possible to bring forward the flowering season by sowing indoors earlier in the year, but, in that case, the plants need to be put out in the garden at the beginning of May because they need a cold period at about 50 °F if they are to flower freely. Early May is

169

Limonium sinuatum 'Qis Rose,' sea lavender

a particularly tense period as the plants barely tolerate frost and may be ruined by unexpected sub-zero temperatures. Sow indoors in February–March at temperatures between 59–71 °F and grow the plants on in a place that is light, airy, and cool – 59 °F.
Limonium likes poor, sandy soil and a sunny position.

[2–3] 4–5

Limonium sinuatum 'Qis Dark Blue,' sea lavender

Limonium suworowii

See *Psylliostachys suworowii.*

Linanthus pacificus

See *Linanthus grandiflorus.*

Linanthus × hybridus

See *Leptosiphon.*

Linanthus grandiflorus

It is rare to see delicacy such as that of *Linanthus grandiflorus*. The stems are somewhat lax and grow to about 16 in in height. They have needle-shaped, divided, and softly hairy leaves that make it appear as if the stems are wreathed in downy whorls. As for the pale flowers with their lilac bloom – they are no

Limonium sinuatum 'Qis Heavenly Blue,' sea lavender

Limonium sinuatum 'Turbo White,' sea lavender

more than ³/₄ in wide, but so very beautiful! They flower from July to September.

Sow the seed directly in the garden from April to May, preferably in loose, well-drained, but nutritive soil in full sunlight. In that kind of position, the plant will remain compact and sturdy.

4-5 !

Linaria alpina

ALPINE TOADFLAX

Alpine toadflax is not necessarily an annual, although it is well known as such. In ideal circumstances, it will survive the winter. This often happens on rockeries with perfect drainage, but the gardener has to wait and see. It is therefore better to regard the small plant – it grows to 4–8 in tall – as an annual.

The stems with their bluish-grey foliage branch out and become pendulous without any support, which makes the plant eminently suitable for hanging baskets. The attractive, violet flowers, ³/₄ in long, with an orange spot, appear continually from June until the end of the summer.

Although it is quite feasible to sow the species oneself, I was unable to find the seed at any of the suppliers. The plants themselves are quite often from growers of rockery plants and suppliers of annuals.

Linanthus grandiflorus

Linaria alpina, Alpine toadflax

171

Linaria genistifolia ssp. *dalmatica*

DALMATIAN TOADFLAX

In the Balkans and southern Italy, this toad-flax grows as a perennial in the mountains. Its leaves are greyish green and its flowers – about $^3/_4$ in long – are an improbable shade of bright lemon yellow, sometimes with an orange spot on their lips. The plant may grow up to 39 in tall, but is usually shorter and very suitable for growing in a container. Sow the seeds outdoors in February for the plant to flower in July–August. By cutting off the dead flower stems, you will force a second flower-ing. Put the plant in a sunny position and in well-drained soil.

[1–3]

Linaria maroccana

MOROCCAN TOADFLAX

The kinds of Moroccan toadflax that are on

Linaria maroccana 'Fairy Bouquet,' Moroccan toadflax

Linaria genistifolia ssp. *dalmatica*, Dalmatian toadflax

sale are nearly always cultivars resulting from crosses between several annual types of toad-flax. The flowers are always small, $^1/_2$–$^3/_4$ in long, and always colorful in shades of red, lilac, pink, and yellow, nearly always with a yellow or white spot on their lips. The plants grow about 12–16 in tall and are often used in compact multicolored groups. When seen flowering among other wild flowers, they lose their somewhat artificial appear-ance.

Sow directly in the garden for the plants to flower in July–August, and sow again for later flowers. Cut off the stems after they have flowered to encourage a second flush.

Linaria maroccana 'Fairy Bouquet' is one of the multicolored mixtures.

3–5

Linaria purpurea

PURPLE TOADFLAX

The stems of this Italian toadflax grow stiffly upright, sometimes to over 39 in tall, with

Linaria purpurea × 'Bowles Mauve,' purple toadflax

Linaria purpurea × 'Canon J. Went,' purple toadflax

small violet-colored flowers at the top. The perennials are on sale, in flower, in spring, but it is also quite feasible to grow them from seed as annuals. Sow indoors in March–April, or scatter the seed outdoors in April–May. In mild climates, especially in England, they will self-seed freely.

Linaria purpurea 'Bowles' Mauve' bears the typical violet-purple flowers of the species. *Linaria purpurea* 'Canon J. Went' has lovely pale pink flowers, but the color is not reliably retained in seed one has harvested oneself. In dry soil, the plants may survive Dutch winters.

It is best to sow directly outdoors in April–May, or else indoors earlier in the year. Put the plants in a sunny position in well-drained soil.

[3–4] 4–5   **!**

Linaria triornithophora

THREE BIRDS TOADFLAX

Each bud of this species resembles a sleeping

Linaria triornithophora, three birds toadflax

pigeon, with its head tucked under its feathers. And because the flowers are always grouped together in spikes of three, the botanist Linnaeus called the species "three birds" (*triornithophora*). As they awaken, purple flowers with a yellow lip unfurl. The plants grow to about 32 in in height and flower in late summer. They like well-drained soil and may survive the winter there in mild climates. In The Netherlands, this is unlikely, and it is better for us to sow annually in April–May.

4-5

Linum grandiflorum

RED FLAX

When red flax starts flowering in June, it seems as if it will never stop. Small pink flowers with darker centers continually open out into saucers almost 1¼ in wide, hence the attribute "large-flowered." Several cultivars have been developed from the species, of which *Linum grandiflorum* 'Bright Eyes' is, in my opinion, by far the most beautiful.

Sow the seed directly in the garden in April–May, preferably in well-drained, nutritive soil. Red flax likes a warm and sunny position. The stems, about 12–16 in tall, are suitable for cutting and drying. You can harvest your own seed from it and enjoy this magnificent plant for many more years to come.

4-5   !

Linum usitatissimum

FLAX

The thin stems and small blue flowers of flax show up best in between other plants. Linseed is often added to blue flower mixtures, but you may also scatter it separately in bare spots in borders. The species is an important agricultural crop, providing linseed oil and flax, as well as other products.

Linum grandiflorum 'Bright Eyes,' red flax

Linum usitatissimum, flax

The plants often grow over 20 in tall, and tend to bend over under the weight of the developing seeds. These are enclosed in spherical capsules which may be used as dried flowers. The small pale blue flowers, however, are the plant's most decorative feature.

Sow the flaxseed at intervals from March until May to provide a succession of flowers that may continue from July until September.

3-5

Lisianthus russellianus

See *Eustoma grandiflorum.*

Loasa lateritia

See *Caiophora lateritia.*

Lobelia erinus

GARDEN LOBELIA

The ancestor of our garden lobelias was a South African plant about 10 in tall, but nurserymen nowadays would be mortified if their labours produced a plant that high. In fact, this rarely happens, since lobelias grown for gardens are very compact or have a trailing habit. The first group is referred to as *compacta* or 'Compacta,' but more precisely as the *Lobelia erinus* Compacta Group. The plants have a compact upright habit and form green tufts 4–6 in high. They are highly suitable for flower-beds, containers, and edging purposes, but may also be planted in the center of a hanging basket.

The second group, *Lobelia erinus* Pendula Group, often referred to as *pendula* or 'Pendulas,' ultimately acquire a trailing habit. As young plants, trailing and upright lobelias are almost indistinguishable from one another. It is not until they start growing vigorously that trailing lobelias reveal their true nature by arching over the rims of window-boxes, pots, and hanging baskets and concealing them with a mass of green-leafed stems and numerous small flowers, usually colored blue, pink, or white.

Trailing lobelias are, in fact, also suitable for flower-beds and borders, where they will cover the soil with their creeping stems.

Large quantities of both groups of plants are always on sale in May and June, having been grown on, usually from seed, in large greenhouse complexes during the preceding two or three months.

Several cultivars that do not remain true to type when grown from seed are propagated by cuttings. In South Africa, lobelias are perennials growing along watercourses and in the shade of bushes where the soil dries up less quickly. In our part of the world, the plant is susceptible to frost and is therefore

Lobelia erinus 'Half Moon' (Compacta Group)

Lobelia erinus 'KaiserWilhelm' (Compacta Group)

cultivated as an annual. Put bought plants in a very light and preferably sunny spot out-of-doors after the last night frost. Make sure the soil does not dry out, because lobelias do not recover well from lack of moisture, however temporary the condition may be. Also make sure the soil is well drained, and do not add much fertilizer. Excessive feeding stimulates

Lobelia erinus 'Regatta Rose' (Pendula Group), trailing lobelia

Lobelia erinus 'Regatta Sky Blue' (Pendula Group), trailing lobelia

Lobelia erinus 'Regatta Sky Blue' (Pendula Group), trailing lobelia

Lobelia erinus 'Regatta Sky Blue' (Pendula Group), trailing lobelia

Lobelia erinus 'Riviera Lilac' (Compacta Group), garden lobelia

leaf formation at the expense of flowers. The flowering season may last from May until September.

Few people sow lobelias themselves, but here are a few tips for those who like a challenge. Sow indoors from February to April at a temperature of just over 68 °F. The very fine seed should not be covered, because it can germinate only in light conditions. It must not dry out either. The seedlings grow on well at 50–59 °F. After hardening off in April–May, they may be planted out-of-doors after the last night frost.

Cultivars belonging to the Compacta Group include *Lobelia erinus* 'Half Moon' (blue with a definite white center, early flowering); *Lobelia erinus* 'Kaiser Wilhelm' (gentian-blue flowers); *Lobelia erinus* 'Riviera Lilac' (a lilac-pink newcomer); and *Lobelia erinus* 'Riviera Sky Blue' Improved, a somewhat

Lobelia erinus 'Riviera Sky Blue' improved (Compacta Group), garden lobelia

taller gentian-blue plant, very suitable for containers.

The trailing lobelias include: *Lobelia erinus* 'Regatta Rose,' an initially very compact cultivar with crimson-pink flowers; and *Lobelia erinus* 'Regatta Sky Blue,' comparable to the previous plant, but bearing sky-blue flowers.

[2–4]

Lobelia erinus 'Emperor William'

See *Lobelia erinus* 'Kaiser Wilhelm' (Compacta Group).

Lobelia 'Richardii'

TRAILING LOBELIA

The stems of this trailing lobelia are longer and sturdier than those of the plants belong-

Lobelia 'Richardii,' trailing lobelia

ing to the Pendula Group of *Lobelia erinus*. Other lobelia species were crossed in to achieve this remarkable result. 'Richardii' is very suitable for trailing over the edges of larger pots and for hanging baskets. It is propagated by cuttings.

Lobelia × *speciosa*

LOBELIA

With stems rising up to 2–3 ft, and full of brightly colored flowers, $1^1/_4$ in wide, these lobelias are genuine eye-catchers in a garden. The cross was first achieved in Canada by crossing three species of lobelia. This resulted in a perennial that tolerates a fair amount of frost and which you will therefore still be able to admire after its first year. In spite of this, the numerous cultivars are being marketed as annuals. The seeds are sown in greenhouses in January, at a temperature of about 68 °F. The seed should not be covered, but must not dry out during the germination

Lobelia × *speciosa* 'Compliment Deep Red,' lobelia

Lobelia × *speciosa*, lobelia

Lobelia × *speciosa* 'Fan Scarlet,' lobelia

178

process either. Flowering plants may then be supplied in early July.

Enthusiasts are likely to do better by sowing later, in March–April. The plants will obviously come into flower later, in August at the earliest. Put the plants in a sunny position in very nutritive soil, which must never be allowed to dry out. Beautiful cultivars have been developed over the years, mostly in shades of red and pink. They provide excellent cut flowers.

Lobelia × *speciosa* 'Compliment Deep Red' was awarded several prizes because of its outstanding qualities. The plant grows about 28 in tall and, in its first year, bears a single flower stem of deep-red flowers, which contrast beautifully with the fresh green, downy foliage. The plant will flower more profusely in its second year.

Lobelia × *speciosa* 'Fan Scarlet' was awarded a gold medal by Fleuroselect in 1995. The plants grow about 24 in tall and bear several stems of flowers in their first year. The individual flowers are slightly smaller than those of the previous cultivar, but they are more striking because of their bright red color.

[1–4]

Lobelia valida

LOBELIA

At 16 in tall, this South African lobelia resembles a specimen of the *Lobelia erinus* Compacta Group that has turned out a little on the crude side. It has an upright habit, rather fleshy leaves, and continues to bear new flowers for many months. They are considerably larger than those of the ordinary garden lobelia, blue to purplish blue with large white centers. These perennials are not fully hardy and are propagated by commercial growers, who market them in full bloom from early summer. On rare occasions, the seed is also on sale. For the method of sowing, see *Lobelia erinus*.

[1–4]

Lobularia maritima

SWEET ALYSSUM

Gardens where sweet alyssum comes up spontaneously are fortunate, for they must have soil that is loose and aerated, sunny, yet moist enough to allow seeds to germinate. Alyssum is a small plant and will not return to hardened, neglected, overgrown soil in a chilly garden. You will have to sow it your-

Lobelia valida, lobelia

Lobelia ×*speciosa* 'Fan Scarlet,' lobelia

Lobularia maritima 'Easter Bonnet Deep Rose,' sweet alyssum

Lobularia maritima 'Easter Bonnet Pink,' sweet alyssum

Lobularia maritima 'New Apricot,' sweet alyssum

Lobularia maritima 'Paletta,' sweet alyssum

Lobularia maritima 'Salmon,' sweet alyssum

self the first time round, because the species originally came from the sunny slopes along the Mediterranean coasts. Warmth is important to germination, which is why the plant often germinates between paving slabs and in cracks in walls.

For hundreds of years, seed merchants have continually introduced new cultivars of sweet alyssum. Most modern cultivars are very compact, often no more than 2½–4 in high when they come into flower. This makes them very suitable for forming part of colored patterns in flower-beds. The old-fashioned taller varieties show up better as edging plants and in containers, but, unfortunately, it is becoming increasingly difficult to acquire them. The rounded heads of small flowers appear at the top of short stems and release a delightfully sweet, honeyed fragrance. The seed will be start to form lower down. That is the time to cut the flowers if you want to enjoy flowering sweet alyssum in late summer; the plants will recover rapidly and flower again.

Sweet alyssum is very easy to sow. Scatter the seed outdoors from mid-April. It is very important to sow *Lobularia* very thinly, because plants that are too crowded will flower poorly and become subject to mildew. Thin

Lobularia maritima 'Tiny Tim,' sweet alyssum

Lopezia racemosa

the seedlings to at least 4 in, and preferably to 6–8 in apart. Sowing indoors earlier in the year is quite feasible. You need not start excessively early, because the seedlings develop into flowering plants within two months. Some people sow *Lobularia* in autumn and provide protection against the worst of the wet cold. The plants will then come into flower very early, but are more likely to be affected by mildew.

Lobularia maritima 'Easter Bonnet Deep Rose' is one of the latest arrivals – it is low-growing, and bears a profusion of small bright pink flowers. *Lobularia maritima* 'Easter Bonnet Pink' belongs to the same series and has lilac-pink flowers.

Lobularia maritima 'New Apricot' is a dwarf, with seemingly white flowers that, on closer inspection, turn out to have a touch of apricot.

Lobularia maritima 'Paletta' has a wide range of colors, several shades of pink – crimson, lilac, brownish – and also white. The small plants have a delightfully old-fashioned look about them, and yet they are only 4 in high. In fact, 'Paletta' is very modern and was introduced in 1997.

Lobularia maritima 'Salmon' has flowers in a currently fashionable color – salmon pink. The small plants grow to about 4 in high.

At 3¼ in high, *Lobularia maritima* 'Tiny Tim' is a genuine miniature, with a spreading habit. The plants themselves are hidden from view by a carpet of small white flowers. One of the Dutch common names for sweet alyssum is "snow carpet," and 'Tiny Tim' shows you the reason.

[3–4] 4–5 ▼

Lopezia coronata

See *Lopezia racemosa*.

Lopezia racemosa

This is one of those "Whatever-is-that?" plants, species which make visitors to your garden stop in their tracks to enquire about their strange appearance. The small pink flowers, 5/8 in wide, have a very remarkable shape resembling that of a small devil with a retroussé nose and ears like table-tennis bats. The British liken it to a mosquito and call the species "mosquito flower." The plant grows to about 20 in in height, and its large leaves are undoubtedly its principal decorative feature. Pinching out the growing tips will encourage the plant to branch out and produce more flower stems.

It is best to sow the seed directly in the garden from the end of April or, alternatively, sow indoors in March–April. The plants dislike full sunlight and keep their looks far better in partial shade.

[3–4] 4–5

Lophospermum atrosanguineum

See *Rhodochiton atrosanguineus*.

Lophospermum erubescens

See *Asarina erubescens*.

181

Lopezia racemosa

Lotus berthelotii

Lotus berthelotii

The pendulous stems of needle-shaped foliage superficially resemble those of ornamental asparagus. The flowers of *Lotus* make you open your eyes – what a magnificent display of red, orange, or yellow! The plants are widely propagated by cuttings nowadays, and the flowers are no longer the preserve of those with greenhouses. You can buy the plants in flower in late spring.

Make sure you have a very warm and sheltered spot for it, but preferably not in full sunlight. The soil should be well drained, so that it does not stay wet in cool weather. It should not, however, dry out entirely. If your green fingers can ensure all that, the plant will flower until far into autumn. You can then, if you wish, keep it in a light position at a temperature between 41 °F and 54 °F until the following spring.

Lotus berthelotii

Lipinus cruckshanksii

See *Lupinus mutabilis* var. *cruckshanksii*.

Lupinus mutabilis var. *cruckshanksii*

LUPIN

In the Peruvian Alps, these shrublike lupins make the slopes turn blue. In The Netherlands, the plant is cultivated as an annual since it cannot survive the winters. As an annual, the plant stays beautifully green and succulent, with flower stems reaching 28–39 in in height. Bright blue predominates in the keel but, above them, there is a yellow blotch and an upper petal in palest lilac. The blue of the keel gradually changes to red as the flower ages.

The care of this magnificent species is very simple. Sow the seed directly in the garden in April–May, and thin the plants to a distance apart of at least 12 in. From June on-

Lupinus mutabilis var. *cruckshanksii*, lupin

wards, the plant will flower for about two months.

4–5

Lupinus nanus

SMALL LUPIN

The small lupin, a most rewarding plant for a blue annual border, is one of my personal favorites. It adorns entire areas with its fragrant shade of blue, capped with yellow. The individual plants grow to 6–20 in in height, depending on the soil. In poor soil, they remain compact and particularly beautiful, and the foliage acquires a greyish-green color. Make sure you allow an adequate distance between the individual plants. Rob Leopold, the man who promoted the subtle new range of annuals, even plants them as much as 20 in apart, so that they can achieve their maximum spread. In that way, the lupins do not restrict themselves to single upright flower stems. Instead, they spread out into complex flowering organ-like structures and also go on flowering for a longer period. The flowers, however, come to an end after barely two months, and then the seed pods ripen. The seeds are quite easy to harvest. Sow them directly in the garden during the subsequent months of April and May for flowers from the end of June until far into August.

4–5   !

Lupinus nanus, small lupin

Lupinus nanus, small lupin

Lychnis coeli-rosa

See *Silene coeli-rosa.*

Lysimachia congestiflora 'Lyssi,' loosestrife

Lysimachia congestiflora 'Lyssi,' loosestrife

Lysimachia congestiflora

LOOSESTRIFE

One of the most rewarding patio plants has been available from specialists ever since 1992, but it still has not managed to achieve a large-scale breakthrough. Perhaps it is the yellow flowers that prevent it from becoming popular, or perhaps the intervals following the various periods of flowering. Still, this particular loosestrife should attract far more interest. The plant has a spreading habit and half trails over the rim of a pot. Its dense foliage makes a splendid filler.

The cultivar *Lysimachia congestiflora* 'Lyssi' is the version most frequently available. Its small flowers have red centers.

The plant is propagated by cuttings, but it grows slowly and takes a long time to cultivate, and that makes it pricey. Stand the plant in a place that is warm but not too sunny – to prevent scorching – and then water normally.

Majorana hortensis

See *Origanum majorana*.

Malope trifida

The buds of *Malope trifida* are blinkered. They are enclosed not only by their calyces, but also by axillary leaflets immediately below the buds. As they open, trumpet-shaped flowers, about 2³/₄ in wide, unfurl. Those of the species are purplish red, but other colors are also available now.

The trumpet-shaped *Malope trifida* grows as an annual in western Mediterranean regions. It likes a sunny position, nutritive soil, and adequate moisture. Sow the seed indoors in March–April, or scatter it directly in the garden after mid-April. The plant comes into flower in July and just goes on flowering. More and more blooms are carried at the top of the approximately 32-in tall plant, and attract huge numbers of butterflies.

Malope trifida 'Vulcan' grows vigorously and bears magnificent crimson flowers, 3¹/₄ in wide. The flowers of *Malope trifida* 'White Queen' are slightly smaller and snowy white.

[3–4] 4–5

Malope trifida 'Vulcan'

Malope trifida 'White Queen'

Malva 'Gibbortello'

MALLOW

The various species of mallow grow mainly in southern Europe, but have a long history fur-

Malva 'Gibbortello,' mallow

ther north. Their leaves are edible, and some species were used as medicine. The species mentioned here are grown as biennials or perennials in the south. They survive the winter in mild climates, but in regions where the temperature can drop to 5 °F or even lower, they cannot live through an average one, and it is therefore better to grow them as annuals. They are propagated by cuttings or seed in early spring. Anyone wanting to grow them from seed should start early, because the seedlings need about four months to come into flower.

'Gibbortello' may be propagated by seed or cuttings. Growing it as a biennial – sow in late summer – is also quite feasible. The plant grows about 4 ft tall. Its purple flowers fade to lilac mauve. After it has flowered, the plant usually dies.

[2–3] 4–5 7–9 🖌 € 🌼 🐝

Malva mauritiana

See *Malva sylvestris*.

Malva neglecta

DWARF MALLOW

The stems of dwarf mallows are almost prostrate initially, and then rise up to a maximum height of 20 in. The annual species grows wild almost throughout Europe, including The Netherlands. From June until September, the leaf axils are adorned with whitish pink flowers with mauve stripes. At more than ³/₄ in wide, the flowers are considerably smaller than those of its close relative, *Malva sylvestris*. Sow directly in the garden in April for flowers from July onwards.

4–5 🌼 🐝

Malva sylvestris

COMMON MALLOW

The common mallow is a native perennial in The Netherlands, but its widest distribution is in countries farther south. Here, it is margin-

Malva neglecta, dwarf mallow

Malva sylvestris, common mallow

ally hardy and the vulnerable cultivars are therefore grown mainly as annuals. Because it takes about four months for the seedlings to come into flower, commercial growers sow very early in the year and can therefore supply flowering plants by the end of May. The flowers are about $1\frac{1}{2}$ in wide. If you sow the seeds yourself, the plants usually come into flower in late summer, but they will go on flowering for much longer. The plant continues to grow while it is in flower, and, depending on its position, ultimately reaches a height of 3–5 ft. It does best in loose, warm, and nutritive soil.

The characteristic "cheeses" are formed lower down the stems. Inside them, the disc-shaped seeds are packed close together like rolls of sweets, but in circular capsules.

To ensure early flowering, the seeds may be sown indoors in the first months of the year. For flowers in late summer, sow directly in the garden in early April.

Among the many cultivars, the following are currently very popular: *Malva sylvestris* 'Moravia,' because of its extra-large dark mauve flowers with deep-red veins; *Malva sylvestris* 'Primley Blue,' which has a spreading growth and does not grow more than 39 in tall. The lavender-colored flowers have mauve veins.

Malva sylvestris 'Zebrina' has large, very pale pink flowers with strongly contrasting purplish-red stripes.

[2–3] 4–5

Malva sylvestris 'Primley Blue,' common mallow

Malva sylvestris Zebrina,' common mallow

Malva sylvestris 'Moravia,' common mallow

Malva verticillata 'Crispa'

Matricaria recutita, real camomile

Matricaria recutita, real camomile

Malva verticillata 'Crispa'

The beautifully shaped and prickly foliage is
very popular as ornamental greenery in bouquets and as a base for the elegant decoration
of a dessert – it is edible. The plant may grow
as tall as a man and is therefore also used as
an annual screen. The small flowers emerge
from clusters in the axils of the leaves. They
are only 5/8 in wide, but very lovely.

Sow this mallow directly in the garden from
March onwards. The plants have no special
requirements.

3-5

Matricaria capensis

See *Tanacetum parthenium.*

Matricaria chamomilla

See *Matricaria recutita.*

Matricaria inodora

See *Tripleurospermum inodorum.*

Matricaria maritima ssp. *inodora*

See *Tripleurospermum inodorum.*

Matricaria perforata

See *Tripleurospermum inodorum.*

Matricaria recutita

REAL CAMOMILE

Large quantities of camomile often spring up
in places where white sand is supplied for de-
velopments such as a new housing estate or
a new fly-over. Having long lain dormant in
deeper layers, the seed germinates as soon as
it comes to the surface. After a few years,

other plants take over and the camomile gradually disappears.

Camomile is also a short-lived summer-flowering plant in a garden. Sow the seed in loose, preferably poor soil in a sunny spot in spring. The plants grow 8–24 in tall, depending on the richness of the soil. They flower between June and August. The small flowers may be pulled off the plants with a fork and dried in the shade before using them for making camomile tea. Check by squeezing or cutting open a few flower heads. Real camomile has a hollow space below the yellow tubular flowers, but in the other species, including false camomile, the space is filled.

Camomile is an ideal plant for temporarily providing a profusion of flowers in natural parts of the garden that have been dug over.

3–4

Matthiola incana

STOCK

From April onwards, florists' bouquets often include stocks. They enchant us with the soft colors of the double flowers, but, above all, with their intensely sweet scent. It has an almost stupefying effect and some people think it is excessively strong. The stems of the varieties grown for cutting are often about 28 in long. Containers full of stocks are also marketed in spring, and are meant for planting out in flower-beds in the garden.

The commercial cultivation of stocks is fairly complicated. Still, you can have a go yourself by sowing them indoors at 68 °F in March–April. Allow the temperature to fall drastically after that, and note which seedlings develop a dark green color – these are the single-flowered plants – and which remain light green – the double-flowered varieties. Then you can select them to suit your own taste. Grow the plants on at about 50–59 °F, and plant them out-of-doors after mid-May. Find a sunny position for them in well-drained soil. If seeds are sown directly in the garden in April–May, the plants will come into flower in July.

Matthiola incana 'Miracle Ball Pink' with 'Miracle Gold,' stocks

Matthiola incana 'Miracle Crimson,' stock

Matthiola incana 'Miracle Lavender,' stock

Matthiola incana 'Miracle Lavender,' stock

Melampodium paludosum 'Discovery'

The varieties in the Miracle Series are specifically cultivated for cutting. They do not branch out, but grow neatly upright to about in. *Matthiola incana* 'Miracle Ball Pink' has soft pink flowers, those of *Matthiola incana* 'Miracle Crimson' are crimson, those of *Matthiola incana* 'Miracle Gold' are buttery yellow, and those of *Matthiola*

Medicago sativa, lucerne

incana 'Miracle Lavender' are lavender blue.

[3–4] 4–5

Maurandya erubescens

See *Asarina erubescens*.

Maurandya scandens

See *Asarina scandens*.

Medicago sativa

LUCERNE

Lucerne is known mainly as a garnish for salad (alfalfa), a fodder plant, a green fertilizer, and a crop for bee-keeping. It is also, however, a very attractive plant that will brighten up a small patch in a natural garden. It will also attract many bees and butterflies. Sow directly in the garden in early spring. For use as a green fertilizer, the plants are dug over just before they come into flower – after about three months. Otherwise you may enjoy its flowers in July–August. The perennial forms small tubercles in the soil, from which it will sprout again the following spring.

3-4

Melampodium paludosum

A lot of foliage combined with golden yellow flowers is something that most keen gardeners do not like very much. Yellow is not very easy to combine with other colors. If, however, you put this American plant in a container, its image will suddenly change. The green foliage will cover the pot and grow to 10 in in height, and the yellow flowers will look bright and cheerful on a patio. The plants do not flower profusely, but keep on

flowering from the time of purchase in May–June until well into October, when the first sharp frost will kill them off. There will be new ones on sale the following year. Wait until June before putting them out-of-doors in a sunny position, because the plants dislike the cold and permanently wet soil.

In the brief period that the plant has been increasing in popularity, quite a lot of cultivars have been developed. *Melampodium paludosum* 'Discovery' and *Melampodium paludosum* 'Medallion' both have fairly coarse foliage. *Melampodium paludosum* 'Derby' has smaller leaves, and those of *Melampodium paludosum* 'Showstar' have a very regular shape.

[2-4]

Mesembryanthemum cordifolium

See *Aptenia cordifolia.*

Mesembryanthemum criniflorum

See *Dorotheanthus bellidiformis.*

Million Bells Blue

See *Petunia* 'Sunbelbu.'

Million Bells Pink

See *Petunia* 'Sunbelpi.'

Melampodium paludosum 'Medaillon'

Mimulus aurantiacus (with *Oxalis vulcanicola*), monkey flower

Mimulus aurantiacus, monkey flower

Mimulus aurantiacus

MONKEY FLOWER

The sticky branches of this shrubby monkey flower eventually grow to about 39 in in length. The plant is indigenous in the south-western regions of the United States and likes warm, sunny weather. Its dark green leaves are coated with a shiny, sticky layer. The orange to salmon-pink flowers, $1^1/_2$ in wide, are carried from late spring until early autumn. The stems grow in all directions and, unless supported, will eventually begin to trail beautifully. This makes the plant particularly suitable for hanging baskets and large pots, in which the plant goes well with all kinds of more compact summer-flowering species.
Mimulus aurantiacus is propagated by cuttings. Flowering plants are available from specialist patio plant firms from May. It is possible to overwinter them if you can provide a light, cool, and frost-free place.

Mimulus aurantiacus var. puniceus

See *Mimulus puniceus*.

Mimulus glutinosus

See *Mimulus aurantiacus*.

Mimulus × hybridus

MONKEY FLOWER.

Monkey flowers are on sale at the markets in April–May. They are intended to be used for planting up containers. Do not, however, stand them in full sunlight, as the soil will dry out too quickly and the sunlight is too strong for these moisture-loving plants. A position on a shady patio or balcony is far more suitable. When the plants have finished flowering several weeks later, cut them back hard and water them with liquid fertilizer to encourage a second flowering.
Monkey flowers are actually more suitable for open ground and especially for moist soil – along the edge of a pond, for instance. Some species will self-seed spontaneously in

Mimulus × hybridus (Tigrinus Type), monkey flower

Mimulus 'Andean Nymph,' monkey flower

Mimulus 'Highland Hybrids,' monkey flower

Mimulus puniceus, monkey flower

those conditions and it is a well-known fact that some people begin to regard the yellow monkey flower (*Mimilus luteus*) as a weed. But what a weed!

The seed is quite easy to sow yourself, even though it is very fine. Sow indoors early in the year or directly in the garden from April. The ideal temperature for germination is about 59 °F. The small plants are grown on in cool conditions (at about 50 °F), and may be put out-of-doors after the last night frost.

Mimulus × hybridus is the collective name for the innumerable hybrids developed by crossing the yellow monkey flower and *Mimulus guttatus*. The spotted hybrids are sometimes called *Mimulus × tigrinus*.

Mimulus 'Andean Nymph' is a very remarkable mixture of colors. The original species comes from the mountainous regions of Chile.

Mimulus 'Highland Hybrids' is the collective name of some very diverse and always rewarding cultivars.

Mimulus 'Twinkle' provides a mixture of shades of bright red, pink, and yellow.

[3] 4–5

Mimulus puniceus

MONKEY FLOWER

This mimulus differs very little from *Mimulus aurantiacus*. The species is a small bush in the slightly warmer parts of California and the adjoining regions of Mexico. Its flowers are a lovely shade of deep red with orange throats. For notes on uses and care, see *Mimulus aurantiacus*.

   !

Mimulus 'Twinkle'- mix, monkey flower

sible to overwinter the tubers that develop in the soil in the same way as dahlias, but sowing is so easy that it is hardly worthwhile. *Mirabilis jalapa* 'Tea Time Formula Mixture' provides flowers in all manner of colors. Those of *Mirabilis jalapa* 'Tea Time Red' are rose-red.

[3–4] 4–5

Mirabilis jalapa, four o'clock flower, marvel of Peru

Mirabilis jalapa 'Tea Time Formula Mixture,' four o'clock flower, marvel of Peru

Mirabilis jalapa

FOUR O'CLOCK FLOWER, MARVEL OF PERU

Four o'clock flowers open towards evening and, eventually, a delightful sweet scent will betray their presence. Moths buzz around in search of the nectar in their long calyces. In hot weather, the flowers will have faded by morning, but on sombre days they cheer us up until far into the afternoon.

The other name for the species, Marvel of Peru, is based on the extraordinary phenomenon that a single plant often bears flowers in different colors. They usually vary between pink and crimson, but they may also be white or yellow, or have multicolored stripes.

Sow directly in the garden in April–May, or directly in the pot where they are to flower, in March–April. They are difficult to transplant. The plants grow rapidly to about 32 in tall, and may come into flower after two months. They subsequently go on flowering until the first night frost. Basically, it is pos-

Mirabilis jalapa, 'Tea Time Red,' four o'clock flower, marvel of Peru

194

Monarda citriodora, bergamot

Monarda 'Lambada,' bergamot

Momordica elateria

See *Ecballium elaterium.*

Monarda citriodora

BERGAMOT

Among the monardas, this is the odd one out. Almost all the others belong to the American perennials, but *Monarda citriodora* is an annual. It is best to sow the seeds indoors in March, or directly in the garden in mid-May. Choose a sunny position, with as loose and sandy a soil mixture as possible. If sown early, the plants, about 20–36 in tall, will reward you from July until well into autumn with whorls of old-rose-colored blooms – labiates with stipules. The young leaves are lemon- scented and may be added to tea.

[3–4] 5

Monarda 'Lambada'

BERGAMOT

'Lambada' is a hybrid from the Citriodora Group and its relationship with *Monarda citriodora* is not only visible, but the young leaves also have the characteristic lemon scent. Kieft Seeds Holland, the firm which developed 'Lambada,' did this specifically for the market in cut flowers.

It is rarely on sale as a border plant, which is partly due to the difficulty in transplanting it. Even so, if you sow indoors in small pots in March, you can plant out the seedlings in the garden, rootball and all, after the last night frost. They will come into flower just over four months after they were sown (during July in this case), but will go on flowering until the end of September. By then, the plants will be about 3 ft tall, and consequently very suitable for background planting, partly because the deep pink shade of the flowers goes very well with other colours.

[3]   !

Monarda punctata, bergamot

Monarda punctata, bergamot

Monarda punctata

BERGAMOT

In the case of *Monarda punctata* it is not so much the flowers that provide color, but the whorl of leaves below them. They are salmon pink and support flowers in very subtle color combinations – ochre yellow and creamy white with brownish-purple spots. The plants, about 32 in in height, are suitable for borders as well as for large pots. They flower from July until September. It is best to sow the seed indoors in small pots in March, and to plant the seedlings out in the garden in mid-May.

[3]   !

Monopsis 'Kopablue Papillio'

CAPE LOBELIA

Amidst the trailing stems of lilac-blue *Scaevola* in the photograph, you may just distinguish the true blue of a new plant propagated by cuttings, 'Kopablue Papillio,' which is also supplied under the names *Monopsis* 'Kopablue Blue Papillio' and *Monopsis* 'Papillio Blue.' The greenery looks very fragile, but is amazingly strong. If you forget to water it just occasionally, which may happen in the case of hanging baskets, the small plant will recover well.

If the trailing stems stop flowering, you may cut them back hard, after which the plant will sprout again and bear more flowers. The only drawback is its slow start. Professional grow-

Monopsis 'Kopablue Papillio' (with *Scaevola* in a hanging basket), Cape lobelia

Monopsis lutea, Cape lobelia

ers need to pinch out the tip regularly to be able to supply satisfactory plants. They are on sale in spring.

Monopsis lutea

CAPE LOBELIA

Why the shelves of the garden center are not overflowing with Cape lobelias is a mystery to me. The plant is a winner for hanging baskets, but there are a few specialist suppliers. Early in its development, the stems grow in a loose dome shape to about 12 in in height and the small leaves sometimes press close to them.

The real surprise, however, is to see the stems grow longer throughout the season, their tips adorned with small golden-yellow flowers. Flowering continues unceasingly from May until September. They eventually hang down for over 39 in, a wonderful sight. You can also stand the plant on a low wall, or plant it on a rockery. In South Africa, it and may be propagated by cuttings and overwintered in a dry and frost-free place. It is possible to grow the plant from seed.

Myosotis arvensis

FIELD FORGET-ME-NOT

The field forget-me-not is one of our loveliest wild plants. It sometimes turns up spontaneously in fields, and spreads capriciously through a garden if you ever sow it there. Just pull the plants out of places where you don't want them. They will, in fact, germinate only in loose soil, preferably after it has been dug over.

Just sow a patch of them in spring, and enjoy the minute sky-blue flowers with their golden eyes. If you sow directly in the garden in April, the plants, 8–20 in tall, will flower from July. They are ideal for a natural garden.

4–5

Myosotis arvensis, field forget-me-not

Nemesia caerulea

The 'blue' nemesia is propagated either by seed or by cuttings. Plants grown from cuttings of 'Joan Wilder' and 'Woodcote' are available from specialized nurseries as early as May. They are then in full flower. The flowers, always with a yellow spot on their lips, are relatively small, about 5/8 in long. The plants themselves have an upright habit. Their stems grow to about 16 in in length, and, later on in the season, often begin to bend over under their own weight. In South Africa, the species grows as a perennial. It

Nemesia caerulea 'Joan Wilder'

Nemesia caerulea 'Woodcote'

Nemesia caerulea 'Joan Wilder'

Nemesia caerulea 'Pallida'

Nemesia floribunda

Nemesia strumosa 'Fire King' with *Senecio*

likes sunlight as well as fresh air. Avoid permanently wet soil. If you sow varieties propagated by seed, you can enjoy flowers from July until September.

Nemesia caerulea 'Pallida' is featured in most seed catalogues under the name *Nemesia foetens* 'Pallida.' *Foetens* means stinking, whereas the small flowers have a delightful scent. They vary considerably in color: lavender blue, pink, and almost white.

Nemesia carulea 'Woodcote' has mauve flowers.

[2-4] 4-5 / € ☘ ▼ ⚘

Nemesia floribunda

This is something of a maverick. The plant grows taller (up to 16 in) and has smaller flowers than most other nemesias. This does not appear to be a recommendation, but the species has a very subtle appeal and may become the favorite of garden lovers with sophisticated natural tastes. The seed, unfortunately is rarely on sale.

[2-4] 4-5 ☘ ▼ ⚘

Nemesia foetens HORT

See *Nemesia caerulea*.

Nemesia fruticans HORT

See *Nemesia caerulea*.

Nemesia 'Fragrant Cloud'

This is one of the many new varieties propagated by cuttings. They tend to be a little secretive about origins, as openness might give their competitors some ideas. It is likely that *Nemesia denticulata* features somewhere in their ancestry and, according to specialist Koen Delaey of the Sollya nursery in Hertsberge in Belgium, the same probably applies to *Nemesia caerulea* 'Innocense.' 'It smells exactly the same,' Koen says.

'Fragrant Cloud' comes from England, where it is sold as a hardy plant. In well-drained soil, it may indeed tolerate 14 °F–10 °F. In The Netherlands, however, that means that you will be obliged to buy a new specimen after the winter.

The plant grows to about 8 in high and starts drooping slightly as it ages. Cut back the stems as soon as they start running to seed. 'Fragrant Cloud' will then branch out beautifully and flower all the more profusely in late summer.

/ € ☘ ▼ ⚘ !

Nemesia 'Fragrant Cloud'

Nemesia strumosa 'Fire King'

Nemesia strumosa

Although nemesias like sunlight, they have a strong dislike of very hot weather. The plants will begin to wilt and, if the warm soil surrounding the roots are dries up, the plant will collapse altogether. You should therefore find an airy position for them and make sure that the soil in pots and other contain-

Nemesia strumosa 'Orange Prince'

ers never dries up entirely. If you bear this tip in mind, things can hardly go wrong. The small plants are on sale at markets and garden centers as early as May. They are often sold in the same packs in which they were sown, as the roots of seedlings cannot tolerate much in the way of damage. They were sown in greenhouses more than three months prior to being sold. If you want to sow them yourself, you may opt for early flowering. In that case, you should sow indoors in February–March; the temperature for germination is 68 °F. The seeds may be covered lightly. Sow directly in small pots, or prick them out as soon as they are manageable. In that way, you will prevent damage to their roots. After the last frost, they should be planted out with their rootballs intact and pre-soaked.

You can make things easy for yourself by sowing directly in the garden from the end of April and thinning the seedlings when they have come up. In that case, they will not flower until July. If they threaten to stop flowering, cut them back hard and give them some fertilizer. They will then start flowering again and may go on until early autumn.

The individual flowers are $3/4$–$1 1/4$ in wide on plants 8–12 in high.

Nemesia strumosa 'Fire King' forms compact little tufts of light green with, above them, striking red flowers with orange and black in their throats.

Nemesia strumosa 'National Ensign' was known over a century ago, but was subsequently forgotten. Now it has rightly been revived to provide a cheerful note in the gar-

Nemesia strumosa 'National Ensign'

Nemesia 'Thumbelina'

Nemesia versicolor 'Blue Bird'

den. The flowers are strikingly bicolored – red at the top, with a white bottom half. Very similar plants are marketed under the following names: *Nemesia strumosa* 'Aurora,' *Nemesia strumosa* 'Danish Flag,' *Nemesia strumosa* 'Mello Red and White,' and *Nemesia strumosa* 'Red and White.'
Nemesia strumosa 'Orange Prince' bear a profusion of orange flowers.

[2–4] 4-5

Nemesia 'Thumbelina'

'Thumbelina,' is one of the current novelties: a plant, 6–8 in high, with lavender-blue flowers, almost 1¼ in wide. They appear at the tips of somewhat leggy stems, which makes 'Thumbelina' highly suitable for trailing over the edges of containers and hanging baskets. Flowering plants appear on the market from May onwards, and continue to flower throughout the summer, even without being cut back.

Nemesia versicolor

Along with *Nemesia strumosa*, *Nemesia versicolor* was in at the birth of most of the cultivars described above. The differences between the two species are not very great. The flowers of *Nemesia versicolor* are somewhat smaller and have distinct spurs at the back. The plants grow to a maximum

height of 10 in. For cultivation, see *Nemesia strumosa*. *Nemesia versicolor* is the form sold most frequently. It has intensely blue flowers, with a white or yellow spot on their lip.

[2–4] 4-5   ▼

Nemophila insignis

See *Nemophila menziesii*.

Nemophila maculata

FIVE-SPOT BABY

The mauve veins on each of the five petals end in a purplish-blue spot, hence the common name of this small plant. It can flower for months on end, bearing relatively large blooms almost 1½ in wide. The plant itself reaches a maximum height of 8 in and has a considerable spread. If there is nothing to

Nemophila maculata, five-spot baby

Nemophila menziesii, baby blue-eyes

Nemophila menziesii, baby blue-eyes

support them, the lax and watery stems become pendulous, splendid for the "front row" of flower-beds and borders, and perhaps even more so for containers or hanging baskets. Make sure that the succulent foliage never dries out. Always give it plenty of water, otherwise you will definitely lose the plant,

and shelter it from fierce sun and drying winds.

For further care and cultivation see *Nemophila menziesii.*

8-9 3-6 🌸 🌼 ▼ !

Nemophila menziesii

BABY BLUE-EYES

The watery stems of baby blue-eyes grow in all directions. In a border, the plants will grow to 4–8 in tall, but they form mats about 20 in in diameter. They are highly suitable for pots and hanging baskets and trail gracefully over their rims. The flowers are about $^3/_4$–$1^1/_4$ in wide, but they are far more striking than might be thought in view of their size. They are sky blue with white centers, which inspired those who named the plant to dream up the common name "baby blue-eyes."

Baby blue-eyes are near-hardy plants from North America. They are easy to sow and

Nemophila menziesii, baby blue-eyes

may flower within two months. In ideal circumstances, they may flower for a long time, but their flowering season may also be extended by repeated sowing. If sown in autumn, the plants will be in flower in April. If they are sown directly in the garden in April, flowering will begin in July.

Baby blue-eyes like moist soil and will disappear for good if the soil in a pot is left to dry out entirely. The plants should therefore be grown in containers or hanging baskets in places that are light but shady.

Nemophila menziesii var. *atromaria* 'Snowstorm' is the long name of a very delicate little plant. Its small flowers are a mere $\frac{1}{2}$ in wide, but incredibly beautiful – white, with tiny dots of deepest purple. As a result of a onetime spelling error, the same plant is frequently on sale as *Nemophila* 'Atomaria.'

[8-9] 3-6   **!**

Nemophila menziesii var. *atromaria* 'Snowstorm'

Nepeta nervosa, catmint

Nepeta nervosa

CATMINT

Although this plant from the Himalayas is a hardy perennial, it is quite frequently cultivated as an annual. Flowering plants are on sale as early as May. They grow to about 10 in in height, and bear racemes, over $3\frac{1}{4}$ in long, of lilac-blue flowers. The foliage is prominently veined (*nervosa*). Plant catmint at the front of a border, or in a pot, to provide months of enjoyment. If the seed is sown directly in the garden in autumn, a first flowering is likely by the end of May. If it is sown indoors in early spring, the plants will flower from June until September.

8–9 [2–3]

Nicandra physalodes

APPLE OF PERU, SHOOFLY

The apple of Peru is a fast-growing plant, with strong stems and coarse foliage. It often

Nicandra physalodes, 'Apple of Peru,' 'shoofly'

Nicandra physalodes, 'Apple of Peru,' 'shoofly'

Spontaneous *Nicotiana* hybrid

grows to the height of a man in the course of the summer, particularly if it was sown in nutritive, moisture-retentive soil. In poor soil, it will remain considerably shorter.

The stems spread almost as wide as they are tall, so it will require plenty of space. Other annuals may be grown at its base. The first flowers will appear by the end of June. They are more than $1\frac{1}{4}$ in wide, and lilac to blue with white centers.

The flowers fade rapidly, but then, the calyces join up to form a winged "balloon," which contains a pouch holding the seeds. The stems with the fruit are eminently suitable for drying.

Sow *Nicandra* directly in the garden from March onwards. The seed will remain capable of germination for decades. It often self-seeds in the garden, particularly after the soil has been dug over.

Nicandra physalodes 'Black Pod' has fruit tinged with inky black.

3–5

Nicotiana

TOBACCO PLANT

In America, nearly all species of tobacco plant grow as annuals or perennials. In our part of the world, they are cultivated almost exclusively as annuals. The various species of ornamental tobacco are among the most rewarding summer-flowering plants for borders, pots, and other containers. They are very easy to grow from seed and flower over a long period – no wonder they are so popular! Of course, there is always a price to pay. New cultivars are continually appearing on the market, always bearing new names, but the germinated plants are often not quite like the picture on the seed packet. The main reason for this is that the tobacco species are inclined to cross-fertilize one another and often produce unwanted hybrids. It is therefore advisable to buy seed from reliable suppliers.

Sow the seed indoors in March–April, or directly out-of-doors from early May. Cover very sparingly or not at all, because the seeds need light to germinate. Growing the seedlings on is nearly always straightforward, although the mosaic virus occasionally rears its ugly head. Yellow patches appear on the leaves, which begin to curl up. There is no cure for the mosaic virus causing the disease, and it is therefore best to burn seriously affected plants.

Another disease is easily prevented. Tobacco belongs to the Solanaceae family, which also includes the potato. If you plant tobacco in the same soil year after year, eel worms may well increase on a massive scale, and obstruct the plants' growth. In potato-growing circles, this is referred to as 'potato disease,' or 'potato root eelworm disease.' The solution is a simple one: grow tobacco in a different part of the garden every year.

Tobacco plants like loose but nutritive and moisture-retentive soil. Most of them like sunlight, but some do better in partial or full shade. All tobacco plants contain nicotine to a greater or lesser extent, and the substance is highly toxic.

Nicotiana alata 'Grandiflora,' ornamental tobacco

Nicotiana affinis T. MOORE

See *Nicotiana alata* 'Grandiflora.'

Nicotiana alata

ORNAMENTAL TOBACCO

The seed of the species is hardly ever on sale, unlike that of the cultivars. The height of the plants depends very much on their position,

Nicotiana alata 'Grandiflora,' ornamental tobacco

Nicotiana alata 'White Bedder,' ornamental tobacco

Nicotiana alata 'White Bedder,' ornamental tobacco

the nutritive condition of the soil, and, above all, the actual moment during the season. The plants come into flower when they are about 8 in high. They subsequently go on flowering until far into September, and continue to grow inch by inch as more flowers are borne. In rich soil, the perennial plant may, in theory, grow to about 5 ft tall but, because they are always grown as annuals in The Netherlands, they never have time to reach that height, and often remain at less than 28 in.

See *Nicotiana* for sowing and cultivation.

Nicotiana alata 'Grandiflora' is one of the best scented flowers in existence. When the flowers open in the evening, they emit a delightful fragrance. Breaths of cool evening air waft the strong sweet aroma across the patio or through the open windows of the house. It is quite all right to put the 24-in tall plant towards the back of the border, because the flowers droop like damp dishcloths during the day and do not open again until sunset. That is when the moths arrive. They hover like humming-birds in front of the flowers and push their long tongues into the nectar at the back of the trumpet-shaped flowers – these, incidentally, are not suitable for cutting.

Nicotiana alata 'Red Devil' bears intensely red flowers at the end of stems about 20 in long. The flowers stay open in the daytime, but are hardly scented.

Nicotiana alata 'White Bedder' is less fragrant than 'Grandiflora.' However, because its flowers stay open during the day, it merits a position by the edge of the patio, from where its delightful gentle fragrance will drift

across the garden in the evening. This plant grows up to 39 in tall.

See *Nicotiana* for sowing and cultivation.

[3–4] 5   !

Nicotiana glutinosa

ORNAMENTAL TOBACCO

The plant's Latin name refers to the sticky stems of this approximately 39-in tall plant. It reminds one strongly of *Nicotiana rustica*,

Nicotiana alata 'Red Devil,' ornamental tobacco

Nicotiana glutinosa, ornamental tobacco

although the petals of that species have fused to into a rotate corolla. The flowers of *glutinosa* are more pointed, and over 5/8 in wide. From June to September, they appear at the top of the plant, along with large leaves that feel downy and sticky at the same time. The whole plant emits an unpleasant odor. See *Nicotiana* for sowing and cultivation.

[3–4] 5

Nicotiana 'Havana Appleblossom'

ORNAMENTAL TOBACCO

White flowers emerge from rose-red buds and, in that respect, this prize-winning variety resembles apple blossom in spring. The flowers of 'Havana Appleblossom,' however, are 2½ in wide and, if you sowed them yourself, may be admired on the compact plants from late June until well into October. They are very suitable for flower-beds and borders, but particularly for growing in pots. When you buy the plants, they will be about 4–8 in

Nicotiana 'Havana Appleblossom,' ornamental tobacco

Nicotiana knightiana, ornamental tobacco

Nicotiana langsdorffii, ornamental tobacco

high, after which they may grow to about 20 in in height as they flower. They branch out vigorously and therefore flower freely. Flowering plants are on sale from the end of May, but seed is available only in a few places. See *Nicotiana* for sowing and cultivation.

[3-4] 5

Nicotiana knightiana

ORNAMENTAL TOBACCO

Because of its loose type of inflorescence with long green flowers, only 1/8 in or so wide, it is easy to overlook this ornamental tobacco. In a lovely border of mixed annuals, however, it struck me at once because of its elegant appearance and its usefulness as an "accompanying" chorus to other annuals. The yellowish green of the small flowers goes with everything. It is also splendid as a filler in containers and bouquets. It goes on flowering freely over a long period from the end of June until far into September. For care, see *Nicotiana*.

[3-4] 5

Nicotiana langsdorffii

ORNAMENTAL TOBACCO

After you have sown this ornamental tobacco

Nicotiana langsdorffii, ornamental tobacco

Nicotiana langsdorffii, ornamental tobacco

Nicotiana 'Lime Green,' ornamental tobacco

Nicotiana 'Lime Green,' ornamental tobacco

out-of-doors, it will be a long time before you see anything. Just as you were beginning to lose hope, however, you will find some small green mints on the soil – the round seed leaves. The plants develop slowly until they move up a gear or two in August. The stems will suddenly start shooting up and – depending on their position – grow to 39 in or even as tall as a man. Whole rows of the most delicate-looking bell-shaped flowers dangle on the stems until well into October. They are apple green with mauve stamens and although they are no more than $^1/_2$ in

Nicotiana 'Lime Green,' ornamental tobacco

wide, they will steal the show in late summer. In a mild autumn, you can pick little bunches of them until well into November. Sow *langsdorffii* indoors earlier in the year if you want to enjoy the flowers sooner. See *Nicotiana* for sowing method and further cultivation.

[3–4] 5   !

Nicotiana 'Lime Green'

ORNAMENTAL TOBACCO

The more rewarding a plant is, the more fervently plant breeders rush into attempts to introduce slightly different forms. 'Lime Green' is simply one of the most rewarding plants for a border of annuals. It grows about 30 in tall, bearing lime-green flowers, a color which really may be combined with those of any other summer flower. Contrary to all the rules, deviant forms and colors of this plant – so rewarding for flower-beds, borders, pots, and vases – are on sale labelled 'Lime Green.' Sometimes, they are little more than a drab yellowish green. If you want to be assured of a good color, wait until mid-May when flowering plants will be available from specialists.

[3–4] 5   !

Nicotiana rustica

The European conquerors of America watched in amazement when smoke emerged from the mouths of American Indians. Not long afterwards, Europe, too, was smoking. Genuine tobacco, with its more refined taste,

Nicotiana rustica

Nicotiana rustica

Nicotiana rustica 'Mon Cap'

was discovered later. In World War II, when supplies from the tropics came to an end in The Netherlands, people grew *Nicotiana rusticana,* which is easier to cultivate in this climate, to roll into cigarettes.

Give it a try as an ornamental plant in a border of annuals. The flowers are only ³/₄ in wide and, although they are open during the day, they are not very striking. It is the leaves, up to 12 in long, that give the plant its decorative appearance. It usually grows to between 32 in and 48 in tall.

Nicotina rustica 'Mon Cap' was featured in the Plant World Seeds (New Abbot) catalogue as *Nicotiana* 'Mon Cap.' The English grower called it a "mystery plant." The seed came from a customer, and the plants cultivated from it look suspiciously like the common *rusticana.* For cultivation, see *Nicotiana.*

[3–4] 5

Nicotiana suavolens, ornamental tobacco

Nicotiana sylvestris, flowering tobacco

Nicotiana × sanderae

ORNAMENTAL TOBACCO

Nearly all the cultivated varieties that we see nowadays are derived from *Nicotiana × sanderae*. At the beginning of the twentieth century, the nurseryman Sander crossed the seed of *Nicotiana alata* with the newly discovered Brazilian species *Nicotiana forgetiana*. Although the name *Nicotiana × sanderae* should therefore officially precede that of the cultivars derived from it, I decided against it as this practice is not followed in any of the seed catalogues.

Nicotiana suaveolens

ORNAMENTAL TOBACCO

The white flowers of *suavolens* are suspended obliquely from thin, sticky stems. The flower tubes, over 1½ in wide, have wine-red stripes on the outside. There is much to enjoy in the evening, at night, and in the early morning. The flowers are particularly graceful and have

a wonderful scent, but close up in the daytime (earlier and to a greater extent if they are in full sunlight). It is therefore worthwhile to try out planting this species in partial shade, where, at a height of 20–39 in the plants will show up best.

[3–4] 5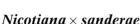

Nicotiana sylvestris

FLOWERING TOBACCO

The sturdy stems of flowering tobacco usually grow to about 5 ft tall in a single season, but they do need time to achieve that. Even if they are sown indoors in early spring, they will not come into flower before the end of July. The plants are sensitive to cold in spring, and should not be put out-of-doors – either in the garden or in a large container – before June. If the seed is sown outdoors at the end of May, the plants will not come into flower until late August. It is possible, however, to over-winter the plants indoors. The temperature must not drop below 23 °F. In spring, the plants will sprout again and come into flower earlier.

Flowering tobacco likes nutritive soil and will achieve impressive dimensions in it: height up to 8 ft, leaves up to 24 in long, and flowers with tubes 4 in long. As well as liking food and moisture, flowering tobacco prefers shade to sunlight. In the shade its flowers remain open during the day. The real treat begins in the evening when they acquire the heavy scent of freesias and entice long-tongued moths to call on them. Flowering tobacco is splendid when grown as a single plant, and visitors will go on talking about it until far into the night.

[2–4] 5   !

Nicotiana tabacum

REAL TOBACCO

Real tobacco is a comfort and a plague at the same time. The long leaves are dried, cut, and fermented to provide the tobacco for cigarettes, cigars, and pipes. In a north European climate, growing tobacco plants just is not worthwhile. The plant grows to over 39 in tall, has a lot of slightly sticky leaves, and, from July onwards, bears 1¼ -in wide flowers in greenish white, pink to red, and every imaginable shade in between. If you insist on red flowers, then choose the cultivar *Nicotiana tabacum* 'Purpureum.'

For cultivation, see *Nicotiana*.

[3–4] 5

Nicotiana tabacum, real tobacco

Nicotiana 'Tuxedo Lime,' ornamental tobacco

Nicotiana tabacum, real tobacco

212

Nicotiana 'Tuxedo Salmon Pink,' ornamental tobacco

Nicotiana 'Tuxedo Salmon Pink,' ornamental tobacco

Nicotiana 'Tuxedo'

ORNAMENTAL TOBACCO

The market is ripe for more and more new cultivars of ornamental tobacco. Usually, they are descendants of *Nicotiana* × *sanderae*. Growers of the bedding plants supplied in such huge quantities ask for compact, more compact, and even more compact still, because that is how they can grow and transport more plants. The plants from the Tuxedo Series are F1 hybrids and therefore turn out conveniently uniform. They grow to about 8 in high and are meant, above all, for flower-beds and containers. They lack the lanky charm of taller strains, but looking after them is very simple. Growing them in pots does not present any problems, and they are not very sensitive to wind or rain.

Nicotiana 'Tuxedo Lime' has greenish-yellow flowers. *Nicotiana* 'Tuxedo Salmon Pink' may well become very popular one day. The salmon-pink shade of its flowers is certainly fashionable at the moment. For sowing and care, see *Nicotiana*.

[3–4] 5   **!**

Nierembergia caerulea

See *Nierembergia hippomanica* var. *violacea*.

Nierembergia frutescens

See *Nierembergia scoparia*.

Nierembergia hippomanica var. *violacea* 'Mont Blanc,' cup flower

Nierembergia hippomanica var. *violacea* 'Purple Robe,' cup flower

Nierembergia hippomanica var. violacea

CUP FLOWER

Small, violet-blue flowers, $^3/_4$–$1^1/_4$ in wide, appear above a compact mat of greenery. This small perennial grows naturally in the cool mountains regions of Argentina, but it is not fully hardy in The Netherlands. It is therefore cultivated as an annual here. Anyone wishing to sow it, should start early – in February or March for flowers from July onwards. Professional nurserymen supply the small plants in vast quantities between June and September. Give them a sunny position in moisture-retentive soil, and they will spread as they flower. The plants grow about 6 in high, and are also suitable for containers and hanging baskets. It is essential to prevent the rootball from drying out.

Nierembergia hippomanica var. *violacea* 'Mont Blanc' has pure white flowers with small, yellow centers. *Nierembergia hippomanica* var. *violacea* 'Purple Robe' bears deep-violet flowers, again with small yellow centers. Both may be overwintered in frost-free positions.

[2–4]

Nierembergia scoparia

This splendid little plant is in scant supply, but once you have one, you will want more. Small, pale flowers have yellow centers and veins which look as if they have been colored in a poster-paint shade of lilac blue. In the border regions between Brazil, Argentina, and Uruguay, where this perennial originally came from, it grows up to 20 in tall. The cultivars marketed in The Netherlands, usually stop at a height of about 8–12 in. For care, see *Nierembergia hippomanica*.

Nigella damascena

LOVE-IN-A-MIST

The flowers appear above a whorl of greenery branching like coral. The "love" in the name is a flower just a few centimetres (an inch or so) wide. It may be white, pink, red, blue, or something in between. Even the wild species from southern Europe and North Africa sometimes bear flowers in one color, and

Nierembergia scoparia, cup flower

214

Nigella damascena, love-in-a-mist

Nigella damascena, love-in-a-mist

Nigella hispanica, love-in-a-mist

sometimes in another. The annual plant grows about 12–20 in tall.

Sadly, they flower but briefly – just four weeks or so. Fortunately, however, we do not have to part with them then, because decorative inflated seed pods appear in their stead. Cut them off as soon as they are fully developed, and hang them up to dry upside down. They will provide a delightful memento of the summer later on.

If, however, you want to see flowers over a longer period, sow at intervals of about a month. The plants like sun, but do not have any further requirements. It is best to sow di-

rectly in the garden between March and June, or in the pot where they are to flower, because they dislike having their roots disturbed. Unfortunately, there are also some very ugly specimens on the market. One example of a real hobgoblin is *Nigella damascena* 'Baby Blue,' in which the lovely airy look of the species has been replaced by a plug of greenery barely 6 in high, with tiny flowers and inflated seed pods like little horned devils. It is suitable for pots – but one to avoid, I think. Consider instead *Nigella damascena* 'Cambridge Blue,' a slender plant which may grow to 3 ft tall, with sky-blue semi-double flowers, a real treasure for mixed borders and bouquets, and also for drying.

Nigella damascena 'Miss Jekyll Rose' is a variety from the Miss Jekyll Series, with deep-red flowers. The plants grow to about 20 in in height, and were developed specially for the cut-flower and dried-flower trade. The stems are consequently straight, and perhaps too stiff for a natural border. Even so, they are good for filling a bare patch. The flowers are semi-double, and – depending on the strain – white, violet-blue, sky-blue (this is the original *Nigella damascena* 'Miss Jekyll'), or pink to red. They have splendid inflated seed pods.

3-6 🌱 🏺 ⚱ 🐝 !

Nigella hispanica

The flowers of this Spanish *Nigella* are carried well above its foliage. The entire plant, which also grows to about 20 in in height, looks coarser, and its lilac-blue flowers lack the heavenly reflection of love-in-a-mist.

There is, however, a lot going on in the center of this Spanish relative – a whorl of stamens and a reddish ovary that quickly develops into a remarkable inflated seed pod, wonderful for drying. For sowing and cultivation, see *Nigella damascena*.

3-6 🌱 🏺 ⚱ 🐝

Nigella damascena 'Cambridge Blue,' love-in-a-mist

Nigella damascena 'Baby Blue,' love-in-a-mist

Nigella damascena 'Miss Jekyll Rose,' love-in-a-mist

216

Nigella sativa, black cumin

Nigella sativa

BLACK CUMIN

The greenish-yellow or blue-tinged white flowers of black cumin are scarcely noticeable among its feathery foliage. It is so finely divided and such a beautiful shade of light green that the plants, 12 in tall, make wonderful fillers in bouquets of wild flowers. The fragrant seeds were, and still are, used as aromatic herbs for flavouring all kinds of dishes.

For sowing and cultivation, see *Nigella damascena*.

3–6

Nolana atriplicifolia

See *Nolana paradoxa.*

Nolana grandiflora

See *Nolana paradoxa.*

Nolana humifusa

The seed of this *Nolana* is available only from specialists, which is strange, because it merits a place in almost every garden. *Nolana humifusa* is a spreading, prostrate plant and therefore one of the most rewarding kinds of annual ground cover (in Peru it grows as a perennial). Small new flowers, $^3/_4$–$1^1/_4$ in wide, are formed continually above the greyish-green mat of small succulent leaves from July until the first serious frost. Its appearance alone indicates that the species likes well-drained soil, but it also does quite

Nolana humifosa, Chilean bellflower

Nolana humifosa 'Little Bells,' Chilean bellflower

Nolana paradoxa 'Sky Blue'

well in average kinds of garden soil. In fertile soil, the shoots will take off and cover $10^3/_4$–$21^1/_2$ sq. ft of soil by the end of the summer. The lavender-blue flowers have a subtle pattern of small, deep-purple lines that entice innumerable insects to the heart of the flower. Sow indoors in March–April, or outdoors from April onwards.

Nolana humifusa 'Little Bells' bears light blue flowers, over $^3/_4$ in wide, which also have a deep-purple nectar guide. The plant is eminently suitable for hanging baskets.

[3–4] 5   !

Nolana napiformis

See *Nolana paradoxa.*

Nolana paradoxa

This is a splendid plant for flower-beds, borders, pots, troughs, and hanging baskets. What would you say to blue flowers with the respectable width of $1^1/_2$ in, each with a white zone and yellow throat in its center? These treasures are borne on ground-cover plants which, if there is nothing to support them, trail over the rims of pots.

The species comes from the coastal deserts of Peru and Chile. It likes a warm position in well-drained soil, but also does well in richer soil and even manages to flower in our wettest summers. In really gloomy weather, however,

it shows its aversion to the Dutch climate by half-closing its flowers. Sow indoors in March–April, or outdoors in May. It may be expected to flower from July until September. *Nolana paradoxa* 'Blue Bird' and *Nolana paradoxa* 'Sky Blue' are two names for plants that are scarcely distinguishable from the species. Genuinely divergent forms have lavender-blue flowers or pure-white ones, as in the case of *Nolana paradoxa* 'Snow Bird.'

[3–4] 5   ▼ !

Nolana prostrata

See *Nolana humifusa.*

Nycterinia capensis

See *Zaluzianskya capensis.*

Ocimum basilicum, basil

O

Ocimum basilicum

BASIL

Basil is cultivated because of the delicious aroma of its foliage. Anyone who has sown the herb for that reason will be pleased with the decorative appearance of the plant and the long spikes of small, white to rose-red flowers. Basil is a highly variable plant, with innumerable subspecies and cultivars. Leaf color and leaf size may differ dramatically. *Ocimum basilicum* 'Dark Opal,' for example, has purplish-red leaves. The photograph shows a form that closely resembles *Ocimum sanctum,* the sacred basil from India.

Wait until the end of May before sowing basil outdoors, but preferably in a greenhouse or cold frame. The plants like shelter and warmth, and are most satisfactory if grown in a greenhouse.

[3–5] 5–6

Oenothera pallida

EVENING PRIMROSE

The white flowers, over 2 in wide, of this perennial from the west of the United States open in the evening, attracting moths with their delightful fragrance. Their coarse stems

Oenothera pallida 'Innocense,' evening primrose

grow about 20 in tall, and spread in all directions. Plant evening primroses along the edges of a patio to enjoy scented summer evenings. There will be fresh flowers daily from the end of June until early October. The flowers turn pink in the course of the morning (as a sign to insects that they are no longer welcome), and droop in the afternoon, early on if it is hot.

Sow indoors in March–April, or out-of-doors from April. If conditions are favorable, the plants will come into flower two months later.

Oenothera pallida 'Innocense' does not differ much from the species, and is sometimes available as a plant.

[3–4] 4–5

Omphalodes linifolia, Venus's navelwort

Origanum majorana, marjoram

Orlaya grandiflora

Omphalodes linifolia

VENUS'S NAVELWORT

The small flowers of Venus's navelwort will disarm the most persistent grumbler. There are few plants that flower as sweetly. Unfortunately, the treat does not last for long. After three to five weeks, the flowers will have worked their way up the 16-in stems and opened, then closed and set seed. It is possible to extend their flowering season by sowing in situ at intervals of about a month between March and June. In loose, well-drained soil, the plant may start behaving like an agreeable weed by self-seeding, surviving the winter, and coming into flower as early as May–June. If you want them for a container, sow the seed directly in it, because the seedlings dislike being transplanted.

3-6

Origanum majorana

SWEET MARJORAM

The minuscule flowers of marjoram emerge from tiny spheres smaller than the smallest

Orlaya grandiflora

pea, and large numbers of them are to be seen on stems above the greyish-green foliage throughout the summer.

On average, the plant grows to a height of 12 in, but spreads more widely than that, and its stems trail beautifully over the rim of a pot. Marjoram has an unsurpassed fragrance and is a favorite culinary herb. It has a mildly sweet flavour and is often added to roasts. Cut off the tops of the plants and dry them in sweet-scented bunches, or shred them into the potpourri.

Marjoram is a perennial that is not quite able

Orlaya grandiflora

220

Osteospermum 'Bamba'

bels. Superficially, they resemble *Ammi majus*, but the outer flowers are larger and look like small white pendent hearts. It makes a suitable filler in a natural garden and a splendid cut flower. The plants self-seed in suitable places and germinate in autumn. It is therefore best to sow them in autumn. In the Dutch climate, the seedlings survive most winters as small rosettes. They shoot up rapidly in spring and may come into flower by early June. The flowers last for two months at the most, but you may still enjoy the umbels of extremely bristly seeds for a while after that.

Orlaya grandiflora does best in fairly dry sandy soil, or clay that is kept loose. In very humus-rich or fertilized soil, there is a considerable likelihood of infestation by carrot fly. It is therefore simply a matter of trying out whether the plant does well in a particular spot. If it does, you will see *Orlaya grandiflora* again every year.

8-9 3-5   !

to survive Dutch winters. Sow indoors in March–April, or outdoors from the end of May. Find a sunny and sheltered position for the plants, preferably in loamy soil.

[3–4] 5–6]

Orlaya grandiflora

Plants that are called new are often rediscovered treasures. This is true of *Orlaya grandiflora*, which may be included in books on the wild plants of Europe, but is not to be found in even the very fattest volumes on plants for the garden. It self-seeded freely in the olive groves of Tuscany, and on other dry, warm hillsides in southern and central Europe, but nobody made the effort to market the seed of this annual plant for growing in a garden. Those days are now past, and it looks as though *Orlaya grandiflora* has a golden future in the garden.

The plants grow to about 32 in tall, producing bipinnate foliage and bearing white (or sometimes pale pink) ray flowers in full um-

Osteospermum 'Buttermilk'

221

Osteospermum

Osteospermum 'Congo'

Osteospermum is a real maverick among the compositae family. Usually, a border of sterile ray flowers – those of a marguerite, for example – attracts insects to the center of the flower with its tubular florets; these are fertile and develop the seed. In osteospermums, however, the tubular florets are sterile and the seed is formed in the fertile ray flowers. You can see this phenomenon yourself after the plants have flowered. The brownish-black seeds, which are very large and hard, develop into wreaths round the centers of the faded flowers. This characteristic distinguishes *Osteospermum* from *Dimorphotheca*, a genus dealt with elsewhere in this encyclopedia, with flowers that in other respects closely resemble those of *Osteospermum*.

For several years now, these magnificent plants have been on sale on a quite a large scale from March onwards. Plants that have been properly hardened off will tolerate a few degrees of frost. The wild species and older cultivars do not flower until after a cold period. More modern cultivars do not need that cold induction. They also stay far more compact than the bushy plants from South Africa.

Chemical growth inhibitors are still used to keep the plants compact, but they are no longer required for all cultivars. They are on sale as flowering plants with a height and spread of about 8 in. When in flower, plants in a sunny position grow to about 20 in tall, sometimes to about 39 in in the shade. Their main flowering season is in spring, but they continue to bear flowers well into autumn. It is therefore important to ensure that they have a very sunny position in loose, well-drained soil. If you are growing them in pots, avoid letting the soil dry out completely and provide some extra food to extend the flowering season.

Osteospermum 'Lusaka'

Osteospermum 'Zulu'

Osteospermum 'Volta'

Oxalis vulcanicola

Osteospermum ecklonis is the main ancestor of the current hybrids, but other species such as *Osteospermum jucundum* were bred in as well. Although some cultivars may be propagated by seed – sown under glass in March–April – those mentioned below are typical plants grown from cuttings. In that way, their essential characteristics are best retained, and improvers can secure their plant breeder's rights to their products. Only licence-holders are entitled to cultivate the plants on a commercial scale. In my opinion, the plants will, under glass, tolerate temperature of about 14 °F.

Osteospermum 'Bamba' : broad ray flowers, almost white as they emerge from the buds, but soon changing to violet.

Osteospermum 'Buttermilk' : pale yellow flowers developing from brown-striped buds.

Osteospermum 'Congo' : relatively small, pale violet-pink flowers with blue eyes.

Osteospermum 'Lusaka' : ray flowers more oblong than those of 'Bamba', and slightly lighter in color.

Osteospermum 'Pemba' : the ray flowers are pressed together to form tubes halfway along.

Osteospermum 'Volta' : lilac pink, subsequently paling to almost white.

Osteospermum 'Zulu' : soft yellow.

Oxalis vulcanicola

This plant, which is suitable for pots and hanging baskets, is adorned with small yellow flowers for months on end. Its foliage forms a dense tuft with a little brown mixed in with it. The small stems are always red and hairy. The plant grows to about 6 in high and eventually spreads farther and farther. On a rockery it will embrace a stone; in a border it will form a mat; and in a pot or a hanging basket, the stems will trail over the rim or edge. Indeed, that is how we see it most frequently, on sale as a trailing plant, bearing- a profusion of flowers.

The plant's natural habitat is on the slopes of volcanoes in Central America – about 9,840 ft high. It is often very damp there but, because of their situation, frosts are rare. Consequently, this particular oxalis really cannot tolerate frost. Keep it well watered in summer and keep it in light and frost-free place in winter. Alternatively, buy new plants in spring.

Oxypetalum caeruleum

See *Tweedia caerulea*.

Oxalis vulcanicola with *Mimulus aurantiacus*

Papaver commutatum

POPPY

The black blotches on our native poppies are situated right at the base of the petals. Those on their relative from the Balkans and Asia Minor have moved farther towards the center of the petals. The flowers resemble lady-birds, red with black dots, and the cultivar most frequently available is therefore called *Papaver commutatum* 'Lady Bird.' The blotches on this cultivar are slightly larger than those of the species, and appear on flowers 2 in wide, which are borne on knee-high plants. For sowing and propagation, see *Papaver rhoeas*.

3-5

Papaver nudicaule

ICELAND POPPY

Flowers, including Iceland poppies, give the northern tundras some color during their brief summers. It was discovered long ago that the perennial also does very well in other parts of the world. It has been hybridized for centuries, so that the ancestry of the plants in our gardens is no longer known precisely. The light green foliage rarely exceeds 12 in in height, but the flowers sometimes grow more than 39 in tall. They flower on long hairy

Papaver nudicaule, Iceland poppy

Papaver commutatum 'Lady Bird'

stems in all manner of colors – white, pale pink, salmon pink, apricot, red, but usually yellow or orange.

Iceland poppies are often sown in late summer and may then flower as early as the following May–June. It is also possible to sow in early spring, in which case the first flowers may be expected to appear in late summer.

7-9 3-4

Papaver nudicaule 'Solar Fire Orange,' Iceland poppy

Papaver rhoeas

FIELD POPPY

Poppy seed remains capable of germination for a very long time and may continue to rest in deep soil layers for decades. If it is then brought to the surface during digging work, it will germinate, and that is why soil excavated for the banks of motorways or building sites is so often covered in a blaze of red poppies. In subsequent years, they are gradually

Papaver rhoeas, corn poppy, field poppy

Papaver rhoeas, corn poppy, field poppy

ousted by other wild plants. Sow poppies directly in the garden in loose soil and in a sunny spot, and thin out the seedlings to a distance of 8 in apart, so that the remaining plants can develop properly. Common poppies grow about 24 in tall and flower quite briefly in July and August. Repeated sowing will extend their flowering season. In addition to the original red-flowered species, numerous selections of single to semi-double flowers in a whole range of colors were developed.

Papaver rhoeas 'Parelmoer' (also called *Papaver rhoeas* 'Fairy Wings' and *Papaver rhoeas* 'Mother of Pearl') has flowers in lovely pastel shades of soft lilac, a hint of blue, dove grey, subdued pink, apricot, but also soft red and greyish white. If you want to obtain seed from them, pull out the plants with deviant colors. Poppies have a tendency to return ultimately to the original red.

9–10 3–5

Papaver rhoeas 'Mother of Pearl,' corn poppy, field poppy

Papaver somniferum, opium poppy

Papaver somniferum, opium poppy

Papaver somniferum 'Danish Flag,' opium poppy

Papaver somniferum

OPIUM POPPY

Opium poppies are cultivated on a large scale, for oil extraction, among other reasons. The ripe poppy seed is also used for scattering on bread rolls before they are baked. In the old days, children used to be given an infusion of the dried seed capsule to get them to sleep (hence the Dutch common name *slaapbol* – "sleepy head"). With the exception of the ripe seeds, the entire plant contains opium, a narcotic once smoked on a large scale in China to forget the anxieties of the day. Opium formed the base for morphine, one of the principal analgesic medicines. Morphine in the form of heroin is widely used as a drug nowadays.

Fortunately, the opium poppy is also an intriguing garden plant, which will self-seed year after year. The original species usually has mauve flowers – rarely white or red. There are now, however, numerous lovely cultivars available with single to fully double flowers in many different colors.

Papaver somniferum 'Danish Flag' has bright red flowers, usually with a black (deep purple) blotch at the base of each petal. In 'Danish Flag,' the blotch is white, thus creating the colors of the Danish flag. The same colors occur in *Papaver somniferum* 'Daneborg,' except that there the petals look somewhat frayed.

Papaver somniferum 'Hen&Chickens' is remarkable, not so much for its flowers as for the misshapen seed capsules surrounded by irregularly shaped mini-capsules.

The ripe seed capsules of all poppies are very suitable for drying. They are formed in such a way that a vortex is created on the inside whenever the wind blows in through the openings. The seeds are then blown out on the other side. Children love trying this out and sow the plants for the following season in that way.

Papaver somniferum 'Rose Paeony' is one of the fully double opium poppies and is also known as *Papaver paeoniflorum* or peony-flowered poppy.

Papaver somniferum, opium poppy

Papaver somniferum 'Hen&Chickens,' opium poppy

Papaver somniferum 'Rose Paeony,' opium poppy

Sow poppies directly in the garden in late summer and autumn or else in early spring, and then repeat the operation to extend the flowering season.

The seedlings cannot be transplanted.

Thin them out to distances of 8 in apart for best results.

9–10 3–6

Pelargonium

GERANIUM

Geraniums do not primarily suggest plants for just one season. Genuine enthusiasts bring them indoors before the first night frost and put them, almost dry, in a cool, frost-free place, either indoors or in a greenhouse. Even without such facilities, it is still possible to enjoy the plants – huge quantities are propagated by seed or cuttings to provide flowers for a single summer. Geraniums cost less than a bunch of flowers and you can enjoy them for much longer. In May, flowering plants are on sale everywhere. Do not put them out-of-doors until all danger of frost has passed, because just a few degrees of frost are fatal to the plant. From the end of May, they will flower non-stop until they are killed by the first frost in October, or sometimes later.

Geraniums are ideal plants for all kinds of containers, even for hanging baskets. Their roots dislike permanent moisture, and it

Pelargonium × *hortorum* 'Multibloom Pink,' zonal geranium

therefore does not matter if the soil dries up occasionally. Don't water them until the soil feels dry. The leaves will remain smaller, but the plants will flower all the more freely. Do not give them plant food with a high nitrogen content. It is better for flowering plants to use special fertilizers containing very little nitrogen (N) and a relatively large amount of potassium (K). Geraniums like a sunny position, although trailing geraniums are quite happy with less sunlight. The geraniums on the market are all hybrids derived from several South African species. They are divided into upright (zonal) and trailing (ivy-leafed) geraniums. The former have roughly rounded, horseshoe-shaped leaves, often with margins in a different color. The plants grow straight upwards. Trailing geraniums have spreading shoots that may cover the soil. If they cannot find any support, they become pendulous, and are therefore often used in containers. The leaves are a smoother, fresher green, of-

Pelargonium × peltatum, Austrian trailing geranium

ten five-pointed, and somewhat resembling those of ivy.

Pelargonium × hortorum 'Multibloom Pink' is one of the zonal geraniums grown from seed that are on sale, in flower, from April onwards. Plants from the Multibloom Series flower early, have a compact growth (about 25 cm/10 in high) and branch out vigorously.

Pelargonium × hortorum 'Multibloom Salmon,' zonal geranium

Pelargonium × peltatum 'Tornado Rose Nobix,' trailing geranium

Pelargonium × peltatum 'Summer Showers Burgundy,' trailing geranium

Pelargonium × hortorum 'Multibloom Salmon' is another freely flowering variety from the same series.

The seeds of Pelargonium × peltatum 'Tornado Rose Nobix' are planted as early as December. The plants will be in flower by April–May, and are then sold as pink-flowered trailing geraniums.

Pelargonium × peltatum 'Summer Showers Burgundy' can be sold as a flowering plant only three-and-a-half months after it was sown. This new variety has lovely, wine-red flowers.

Pelargonium zonale

See Pelargonium × hortorum.

Penstemon

BEARD TONGUE

Species of Penstemon are natural perennials from North and Central America. In European countries like The Netherlands, however, most species are nearly always lost during the winter as a result of the combination of frost and a wet soil. They are therefore usually cultivated as annuals. There are cultivars which were developed mainly from hybrids of Penstemon hartwegii and Penstemon coboea. Although they flower beautifully, they are still not really popular. This may be due to the long period of cultivation. Depending on the species, it takes three to five months to grow flowering plants from seed. Even so, the plants are often on sale at moderate prices. They flower mainly in late summer, although professional growers sow them in greenhouses very early in the year in order to have them in flower and on sale by May. If you want to sow them yourself, it is better to wait until March–April. Sow indoors at that time, or outdoors in May. Do not move them out-of-doors until after mid-May, and then put them in a sunny spot in well-drained soil or in a pot. It is all right for the soil to be dry. It is best to look for the plants at specialized sup-

Penstemon barbatus 'Dwarf Cambridge Mix,' beard tongue

Penstemon 'Evelyn,' beard tongue

Penstemon barbatus 'Dwarf Cambridge Mix,' beard tongue

Penstemon 'Garnet,' beard tongue

pliers of container plants, because they are rarely on sale at garden centers. The stems are very suitable for cut flowers.

Penstemon barbatus 'Dwarf Cambridge Mix' provides a mixture of pink, red to blue shades. The plants grow about 12 in tall. They should be sown early, as they need four to five months to come into flower.

Penstemon 'Evelyn' is usually available from suppliers of perennials. It is, in fact, one of the cultivars that are least sensitive to frost and may, in the coastal regions of The Netherlands, survive the winter in soil that is not excessively wet. The pale pink flowers grow on stems about 20 in tall.

Penstemon 'Garnet' has a sturdier growth, up to 30 in in height, with wine-red flowers. It is on the borderline between half-hardy and hardy.

Penstemon hartwegii 'Tubular Bells Red' is cultivated exclusively as an annual bedding and potted plant. Commercial firms sow in January to be able to supply flowering plants

Penstemon hartwegii 'Tubular Bells Red,' beard tongue

in April–May. They will then continue to bear red flowers on stems over 20 in high throughout the summer. *Penstemon hartwegii* 'Tubular Bells Rose' has slightly larger flowers with pink and cherry-red markings on a white background.

Even in the milder Dutch province of Zeeland, *Penstemon* 'Mother of Pearl' proves to be insufficiently hardy to survive the winter. It is simply better to grow it as an annual, be-

Penstemon 'Mother of Pearl,' beard tongue

Penstemon hartwegii 'Tubular Bells Rose'

cause it is a lovely cultivar with flowers in mother-of-pearl pink and blue. It grows about 28 in tall.

[3–4] 5

Penstemon 'Andenken an Friedrich Hahn'

See *Penstemon* 'Garnet.'

Penstemon gentianoides

See *Penstemon hartwegii.*

Pentas lanceolata, Egyptian star, star-cluster

Pentas carnea

See *Pentas lanceolata.*

Pentas lanceolata

EGYPTIAN STAR, STAR-CLUSTER

Pentas is usually on sale in the indoor plant section. However, this East African plant likes warmth, but also light, and they suffer from a lack of that in most living-rooms. They get enough light as container plants, but then the problem of overwintering looms up in autumn. The plants do not really tolerate temperatures below 50 °F. Should they therefore be cultivated as annuals? Professional growers sow the species in January to be able to market flowering plants in May. *Pentas* is well known as a bedding and container plant, but we need an exceptionally fine summer for growing them in flower-beds, since the plants fail to do well in cold wet weather. It is better to put them in a pot or other container which is not taken out-of-doors until the temperature remains above 45 °F at night. Then you will be able to enjoy the spherical heads of white, pink, red, or violet flowers.

Pentzia grandiflora

See *Tripleurospermum inodorum.*

Perilla frutescens

Although *Perilla frutescens* flowers in late summer and autumn, we are not really interested in those small, pale mauve flowers. Its true value as an ornamental plant is based on the – edible – deep red foliage of the varieties and cultivars on the market. In red borders in particular, they will provide a perfect background for the dazzling flowers of other plants.

Perilla frutescens 'Atropurpurea,' black nettle

Perilla frutescens var. *nankinensis* 'Atropurpurea Laciniata,' black nettle

Petunia Grandiflora Group

Sow indoors in March–April or out-of-doors from mid-May. Even young plants are highly decorative. They ultimately grow to about 24 in tall. The species itself has greenish foliage, sometimes with purple blotches. *Perilla frutescens* 'Atropurpurea' produces deep purple leaves. Those of *Perilla frutescens* var. *nankinensis* 'Atropurpurea Laciniata' are also irregularly pointed.

[3–4] 5

Persicaria capitata

See *Polygonum capitatum.*

Petunia

In the tropical regions of South America, there are about 35 species of wild petunia. Several of the perennial petunias formed the starting point for all the cultivated plants so

Petunia Grandiflora Group

Petunia Multiflora Group

Petunia Multiflora Group

familiar in Europe nowadays. These cultivars, too, are basically perennials, but they are grown as annuals because they cannot stand any frost. More attention has recently been devoted to other species long forgotten by plant breeders. This has led to a new wave of petunias that are genuinely different.

Petunias belong to the rare botanical genera that bear flowers in any one of the primary colors – red, blue, yellow, or any shade in between and also white. They are often bicolored or multicolored, sometimes with picotee margins or longitudinal stripes like old-fashioned sunshades. Their throats often have different colors, and their dark veins sometimes stand out against lighter backgrounds.

Cultivated petunias can no longer be traced back to their original species. They have been crossed too often for their ancestry to be known and plant breeders often kept their

Petunia 'Blue Daddy'

Petunia 'Fantasy Ivory'

Petunia 'Fantasy Pink Morn'

Petunia 'Brassband' with *Euryops chrysanthemoides* 'Sonnenschein'

hybridization recipes a secret – and still do. Petunias are currently divided into three groups. The Petunia Grandiflora Group has the largest flowers, which may grow to 4 in wide. The enjoyment of these flowers is often marred by wind and rain in a climate like that of The Netherlands. The flowers prove to be very limp and are easily blown to shreds. A severe thunderstorm may flatten them. In our climate, they are really most suitable for greenhouses or very sheltered warm places – for instance, under the eaves.

The Petunia Multiflora Group has smaller flowers, although the difference is not always noticeable. The flowers are less floppy and vulnerable. A single plant will bear more than one flower, so that even the Multifloras largely cover their greenery with blooms. The group is sometimes referred to as *Petunia floribunda*. Then there is another new group: The Petunia Milliflora Group, which has considerably smaller flowers. They are about 1¼ in wide, and more funnel-shaped. They are also more resistant to poor weather conditions.

There are also double petunias. They lack the appeal of the single varieties and prove to be

Petunia 'Focus Burgundy'

Petunia 'Focus Pink Morn'

Petunia 'Focus Sky Blue'

Petunia 'Fortunia Pearly Wave'

Petunia 'Fortunia Red Rising Sun'

Petunia 'Hurrah Rose Star'

extremely sensitive to bad weather, so it is better not to buy them.

Petunias like a warm and sunny position. Most of them prefer poor, loose soil, where they will flower in greater profusion and develop a more compact habit. For very freely flowering petunias cultivated in pots or other containers, the rule is that they must be given extra fertilizer to keep them flowering. They will continue to flower from the date of purchase in May – or from June if you have sown them yourself – until the first night frost.

Unfortunately, it is not very easy to sow petunias. Professional nurserymen have better facilities for adapting conditions, and they grow them by the millions so that you will not be left without them. The appropriate rules are: sow under glass, but not before March. Professional nurserymen start sooner, but are then obliged to take further measures against fungous diseases which may destroy all that was sown. You should therefore provide sterilized, poor soil or cocopeat and make sure pots and propagator are thoroughly clean. Sprinkle the fine seeds thinly on the surface. Press them down lightly, but don't cover them because they need light to germinate. Then cover the propagator with glass or plastic to ensure a very humid atmosphere. The seeds will germinate at about 71 °F. After the seed has germinated, the humidity must be reduced rapidly to prevent grey mold. Remove the glass or plastic, partially at first, and then, after a few days, altogether. Prick out seedlings as soon as they are manageable, and then grow them on at a relatively cool temperature 59–64 °F. They will then branch out better. The warmth-loving plants should not be put out-of-doors until the end of May.

Anyone with suitable facilities for overwintering plants in light, cool, but frost-free conditions, can take cuttings in late summer.

Petunia 'Blue Daddy' belongs to the Grandiflora Group. With a width of almost 4 in, the flowers are certainly impressive. Their basic color is lavender blue with violet throats, and with violet veins forming a fine network in the flower. All the cultivars in the 'Daddy' Series

Petunia 'Hurrah Salmon'

Petunia 'Million Bells Blue'

Petunia 'Lavender Storm'

Petunia 'Million Bells Pink'

are early flowering, and may, in fact, come into flower about ten weeks after they were sown. The veins always look striking against a lighter background. Try combining the approximately 12-in tall plants with grey-leafed foliage plants. In the photograph, *Petunia* 'Brassband' serves as underplanting for *Euryops Chrysanthemoides* 'Sonnenschein.' The light yellow of the flowers goes very well with golden yellow and other shades of yellow and soft blue. Petunias from the Multiflora Group can be grown from seed.

Petunia 'Fantasy Ivory' has small, trumpet-shaped flowers turned in every direction above the very compact plant, which does not grow much beyond 10 in. The flower color of this variety from the Milliflora Group is ivory white with lemon-yellow streaks. As far as I know, the seed is available only in England. In The Netherlands it is normally purchased as a plant.

Petunia 'Fantasy Pink Morn' grows in much the same way as 'Fantasy Ivory,' except that its flowers are soft pink. They become paler to-

wards the centers, and their throats are yellow. The plant belongs to the Milliflora Group and is a plant to buy rather than to sow.

Petunia 'Focus Burgundy' is a plant from the Milliflora Group and has deep-red flowers. They are relatively large and are borne on a sturdy plant which, according to the catalogue, grows to 10 in, but, in fact, manages to achieve double that height. The Focus Series is propagated by seed.

Petunia 'Focus Pink Morn' has strikingly bright red flowers suddenly paling towards their centers, which makes them look bicolored. There is even some yellow left in the center. The Focus Series flowers early, remains compact, and does well, even in rainy summers. It is, after all, a member of the Multiflora Group.

Petunia 'Focus Sky Blue' does indeed have sky-blue flowers, but they tend to spot in wet weather. There are several other varieties on the market with flowers in the same popular color. They are often called 'Sky Blue' or 'Terrace Blue.'

Petunia 'Million Bells Terracotta'

Petunia 'Prism Sunshine'

Although *Petunia* 'Fortunia Pearly Wave' is marketed as 'Fortunia Pearly Wave,' its official name is *Petunia* 'Pearly Wave.' Other suppliers omit 'Fortunia' and refer only to the Wave Series. In spite of the confusion about names, these are very rewarding varieties from the Multiflora Group. They are grown from seed and are therefore not much troubled by viruses. Their shoots are prostrate and cover the soil in flower-beds. Where sup-

port is lacking, they become pendulous and then form a real curtain of foliage and flowers. They are very suitable for containers and hanging baskets. 'Pearly Wave' has been on the market since 1999. It bears pearly white flowers with just a hint of pink. The variety is not uniform and includes plants with a pink-and-white pattern of stripes. Make sure that the Fortunia Wave Series is always kept moist and has plenty of fertilizer.

Petunia 'Fortunia Red Rising Sun,' which is officially called *Petunia* 'Red Rising Sun,' belongs to the Fortunia Series. For a description and cultivation, see above. The name of this plant from the Multiflora group is very appropriate to its clear, orange-red flowers.

Petunia 'Hurrah Rose Star' also belongs to the Multiflora Group. The plants grow about 8 in high, with flowers, $2^3/_4$ in wide, appearing above them. They are rose red with white bands emerging from the center. Sometimes the bands are wider than the rose-red.

Petunia 'Hurrah Salmon' has the same characteristics as the previous variety, except that

Petunia 'Prism Sunshine'

Petunia 'Summer Sun'

237

Petunia 'Surfinia Blue Vein'

Petunia 'Surfinia Blue Vein'

is *Petunia* 'Sunbelbu' – belongs to the Multi-flora Group. Its lilac-blue flowers with yellow centers are just an inch or so wide, but the plants flower profusely and over a long period. They first grow bushy, then spread, and ultimately become pendulous. Their supplier has recently been providing genuine trailing forms. The term "trailing" is then added to the name of the plants. The more upright varieties are given the description "patio." All of them are propagated by cuttings, which are taken in February–March, and are then grown on in cool conditions, (about 52 °F), after they have rooted. They tolerate a few degrees of frost.

Petunia 'Million Bells Pink' – its official name is *Petunia* 'Sunbelpi' – differs only from the above in the pink color of its flowers.

In 1999, *Petunia* 'Million Bells Terracotta' appeared on the market – its official name is *Petunia* 'Kiebelleye.' Its flowers are a lovely shade of soft yellow. Unfortunately, this cultivar is not (yet) stable, so there are also plants with pink streaks on sale. Some even

Petunia 'Surfinia Pink Mini'

its flowers are dusty pink. This is hardly a description which will sell plants, and the supplier therefore calls them salmon pink.

Petunia 'Lavender Storm' was awarded a Fleuroselect gold medal in 1996, especially because it also flowers well in poor summers, even though it is a petunia from the Grandiflora Group. Its pink flowers are $3^1/_2$ in wide. At a height of 12 in, the plant is small enough for flower-beds.

Petunia 'Million Bells Blue' – its official name

Petunia 'Surfinia Pink Mini'

Petunia 'Surfinia Purple Mini'

plant; the varieties are protected under plant breeders' rights. Petunias belonging to the Surfinia Series have a spreading habit and trail luxuriantly over the rims of pots and other containers. In favorable conditions, they can form a curtain of greenery and flowers as much as 10 ft long. To achieve this, they need a warm summer and plenty of water and fertilizer. In our climate, they are less exuberant, but still very satisfactory in that they provide a wealth of flowers to enjoy throughout the summer. They do not do so well in hanging baskets because of their great need for water and food.

have entirely pink or crimson flowers. So if you want to be sure of the right color, don't buy this petunia unless it is in flower.

Petunia 'Prism Sunshine' is a prize-winning new variety in the Grandiflora Group and won a Fleuroselect gold medal in 1998. Its flowers, $3\frac{1}{4}$ in wide are lemon yellow with lighter margins. The plants are 14 in high and suitable for flower-beds as well as for containers and hanging baskets. They are propagated by seed.

Petunia 'Summer Sun' bears deeper yellow flowers than 'Prism Sunshine' and its shape is somewhat looser. 'Summer Sun' also belongs to the Grandiflora Group and is propagated by seed. *Petunia* 'Surfinia Blue Vein' is officially called *Petunia* 'Sunsolos.' In some shops, you will find petunias belonging to this series which are labelled Surfinias, just as if they belonged to a new botanical genus. These so-called Surfinias, however, are genuine petunias. They are propagated by cuttings which may be taken only by licensees, who pay the breeder of the Surfinias a small royalty for each

Petunia 'Surfinia Purple Mini'

Petunia 'Surfinia White'

Petunia 'Surfinia Pink Mini' (official name *Petunia* 'Suntovan') bears pink flowers with translucent centers. For care, see *Petunia* 'Surfinia Blue Vein.'

Petunia 'Surfinia Pink Vein' (official name *Petunia* 'Suntosol') is a variety belonging to the Multiflora Group with crimson veins in pink flowers. (For care, see *Petunia* 'Surfinia Blue Vein').

Petunia 'Surfinia Purple Mini' (official name

Phacelia congesta 'Blue Curls,' Californian bluebell

Petunia 'Revolution') belongs to the Multiflora Group, and carries flowers in a deep purplish shade of pink with dark centers. For care, see *Petunia* 'Surfinia Blue Vein.'

Petunia 'Surfinia Purple Vein' (official name *Petunia* 'Sunpurve') has the large flowers of the Grandiflora Group. Their color is between lavender and pink with prominently contrasting purple veins. For care, see *Petunia* 'Surfinia Blue Vein.'

Petunuia 'Surfinia White' is officially called *Petunia* 'Kesupite' and belongs to the Grandiflora Group. Soon after the introduction of the petunias in the Surfinia Series, they proved to be highly susceptible to viral diseases and this white-flowered variety was particularly affected. Its leaves turned yellow and ultimately the entire plant died. The infection was transferred when cuttings were taken. Since then, nurseries specializing in cuttings have managed to get the problem under control and it is now possible to enjoy the plants' abundant flowers. For care, see *Petunia* 'Surfinia Blue Vein.'

[2-3] ✏ € 🌱 ▼ ⚘

Phacelia congesta 'Blue Curls'

The pale lavender-colored flowers are only ¼ in wide. They are packed close together, hence the name *congesta*. Together, they adorn the border with a pale blue haze. When the flowers are over, the stems straighten out, with the fruits arranged like seeds on ears of corn. The plant, with its softly hairy, pale green foliage, grows to about 20 in in height and flowers for about two months during the period from June to September. Find the plant a spot in full sunlight and well-drained soil. It has a strong dislike of wet summers and of being transplanted. You should therefore sow it in a pot indoors or where it is to flower out-of-doors.

[3] 4-5 🌱 ▼ ⚘ 🐝

Phacelia purshii

Purshii's soft leaves with downy hairs demonstrate its vulnerability. Find a sunny position sheltered from harsh winds for this

plant, which is over 20 in tall, and you will enjoy the flowers, which are nearly 1¼ in wide, white on the inside and tinged with purple at the margins. The new cultivar, *Phacelia purshii* 'Soft Lavender,' has strongly contrasting flowers with blotches and stripes in shades of blue against a light background. Sow in pots indoors, or outdoors where they are to flower.

[3] 4–5

Phacelia tanacetifolia

This is primarily a utilitarian crop. The flowers provide a lot of nectar. which is converted into excellent honey by bees. In addition, the plant is used as a green fertilizer in agriculture. Its luxuriant greenery is ploughed under to enrich poor soil, because sunlight and poor soil are what the plant likes. It grows about 20–39 in tall and, in midsummer, bears small flowers, almost ¾ in wide, in an almost indescribable shade of bluish grey, which goes very well with

Phacelia tanacetifolia, Californian bluebell

other flower colors.

4–5

Pharbitis purpurea

See *Ipomoea purpurea.*

241

Phlox drummondii Group, annual phlox

Phlox drummondii

ANNUAL PHLOX

Annual phlox is not comparable to the dignified perennial plants. Annual phloxes grow to less than 20 in in height and are used mainly in flower-beds. The medium-sized varieties are also suitable for pots and other containers. Flowering plants are on sale from May onwards.

If you sow indoors in March–April, or outdoors after mid-April, they will begin their

long flowering season after about three months.

Cover the seeds with a thin layer of soil since annual phloxes germinate in the dark. If you sow indoors earlier in the year, the temperature should be dropped from about 64 °F to about 54 °F after germination to prevent the premature production of flowers and seeds. Sowing directly in the garden in April–May does not present any problems.

Annual phloxes are sold in a multitude of col-

Phlox drummondii 'Blue Beauty,' annual phlox

Phlox drummondii 'Blue Beauty,' annual phlox

Phlox drummondii 'Dwarf Beauty Mixed,' annual phlox

ors, often in mixtures, but specific colors are available from specialists.

Phlox drummondii 'Blue Beauty' is a blue selection from the popular Beauty Series which, in most countries, is available only in mixtures. The plants grow about 8 in high and carry an unceasing succession of large flowers fading from mauve to light blue throughout the summer. Don't worry about picking small bunches of them.

Phlox drummondii 'Dwarf Beauty Mixed' should remain small, but sometimes shoots up to about 16 in in height. The mixture includes vivid colors as well as pastel shades, but the overall effect is bright and cheerful.

[2–4] 4–5

Phlox 'Ethnie Light Blue'

ANNUAL PHLOX

Although the phloxes in the Ethnie Series closely resemble *Phlox drummondii*, they are of mixed descent, and were developed specifically for flower-beds. Professional growers like them because of the small areas on which they can be cultivated. They flower long and profusely. Still, in my opinion, they are too diminutive. The small plants grow about 4–6 in high, but have a wider spread. Sow them directly in a sunny spot in the garden. You may opt for pink, several shades of red, white, or the blue *Phlox* 'Ethnie Light Blue' introduced in 1998. A mixture is also available.

4–5

Phlox hybrida 'Ethie Light Blue,' annual phlox

Plectostachys serphyllifolia

Summer flowers look their best against a quiet background, one of the reasons why *Helichrysum* has become so popular as filling material for hanging baskets and containers. *Plectostachys* is closely related and is also referred to as *Helichrysum microphyllum*. Microphyllum means "small leafed" and that is what distinguishes *Plectostachys*. Its small leaves are only ½ in long and are produced on spreading shoots. With adequate nourishment and watering, growth is remarkably rapid. Even though the foliage is white-woolly, a fact that usually indicates plants from dry regions, this South African specimen should always be watered adequately. Professional growers propagate the plants by cuttings. They rarely flower in a climate like that of The Netherlands. The flowers in the photograph are those of *Verbena*.

Plectostachys serphyllifolia 'Aurea' has grey-woolly green foliage with yellow margins.

Plectostachys serphyllifolia 'Aurea'

Plectostachys serphyllifolia

Polemonium caeruleum

JACOB'S LADDER

Jacob's ladder grows as a perennial in hilly grasslands in Europe, especially in loamy soil. Garden soil nearly always turns out to be ideal, and the species usually self-seeds profusely there. Anyone entrusting the seeds to the earth in early spring, will find that the

plants come into flower by the late summer of the same year. The species usually has blue flowers, but on rare occasions they are white. In that case, the name of the plant would be *Polemonium caeruleum* 'Album.' The plants grow 20–39 in tall and like moist fertile soil.

2-6

Polemonium pauciflorum

This relative of Jacob's ladder comes from Mexico and finds it difficult to cope with winters in The Netherlands. That is why the perennial is usually cultivated as an annual here. Very few nurseries grow this 16-in tall plant with its slender pinnate foliage. That may be because of the modest color of the flowers, which are $1\frac{1}{2}$ in long. Their basic color is greenish yellow with red streaks. Personally, I think it is a real treasure.

Sow indoors early in the year for the plant to come into flower in July–August. If sown

Polemonium caeruleum, Jacob's ladder

Polemonium pauciflorum

Polygonum capitatum, knotweed

later, it will flower in autumn. The temperature for germination is about 68 °F.

[2-4] 5

Polygonum capitatum

ASIAN KNOTWEED

Polyganum capitatum is not quite hardy in The Netherlands. This perennial from the Himalayas may survive in an unheated greenhouse, but it is simpler to cultivate it as an annual. Sow the seed early under glass, preferably in February–March, but in April if need be. The plants will bear pale pink flower heads within three months, and will continue to flower throughout the summer and autumn.

The plant grows as ground cover with prostrate stems about 12 in long. The green leaves are marked with a vague black V-sign. The foliage turns red in bright sunlight and in dry soil. The plant does best in partial shade. The color of the stems and foliage of *Polygonum capitatum* is highly variable.

Polygonum capitatum 'Victory Carpet' has strikingly red stems, clear red leaf veins, and a striking V-sign on each leaf.

[2-4]

Polygonum capitatum, knotweed

Polygonum capitatum 'Victory Carpet,' knotweed

Portulaca grandiflora 'Kariba Mix,' sun plant

Psylliostachys suworowii 'Rose Pink,' statice

Portulaca grandiflora

SUN PLANT

Nearly all succulents are perennials. They store water in their thick, fleshy leaves to enable them to survive the dry seasons. The sun plant does the same, but this species from central South America is definitely an annual. Sow this cheerful groundcover indoors in March–April, or outdoors in loose soil in a really warm spot from mid-May onwards. Sow the seeds thinly and don't cover them, as they need light in order to germinate. The plants may flower from June until far into September. They are also very useful in containers and hanging baskets.

The double flowers of *Portulaca grandiflora* 'Kariba Mix' show the entire range of colors displayed by the sun plant: white, yellow, pink to red and every imaginable shade in between. The flowers belonging to the mixture are double and resemble roses.

[3–4] 5

Pratia pedunculata

See *Laurentia fluviatilis.*

Psyllostachis suworowii

STATICE

The flowering spikes of statice make an indelible impression, even in borders, where they may be cultivated as if they were forming part of bouquets. The plant has fairly inconspicuous foliage at its base, but the spikes of pink flowers often grow to over 39 in in height. Even so, it is also quite satisfactory to grow the plants in large pots, troughs, or other containers.

It is best to sow this annual from Asia Minor indoors early in the year, and then let the plants grow on in a cool and airy position. That will make them come into flower sooner. The seeds germinate slowly and the first plants may come into flower by the end of June. They go on flowering until far into October.

[2–3] 4

Rehmannia angulata HORT

See *Rehmannia elata*.

Rehmannia elata

The British call this plant the Chinese foxglove, as it originally came from China. In The Netherlands, the plant is not fully hardy and it is therefore cultivated in greenhouses in winter. Professional growers take root cuttings in autumn and can then market flowering plants in May. Purchasing the plants is by far the easiest way to acquire them. Only gardeners with greenhouses are in a position to take cuttings properly and overwinter them in cool condi-

tions. Without a greenhouse, it is possible to sow indoors at a temperature of about 63 °F. The temperature may be lowered further as the seedlings grow. After the last night frost, the

Rehmannia elata

Reseda alba, white mignonette

Reseda alba, white mignonette

plants may be taken out-of-doors to a spot that is sheltered from the wind and preferably in partial shade to prevent leaf scorch. Give them plenty of water and food. *Rehmannia* will then flower for a very long time, bearing pink flowers, about 3¼ in long, on lanky stems which usually grow to between 16 in and 32 in long.

[1-2]

Reseda alba

WHITE MIGNONETTE

The tall white flower heads rise up grandly amidst the other plants in a border of annuals. White mignonette makes an imposing impression, but remains very ordinary. It benefits all the other flowering plants, which show up far

Rhinanthus angustifolius, greater yellow rattle

better when combined with mignonette. It is strange that the plant is seen so rarely, despite the fact that its flowers are wonderfully fragrant and it is very much an "architectural" plant, a species with a strong, clear form. Do sow this treasure – either directly in the garden in April–May, or indoors in March.

It comes into flower as early as June and goes on until September, at least at the top of the plant, which grows to a height of 20–39 in. By then, the small green fruits will have appeared further down the stems. Sow several times in succession if you would like compact plants over a longer period.

[3-4] 5

Rhinanthus angustifolius

GREATER YELLOW RATTLE

Don't try out the seed in a border that has been dug over, because it will not develop there. The reason is that this annual plant parasitizes the roots of grasses. Try scattering some seed on a poor piece of grassland – not the lawn – in the natural garden. If the seed germinates, the plants will self-seed and return again year after year. You will then be able to collect some seed and pass it on to friends. You will find out why the species is called 'rattle' as you harvest them. The seeds make a clearly rattling sound when the dried fruits are touched.

2-4

Rhodanthe chlorocephala ssp. rosea

See *Acroclinium roseum*.

Rhodanthe manglesii

SUNRAY

The small flowers of *Rhodanthe manglesii* grow – with bent heads – on threadlike stems, as if they might break off at any moment. The stems, which grow about 20 in tall, are in fact remarkably strong. The idea is to cut them off in mid-summer and dry the small flowers quickly. That will make them keep their color.

Rhodanthe manglesii 'Timeless Rose'

Rhodochiton atrosanguineus

They are much in demand for dried-flower bouquets, a purpose for which they are also grown commercially. If you want to try them out for yourself, you will probably find it best to sow directly in the garden in poor, loose, humous soil. Sowing in a pot indoors earlier in the year is also feasible, but then let the plants, which do not like having their roots disturbed, come into flower in the pot.

Rhodochiton atrosanguineus

Rhodochiton atrosanguineus, fallen calyces

Rhodanthe manglesii 'Timeless Rose' has small, pale pink, semi-double flowers.

[2–4] 4–5

Rhodochiton atrosanguineus

In just a few years, this perennial Mexican climber has become very popular among a small group of enthusiasts. They sow it every year to enable them to see it in flower from July until well into October. An aubergine-colored corolla resembling a gnome's cap is suspended from a small inverted pink bowl, the calyx, which continues to adorn the plant long after the corolla has been dispersed. Inside the calyx, a spherical fruit full of small brown seeds is formed. Each one is covered by a membrane that is easily blown away by the wind. The seeds may be sown the following year, but after that will quickly lose their capacity to germinate. It takes about four months to grow

249

Rhodochiton atrosanguineus, the climber above a window

Ricinus communis, castor oil plant

flowering plants from seed. Professional growers start work on them in winter, but it is better for amateurs to entrust the seed to the earth in March–April. The seed germinates at room temperature, after which seedlings are grown on in slightly cooler conditions. By early June, they may be put out-of-doors in a sheltered, sunny position, preferably in a large pot. Provide each plant with a support to enable it to climb to 3–10 ft, depending on the height of the support and the quality of the summer. The plants may be overwintered in a frost-free place, but it is hardly worthwhile.

[3-4]

Rhodochiton volubilis

See *Rhodochiton atrosanguineus*.

Ricinus communis

CASTOR-OIL-PLANT

The oil from the seeds of the castor-oil-plant make both the gastrointestinal tract and racing car engines move faster. Because of its toxicity, castor oil is a tried-and-tested medicine for constipation – the intestines try to get rid of the poison as quickly as possible. At one time, castor oil was also a favorite for racing car engines.

Be careful with the seeds, as they are highly toxic if swallowed. Soak them for 24 hours in tepid water, and then sow them in a warm place indoors, or directly in the garden from mid-May onwards. This small plant of African origin likes to grow in a warm spot in very fertile soil. If you give it liberal amounts of fertilizer, it may grow to a height of 6 ft, with a spread of over 39 in. The foliage is magnificently palm-shaped. You may expect to see the

Rudbeckia hirta, cone flower

plants, 20–36 in tall, bear flowers about 3¼ in wide. The ray florets of the species are yellow with a brown blotch at their base. The centers are dark. There are numerous cultivars, with colors ranging from orange brown to lemon yellow. They are very suitable for rich, late summer flower arrangements.

Rudbeckia hirta 'Irish Eyes' is also called *Rudbeckia hirta* 'Green Eyes' because of its striking light green center in surrounded by bright yellow ray flowers. They are about 4 in wide and highly suitable for vases. The stems are straight and sturdy and grow about 24 in tall.

[3–4] 4

Rudbeckia serotina

See *Rudbeckia hirta*.

Rudbeckia hirta 'Irish Eyes,' cone flower

first flowers – prickly, yellow with a lot of red – after two or three months.

[3–4] 5

Rudbeckia hirta

CONEFLOWER

It takes three to four months to cultivate flowering *Rudbeckia hirta* plants from seed. The species grows as a short-lived perennial in North America, but does not survive the winter in countries like The Netherlands, where it is always cultivated as an annual. Professional growers begin to market the plants, in flower, by the end of April. For amateurs, it is better to start later. If you sow indoors in March or April – the ideal temperature for germination is 60 °F – the first flowers may be expected in April. If you sow outdoors in April, you will see the first flowers in August. The plants will continue to flower incessantly until well into October. The

Salpiglossis sinuata

Salpiglossis sinuata bears flowers about 2 in wide. They have distinctive markings, with contrasting colors along their veins, like ingenious patterns woven into brocade – hence their Dutch common name *brokaatbloem*. They create a very baroque impression. That may account for their lack of popularity among otherwise keen gardeners until they happen to see the plants in someone else's garden. I myself go overboard for the cultivar *Salpiglossis sinuata* with its chocolate-brown veins on golden-yellow and greyish-pink petals.

The plants grow to about 28 in in height. They are usually marketed in multicolored mixtures such as *Salpiglossis sinuata* 'Superbissima,' *Salpiglossis sinuata* 'Casino,' or *Salpiglossis sinuata* 'Bolero.'

The species hails from the Andes Mountains

Salpiglossis sinuata 'Gloomy Rival'

Salpiglossis sinuata 'Superbissima'

Salvia coccinea

Salvia coccinea

Salvia coccinea 'Lady in Red'

Salvia coccinea 'Rose Salmon'

Salvia coccinea 'Snow Nymph'

and is particularly suitable for a sunny position in soil that is not excessively rich or wet. Arrange the plants in groups to create the best effects. If growing them for cutting, plant them at distances of about 20 in apart. If they are cultivated in a greenhouse, the results will be even more abundant. If you sow in April (germination temperature 63 °F), the first flowers will appear in August.

[3–4] 5   🌱   🌸   ▜   🏺   !

Salpiglossis superbissima

See *Salpiglossis sinuata*.

Salpiglossis variabilis

See *Salpiglossis sinuata*.

Salvia coccinea

This sage comes from the warmer regions of America, where it forms a complete shrub

253

with loose growth. Because it is not hardy in north-west Europe and is so easy and quick to grow from seed, it is cultivated as an annual here. That gives it a totally different character, with its black-tinged square stems, their tips ablaze with red flowers, growing to a maximum height of 39 in. The color of the flowers is so blinding that it claims all one's attention, and this form of sage may therefore be used on its own to provide an eye-catching focal point in a boring corner of the garden, or as a showpiece in a pot.

Professional growers sow in January to enable them to supply flowering plants in April. In that case, cultivation takes 10–12 weeks. Amateur gardeners are less likely to have appropriate lighting available, in which case it is better to wait until February or even March before sowing indoors at, for example, 60 °F. Grow the seedlings on at a slightly cooler temperature. This will prevent straggly growth and the plants you have sown will still flower in June. They are on sale in many places to provide earlier flowers.

Salvia coccinea likes warmth, but, in my opinion, looks its best if grown in partial shade, where the plants will be a little taller and acquire their characteristic loose growth. Unfortunately, however, plant breeders have adopted a different course to please the commercial market. Modern cultivars are often considerably more compact and therefore more attractive to professional nurserymen, who can market them in convenient packs. To give these plants back their natural charm, it is therefore best to put them in a slightly shaded spot in very nutritive soil.

Salvia coccinea 'Lady in Red' is a compact cultivar that won a prize in 1992. It grows to a mere 10 in high, according to some catalogues. Fortunately, it does not stay as small as that in all circumstances. In a position away from bright sunlight, and in richly fertilized soil, it will be really beautiful, with flowers that may be even brighter than those of the species.

Salvia coccinea 'Rose-Salmon' is cultivated all too rarely, in my opinion. The flowers of this

treasure are bicolored – white at the top with a touch of pale pink and salmon pink at the bottom. They are magnificent, but it is difficult to get hold of either the plants or the seed, although it is worthwhile hunting for them. *Salvia coccinea* 'Coral Nymph' is a comparable cultivar, with brighter coral pink flowers. *Salvia coccinea* 'Snow Nymph' has genuinely snow-white flowers. The plants grow to about 2–16 in high. They look their best in partial shade, where they will grow a little taller and light up beautifully.

[2-3]

Salvia coccinea 'White Lady'

See *Salvia coccinea* 'Snow Nymph.'

Salvia farinacea

Cultivars of *Salvia farinacea* turn up with increasing frequency in the flower-beds of public parks and gardens. They stand stiffly side by side, filling the various sections with their grey stems and usually blue flowers. In fact, they are perennials, which may survive Dutch winters in a frost-free greenhouse or even under a thick winter cover. In spite of that, the plants, which originally came from Texas and the adjoining part of Mexico, are still mainly grown from seed as annuals. Professional growers sow in February and, after fourteen weeks, can supply flowering plants that will bloom from then onwards until the first frost.

It is best for amateur gardeners to sow indoors in March–April. The ideal temperature for germination is about 64 °F; for growing the plants on, it should be slightly lower to keep them compact. A long summer full of flowers will then begin sometime in June.

This type of sage is remarkably vertical. The flower stems grow straight upwards to 32 in. Modern cultivars stop at less than 20 in, which makes them even less suitable for romantic gardening. Even so, something can be done about it. Stand them in pots in between other plants and the overall effect will be much more attractive immediately.

Salvia patens 'Cambridge Blue,' blue sage

Salvia patens 'Cambridge Blue,' blue sage

Salvia patens 'Oxford Blue,' blue sage

After the last night frosts, *Salvia farinacea* may be put out-of-doors in a sunny to partly shaded position. The species is extremely strong, and exceptionally good at withstanding strong wind, which makes it suitable for growing in containers on balconies.

The white flowers of *Salvia farinacea* 'Porcelaine' grow on stems with downy white hairs. The leaf buds and veins are also beautifully white-haired, so that the plant as a whole makes a greyish impression and is therefore very suitable for combining with other plants in a border.

Salvia farinacea 'Rhea' is especially favored by flower arrangers. The stems themselves are a deep purplish blue. The flowers have the same intense color, just as if they and their stems had been plunged into blue ink, with just two small white spots left at the opening to each flower.

Salvia farinacea 'Strata' was awarded a Fleuroselect gold medal in 1996. The plant grows to a maximum height of 16 in, and carries

blue flowers on strikingly white-woolly stems. New flower stems are added throughout the season.

[3–4]

Salvia grahamii

See *Salvia microphylla*.

Salvia patens 'Chilcombe,' blue sage

Salvia patens 'White Perfection,' blue sage

Salvia splendens 'Salsa Salmon Bicolor,' sage

Salvia horminum

See *Salvia viridis.*

Salvia patens

In areas with a mild climate like south-west England, *Salvia patens* is cultivated as a perennial (if protected in winter). In The Netherlands, however, we are obliged to treat this Mexican species differently. Its radical tubers may be dug up in the autumn and stored frost-free in peat dust in the same way as dahlia tubers. We may take cuttings in late summer and keep them in frost-free conditions, but it is also possible to cultivate the plants as annuals. In that case, they should be sown very early in spring. For most plant lovers, a third method is the most convenient

Salvia splendens 'Flamex 2000,' scarlet sage

Salvia splendens 'Salsa Salmon Bicolor,' sage

Salvia splendens 'Sizzler,' scarlet sage

Salvia splendens 'Sizzler White,' sage

one – buying new plants every spring. They are cultivated by professional nurserymen and sold mainly by patio plant specialists.

Salvia patens is often used in large groups in flower-beds and borders. It serves as a focal point in a border and does spectacularly well in a pot. In Mexico, the plant grows as a shrub. Cultivated as an annual, it grows to a height of 16–32 in, depending on growing conditions. Provide nutritive soil and, preferably, a place in partial shade.

There are some magnificent cultivars with flowers in various shades.

Salvia patens 'Cambridge Blue' has sky-blue flowers. The flowers of *Salvia patens*, 2½ in long, are pollinated by hummingbirds. *Salvia patens* 'Chilcombe' bears lilac-blue flowers. Those of *Salvia patens* 'Oxford Blue' are an intense shade of deep blue, and those of *Salvia patens* 'White Perfection' are pure white.

[2–3]   **!**

Salvia splendens

Some plants are no longer cultivated as individual items, but rather are enjoyed for their collective effect in a planting scheme. Scores of plants of the same species are put close together to form a specific color zone. *Salvia splendens* is a clear favorite in this kind of gardening, and the plants used for it tend to be about 8–12 in high.

At one time, nearly all the specimens of *Salvia splendens* on sale had either red or white flowers. Nowadays, however, they are available with flowers in numerous colors, including pink and mauve, and some plants have bicolored flowers. Cultivars with unusual colors are available in very small quantities from florists and more generally from seed merchants.

Salvia splendens comes from Brazil and cannot tolerate any frost at all. You should therefore wait until May before planting it out-of-doors in nutritive, well-drained soil, preferably in a sunny position.

Salvia uliginosa, bog sage

Salvia viridis 'Blue Bird,' sage

Professional growers start sowing by the end of January, since it still takes these annuals at least three months to come into flower. Amateurs would be well advised to delay sowing until the end of February at the earliest in order to take advantage of the greater intensity of light. *Salvia splendens* needs light to germinate and the seed should not, therefore, be covered.

Sow in a closed propagator or a tray covered with glass or plastic. The seeds germinate best in tropical conditions. At 68–71 °F, the ideal temperature for germination is somewhat high. After germination, the seedlings may be grown on in slightly cooler conditions, but not below about 57 °F. If the temperature is too low, the foliage will turn yellow.

There are many cultivars of *Salvia splendens* on the market. They mostly vary in color. All the major seed merchants cultivate their own series, which are sold as "very early flowering" or "very compact." The continual recurrence of very similar names is of little use to plant lovers. There are cultivars of *Salvia splendens*

in shades of bright red, deep red, purple, pink, old-rose, salmon pink, cream, and white. Some flowers are multicolored.

Salvia splendens 'Flamex 2000' is one of the innumerable red cultivars. At a maximum height of 8 in, it remains very compact.

The bracts of *Salvia splendens* 'Salsa Salmon Bicolor' are a buttery yellow with salmon pink, whereas the flowers themselves are shaded from pink to white. Tubular flowers of that kind may grow to over 2 in long – and that on a small plant about 8 in high.

Salvia splendens 'Sizzler' grows more vigorously and has large healthy leaves. Its flowers are deep purple.

Salvia splendens 'Sizzler White' is the white counterpart of the previous cultivar.

[2–4]   ▼

Salvia uliginosa

BOG SAGE

The sky-blue flowers on long graceful stems

Salvia viridis 'Blue Bird,' sage

Salvia viridis 'Blue Monday,' sage

Salvia viridis 'Pink Gem,' sage

Salvia viridis 'Pink Gem,' sage

Salvia viridis 'White Swan,' sage

convey a sense of harvest-time. Summer is past its peak, but *Salvia uliginosa* will go on flowering until far into autumn.

It is an unforgettable sight, particularly if the plant is grown in a large pot. This perennial originally came from South America, where it grows in swampy ground. As it does not tolerate temperatures below 14 °F in open ground, the plant must definitely be taken indoors in autumn. Many people don't bother, and simply buy a new plant in early spring. Bog sage is available from patio plant specialists. Professional growers usually propagate the plants by cuttings or division. The latter operation is very simple, as the plant develops underground suckering shoots. Sowing is another option, but I am not aware of any address where the seed may be purchased.

Salvia viridis

'Flag–at–the–masthead' might be an appropriate name for *Salvia viridis*. The blue, pink, or white foliage formed at the top of the

plant obviously shares the function of flowers in attracting insects. The latter are happy to respond, but are obliged to drop down a level to enjoy the nectar, as the labiate flowers are borne lower down the stems. These are not very striking.

Salvias can give keen gardeners a lot of enjoyment. They are easy to grow from seed. Sow or plant them in groups to create patches of color in a border. The plants begin to acquire color at a height of about 12 in and continue to grow throughout the summer – up to 30 in. They form a magnificent backdrop to other summer-flowering plants, but only to the extent that the colors go well together. Sow indoors in March or early April or – even better – directly in the garden from mid-April. The plants provide color in the garden between July and October. There are many names of cultivars for plants that look almost identical. There is a choice of blue, pink, or white little flags.

Salvia viridis 'Blue Bird' and *Salvia viridis* 'Blue Monday' are purplish blue, *Salvia viridis* 'Pink Gem' is pink, and *Salvia viridis*

Sanvitalia procumbens 'Aztekengold,' creeping zinnia

Sanvitalia procumbens 'Single Sprite,' creeping zinnia

261

Sanvitalia procumbens 'Golden Carpet,' creeping zinnia

Sanvitalia procumbens 'Yellow Sprite,' creeping zinnia

'White Swan' has white leaves with green venation at the top.

[3–4] 4–5 ⚓ ▼ 🍶 🐝 **!**

Salvia viridis 'Oxford Blue'

See *Salvia viridis* 'Blue Monday.'

Sanvitalia procumbens

CREEPING ZINNIA

The stems of creeping zinnias branch out continually to increase the spread of these plants which, however, do not grow much more than 6 in high. An area full of these plants will create a yellow carpet, since they flower freely and unceasingly from June until well into October. This makes creeping zinnias highly suitable for hanging baskets and containers, in which they add to their charm by trailing over the edges.

Sow indoors in March–April, or outdoors from the end of April. The plants may well come into flower two months later. The species orig-

inally came from the warm south of Mexico and the adjoining regions of Guatemala, and cannot tolerate frost. After hardening off the plants, you should therefore wait until the end of May before putting them out-of-doors. They like sunlight and will put up with any kind of soil provided it is not too wet.

Sanvitalia procumbens 'Aztekengold' is one of the most rewarding cultivars and bears a profusion of little flowers resembling small yellow wheels. They also do quite well in summers that are not so very good.

Sanvitalia procumbens 'Golden Carpet' has yellow flowers with blackish-brown centers.

Sanvitalia procumbens 'Mandarin Orange' closely resembles the above cultivar.

Sanvitalia procumbens 'Single Sprite' is most like the natural species, but has semi-double flowers.

[3–4] 4–5 🐝 🌸 ▼ **!**

Saponaria calabrica 'Hellas Rose'

SOAPWORT

Each small flower of this Greek annual is no more than $1/2$ in wide, but the plant flowers so freely that you can still enjoy a dense pink mound for months on end. The foliage forms a compact background. The leaves grow on a tangle of stems, forming cushions which grow to about 12 in high, with a spread that is at least twice the height. This is an ideal annual for rockeries, low walls, flower-beds, and containers.

Sow indoors in March–April, or scatter the seed outdoors from mid-April. The ideal tem-

Saponaria calabrica 'Hellas Rose,' soapwort

Saponaria calabrica 'Hellas Rose,' soapwort

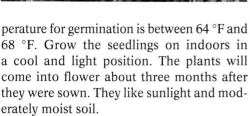

Scabiosa atropurpurea (mixture), sweet scabious

perature for germination is between 64 °F and 68 °F. Grow the seedlings on indoors in a cool and light position. The plants will come into flower about three months after they were sown. They like sunlight and moderately moist soil.

[3–4] 4–5 🌼 ▼ !

Saponaria graeca

See *Saponaria calabrica.*

Saponaria multiflora

See *Saponaria calabrica.*

Saponaria vaccaria

See *Vaccaria hispanica.*

Scabiosa atropurpurea

SWEET SCABIOUS

The scientific and common names for this botanical genus refer to the medicinal use that was made of the plants. The Romans used it for scabies, a form of leprosy, and it was subsequently thought that the plant could be used for all kinds of skin disorders. Meanwhile, we are left with an unpleasant name for a lovely annual, which may grow to 16–39 in tall, depending on conditions. The flowers develop between July and September. Those of the original species are deep purple and about $1\frac{1}{4}$ in wide. The species grows wild in southern Europe. Centuries of crossing and selecting resulted in larger flowers but, unfortunately, also caused the loss of most of its fragrance. In spite of this, even the modern cultivars attract many butterflies.

You are likely to buy a multicolored mixture including white, cream, pale pink, deep pink, red, scarlet, purple, lavender, lilac to pale blue flowers. To have a little more control of the results, it would be better to buy selections in specific colors. The taller cultivars

Scabiosa atropurpurea 'Blue Cockade,' sweet scabious

Scabiosa atropurpurea 'Qis Scarlet,' sweet scabious

are inclined to flop over. Find a sheltered spot for them or provide supports.

Scabiosa atropurpurea 'Blue Cockade' grows to a minimum height of 28 in and carries rounded heads of lavender-blue flowers, over $2^3/_4$ in wide.

Scabiosa atropurpurea 'Qis Scarlet' bears scarlet flowers on stems 32 in long. They are grown mainly for cutting.

It is best to sow indoors in March–April because the plants need at least three months of growth before coming into flower. Sow in pots or balls of earth so that there is no need to disturb the roots – something they dislike. Grow the seedlings on in conditions that are as cool as possible. Alternatively, you may also sow directly in the garden to have flowers in late summer.

[3–4] 4–5 🌱 🏺 🐝

Scabiosa stellata

SCABIOUS

The pale blue of this scabious is a very modest color, but the shape of the flowers is mag-

Scabiosa atropurpurea 'Blue Cockade,' sweet scabious

nificent, like lace. Still, its importance as an ornamental plant is limited, since most people are mainly interested in the fruits, $1^1/_2$ in wide, which are formed when the flowers are over. In the center, there is a five-pointed star

Scabiosa stellata, sweet scabious

Scabiosa stellata, sweet scabious

Scabiosa stellata 'Drumstick,' sweet scabious

Scaevola aemula 'Blue Wonder'

surrounded by a small cup of translucent membrane. It is an ideal flower for drying and that is the principal reason for its cultivation. It is grown in the same way as *Scabiosa atropurpurea.*

Scabiosa stellata 'Drumstick' is the cultivar most frequently available. It grows about 28 in tall, and is also known as *Scabiosa stellata* 'Sternkugel.'

[3–4] 4–5

Scaevola aemula

For some years now, we have been able to enjoy the small fans of *Scaevola*, an Australian plant propagated by cuttings in The Netherlands. Professional nurseries pot up the cuttings between January and March to supply flowering plants three months later.

Taking cuttings yourself is quite feasible. It is best to do that in late summer and then to overwinter the cuttings in a cool, but frost-free and light place.

The plants may be put out-of-doors after mid-May, either as prostrate ground cover along paths, or in flower-beds or pots and are popular among container and hanging-basket enthusiasts. Give the plant a sunny to partially shaded position in nutritive soil, which should never be allowed to dry out entirely. You will then be able to enjoy the $1^{1}/_{4}$-in wide flowers from the time of purchase until the first frost.

Scaevola aemula 'Blue Wonder' is the culti-

Scaevola aemula 'Blue Wonder'

var most often on sale. Until recently, it was called *Scaevola aemula* 'Blue Fan'.

It is just possible that you may come across *Scaevola aemula* 'Petite,' a cultivar with smaller leaves and flowers that are only 5/8 in wide. It flowers freely and beautifully. It just might be the species *Scaevola humilis*.

Scaevola saligna

See *Scaevola aemula*.

Schizanthus pinnatus

See *Schizanthus × wisetonensis*.

Scaevola aemula 'Blue Wonder'

Scaevola aemula 'Petite'

Schizanthus × wisetonensis 'Angel Wings'

Schizanthus × wisetonensis

BUTTERFLY FLOWER

This annual from South Africa, with colorful, orchid-like flowers, is easy to cultivate.

Also known as the poor man's orchid, it is an indoor plant with a great need for warmth. It may flower long and profusely if planted in a sheltered, partly shaded part of the garden, or in a pot or other container from June onwards.

Sow indoors in March–April and grow the seedlings on in a warm position. Make sure they are not allowed to dry out.

Schizanthus × wisetonensis 'Angel Wings' show the rich variety of colors.

[3–4]

Scutellaria alpina

SKULLCAP

Growers of bedding plants are faced with a problem – their greenhouses are empty for a large part of the year. This is expensive, so a clever seed merchant dreamed up a way of keeping greenhouses full, even in summer. Kieft Seeds of Venhuizen in The Netherlands called the programme 'After Holiday Plants,' and *Scutellaria alpina* is one of them. It is a genuinely hardy perennial from the Swiss Alps and other mountainous regions farther east. The seed is sown on the surface and kept thoroughly moist. After about two weeks, the temperature is allowed to fall from about 68 °F to about 35 °F. The seeds germinate after about five weeks and the seedlings are grown on in fairly cool conditions. This is specialist work, but plants are fortunately on sale, in flower, from July. Flowering plants from the previous year are sometimes available even sooner. They look splendid in pots, rockeries, or natural borders. If planted in the garden, they are fully hardy.

Scutellaria alpina 'Greencourt' has bluish-purple flowers with white lips.

Scutellaria alpina 'Romana' has white, blue, or the characteristic bicolored flowers. Both cultivars grow to about 8 in high.

Senecio bicolor

See *Senecio cineraria*.

Scutellaria alpina 'Romana,' skullcap

Scutellaria alpina 'Greencourt,' skullcap

Senecio cineraria

With so much color in our summer gardens, we need a few patches of calm, where we can rest our eyes. Senecio comes in very useful for that purpose. Its foliage is covered with fine white hair and creates a grey impression, splendid when combined with the most difficult shades of red, or orange, or yellow, or any other color for that matter. It will tone

Senecio cineraria 'Silverdust'

Setaria italica 'Macrochaeta,' foxtail millet

Setaria italica 'Max,' foxtail millet

down the brightness of the color, so it is worth adding some of this grey foliage to borders or containers.

Professional nurserymen sow the small plants between January and March. The seed is covered lightly and germinates best at temperatures between 64 °F and 71 °F. The seedlings are grown on at moderate temperatures (about 59 °F) and may be planted out early in May. You may also sow the seed yourself, preferably in February–March, when the light is strong enough. Find a sunny spot for the plants, either in the garden or in a container. Give them adequate water when growing them in pots, even though they originally came from Mediterranean countries. It is best to put the small plants in full sun to keep them beautifully white.

The best-known cultivar is *Senecio cineraria* 'Silverdust,' which has deeply divided leaves.

[2–3]

Senecio cruentus

See *Pericallis* × *hybrida*.

Setaria italica

FOXTAIL MILLET

There are several names for this giant grass, including Italian millet, and it has a long history as a corn crop. These days, we mainly cultivate it for cutting and drying. Scatter the seed in April–May in the place where it is to grow, preferably in a small field or in rows, so that the plants shelter one another. By July–August the grasses will be waist-high and carry handsome panicles that look lovely when added to bouquets and which are also very suitable for drying. In gardens where they are not picked, birds will harvest them, as the seed is delicious. *Setaria Italica* 'Macrochaeta' bears comical thick green panicles that bend over under their own weight. The plant grows to about 32 in in height.

Setaria italica 'Max' may grow to a height of 4¹/₂ ft, but is usually shorter. The flower spikes are at first reminiscent of the female flowers of reedmace. They are a bronze brown color. Pick them in time, because the seeds drop out quite soon.

4–5

Silene coeli-rosa

Silene coeli-rosa grows naturally in south-western Europe and on the other side of the Mediterranean in North Africa. The plants have white, pink, red, lilac, or blue flowers, but most of them are in shades of pink. Their centers are often in contrasting white or black. They grow about 20 in tall. The thin stems carry small flowers, over ³/₄ in wide, in a seemingly casual arrangement that appears to float in the air – a wonderfully beautiful sight. Sow the plants where they are to flower, either in a pot or directly in the garden. If sown in April,

they will flower from early July until the end of August. They subsequently produce an abundance of seed.

There are innumerable cultivars. Seed merchants provide mixtures, or harmonizing shades. *Silene coeli-rosa* 'Blue Angel' grows to a maximum height of 10 in. This compact cultivar bears pale blue flowers until the end of September. It is very suitable for containers.

Silene coeli-rosa 'Blue Pearl'

Silene coeli-rosa

Silene coeli-rosa 'Blue Angel'

Silene coeli-rosa 'Blue Pearl'

Silene pendula, nodding catchfly

Silene coeli-rosa 'Rose Angel'

Silene coeli-rosa 'Pink Pearl'

Silene coeli-rosa 'Blue Pearl' has lilac-blue flowers. It is much bushier and taller than the above plant. It grows to about 16 in in height and its spread is at least as great. Lovely for a large pot and excellent as a cut flower. Definitely starred.

Silene coeli-rosa 'Pink Pearl' is comparable to 'Blue Pearl,' except that the color of the flowers is pink with deep-red centers.

Selene coeli-rosa 'Rose Angel' is the pink dwarf version growing to 10 in high. The eye – spot in the center – is small and dark. It bears flowers over a long period.

[3] 4–5 ⬭ 🌸 ▼ 🏺 🐝 !

Silene pendula

NODDING CATCHFLY

Nodding catchfly originally came from southern Europe, where it germinates in autumn and flowers in May–June. In more northerly parts of Europe, it is best grown as an annual. Sow indoors in March–April, or from early May directly where it is to flower.

The plants then bear their characteristically nodding flowers, about $^3/_4$ in wide, in July and August. The calyx is swollen and delightfully striped, as are the fruits, which continue to adorn the 8-in tall plants for a long time.

There are numerous cultivars on the market. They have pink and white flowers, often single, sometimes semi-double.

The ripe seed may be sown as early as August or September. Put the seedlings in a cold place, but under glass, and they will come into flower in the following month of May. The plants like sunlight and well-drained soil – preferably loamy.

[3-5] 5 8-9

Silybum marianum

BLESSED MARY'S THISTLE

The Blessed Mary's thistle has a liking for the cliffs along the Atlantic coasts of France and the south of England. This outstanding thistle is also found in many places inland, nearly always in sunny spots. Sometimes it grows as an annual, and at other times as a biennial. At first, just a rosette of viciously spiny foliage is formed. It has a beautiful pattern of white blotches (said to be Mary's spilt breast milk). Then the flower stems shoot up, depending on the time of sowing. If sown in summer, the plant will come into flower the following summer. Plants sown indoors in February will flower in midsummer of the same year. If the seed is scattered out-of-doors in March–April, flowers are likely to appear in late summer

Silybum marianum, Blessed Mary's thistle

Silybum marianum, Blessed Mary's thistle

and autumn. Allow for the fact that the plant may self-seed vigorously.

[2-3] 3-4 7-9

Solanum melongena

EGGPLANT

The eggplant is in fact a white aubergine, a vegetable brought to Europe from south-

Silybum marianum, Blessed Mary's thistle

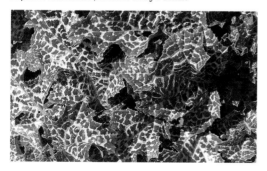

Silybum marianum, Blessed Mary's thistle

271

Solanum melongena, eggplant

Solenopsis axillaris

See *laurentia axillaris.*

Solenopsis fluviatilis

See *Laurentia fluviatilis.*

Solenostemon scutellarioides

ORNAMENTAL NETTLE

Because of their great need for warmth, ornamental nettles are normally marketed as indoor plants in The Netherlands. It is, however, quite all right to put them out-of-doors in summer, either in a flower-bed or a pot, or trailing over the edge of a hanging basket. Choose the warmest part of the garden for them, but avoid long periods of burning sunlight, which causes the foliage and watery stems to lose too much moisture.

Ornamental nettles are typical of the kind of plants that people are likely to buy, even

Solenostemon scutellarioides, ornamental nettle

east Asia as early as the thirteenth century. The eggplant is one of many cultured varieties. The fruits have the shape and, initially, the color of a hen's egg. Subsequently, they turn a bright orange yellow.

The eggplant is sown indoors in February–March at a germination temperature of 68–77 °F. Grow the seedlings on at a warm temperature. The plants should not be moved out-of-doors until early June, preferably to a sheltered spot that is as warm as possible, since only there will it flower freely to make fructification likely. The plants grow about 28 in tall. They flower from July to October and the very decorative fruits are formed afterwards. They may be cooked in the same way as aubergines.

[2-3] 🌼 🏺

Solanum ovigerum

See *Solanum melongena.*

Solenostemon scutellarioides 'Rose Wizard'

Solenostemon scutellarioides 'Carefree Mix'

Solenostemon scutellarioides 'Velvet Red Wizard,'
ornamental nettle

though it is possible to sow them, or propagate them by cuttings, oneself. A cutting in a glass of water quickly develops roots. Sow indoors in February–March at 68–77 °F. Cover the seed very lightly or not at all. Grow the seedlings on in a warm and light position and do not put them out-of-doors until mid-June. The principal feature of ornamental nettles is not their blue flowers, which are small and inconspicuous, but their colorful foliage. You can combine the foliage splendidly with the flowers of other summer-flowering plants.

Solenostemon scutellarioides 'Carefree Mix' is a cultivar that might be used to fill an entire flower-bed. The plants remain very small 8–10 in high – and have small and deeply lobed foliage in diverse colors.

Solenostemon scutellarioides 'Rose Wizard' is a typical tricolor plant, with the fuchsia-red center of the leaf surrounded by creamy white and green. The plants are low-growing, branch out vigorously, and do not flower until late in the season.

Solenostemon scutellarioides 'Velvet Red Wizard' belongs to the same series as the above plant and has comparable features. The leaves are quite variegated in color, but look reddish brown with narrow greenish-yellow margins.

[2-3]

Stachys coccinea

Streptocarpus saxorum, false African violet

Specularia speculum-veneris

See *Legousia speculum-veneris*.

Stachys coccinea

In addition to the hardy species of woundwort, there are some borderline cases that are better to treat as annuals. *Stachys coccinea* tolerates temperatures as low as 14 °F. It comes from the south-east of the United States and from Mexico.

In those countries, the brick-red flowers are pollinated by hummingbirds, since red is a color invisible to insects, but visible to birds. All we need do is enjoy the magnificent combination of the soft red and greyish-green foliage. Put the plant in a (red) border or in a pot. It will come into flower at the end of June and go on flowering until far into September.

Sow indoors in March–April, or outdoors after mid-April. The temperature for germination is 60–68 °F. The young plants may be put out-of-doors at the beginning of May. They will ulti-

mately grow to about 32 in in height, and like sunlight and warmth.

[3–4] 4–5   **!**

Statice perezii

See *Limonium perezii*.

Statice sinuata

See *Limonium sinuatum*.

Streptocarpus saxorum

FALSE AFRICAN VIOLET

The immense popularity of hanging baskets ensured that nurserymen went busily in search of filling material for those hanging mini-gardens. One of their discoveries was this *Streptocarpus*, which had long been cultivated as an indoor plant. Its velvety hairy foliage cannot tolerate fierce sunlight or a lot of moisture, so it is unlikely to have a meteoric career, but it is a lovely little plant for a warm and shady spot – for instance, under the eaves or a verandah. The flowers are carried at the end of bare stems about 8 in long.

Surfinia

See *Petunia.*

Sutera cordata

Unlike *Streptocarpus* (see above), *Sutera* has

Sutera cordata 'Knysma Hills'

Sutera cordata 'Snowflake'

had a meteoric rise in popularity in The Netherlands. The plant emerged from nowhere in 1993 and is now on sale almost everywhere for the purpose of adorning hanging baskets. It is still usually called *Bacopa*, which is actually incorrect, but the name has become established. It forms a dense green tuft, which may grow to about 12 in high, with a much greater spread in borders or flower-beds. If the plant cannot find any support, it begins to trail over edges, and so may easily fill a large hanging basket with greenery and pretty little flowers.

Hang the basket in a light place, but not necessarily in the sun. A sunny position is all right, but it is essential to prevent the soil from drying out, something this South African plant cannot tolerate. It is possible to overwinter *sutera* in a frost-free, cool, and light position, but it is far simpler to buy new plants in spring. Professionals propagate them by cuttings.

Sutera cordata 'Knysma Hills' is one of the cultivars referred to as being blue, of which there are quite a few on sale nowadays. Their flowers are predominantly lilac.

Sutera cordata 'Snowflake' was the first one to be introduced. It was presumably the result of selection of the common species. Its small flowers are white.

Sutera diffusa

See *Sutera cordata.*

Sutera cordata 'Snowflake'

Tagetes anisata

See *Tagetes lucida.*

Tagetes erecta

AFRICAN MARIGOLD

The poor reputation of African marigolds is due mainly to cultivated varieties of *Tagetes erecta.* The cultivars are mostly developed to please nurserymen striving for early-flowering, uniform plants, and huge blooms. In May, the plants are auctioned in packs, usually four pots joined together, since there is still, apparently, a market for these "cheerful monsters." The reason for this is, presumably, that, though the flowers are often fully double and form spongy balls, their shades of lemon yellow, golden yellow, and orange obviously give customers a sense of summer. For propagation and care, see *Tagetes patula.*

Tagetes erecta 'Golden Age' carries yellowy-orange flowers on uniform plants about 12 in high.

Tagetes erecta 'Inca Yellow' is very popular among nurserymen because of the uniformity of the plants, which grow to a maximum height of 12 in. The large yellow flowers, seemingly stemless, jostle for position above the dense greenery.

Tagetes erecta 'Moonbeam': see *Tagetes erecta* 'Mr. Moonlight.'

In *Tagetes erecta* 'Mr. Moonlight,' the greenish center in the yellow double flower is a striking feature. It flowers early and the plants grow to 16 in in height.

Tagetes erecta 'Perfection Yellow' is outstanding because of its beautiful foliage and

Tagetes erecta 'Inca Yellow,' African marigold

Tagetes erecta 'Perfection Yellow,' African marigold

Tagetes erecta 'Golden Age,' African marigold

Tagetes erecta 'Mr. Moonlight,' African marigold

attractive spherical yellow flowers carried on plants that grow about 14 in high.

Tagetes erecta 'Vanilla' is something of an outsider because of its creamy white color. Its flowers grow to a width of $3^{1}/_{4}$ in, and display a certain amount of yellow in their centers. Their height, 20–30 in, is also remarkable.

[2-4] 4-5

Tagetes lucida

'ANISEED MARIGOLD'

The 'aniseed' marigold is a real maverick among African marigolds. Few people will buy the plant for its orange-yellow flowers, which are a mere $^{1}/_{4}$ in wide. What is important about this flower from Central America is the fragrance of its foliage. Pluck up enough courage to crush one between your thumb and index finger, and enjoy the delightful scent of aniseed. Despite the toing and froing of many insect visitors to this plant, no seed is formed in my garden.

4-5

Tagetes erecta 'Vanilla,' African marigold

Tagetes lucida, aniseed marigold

Tagetes patula

FRENCH MARIGOLD

Sowing marigolds is child's play and, in fact, it is a good idea to let children do so on their own. The needle-shaped seeds are easy to handle and, because of the straw color of the floral remains, it is simple to spot where they have dropped on the ground. Tell the children that the seeds must not touch one another anywhere; this will teach them not to sow 'too densely.' Scatter just a minimal layer of sand over the seeds, because they need light to germinate. At about 68 °F and in moist soil, the seeds will germinate in a week's time. The seedlings will be quite strong right away and may be transplanted after several weeks. You can then take hold of them by one of the two seed leaves – teach children never to hold a seedling by its stem. After a few months, the first buds will appear at the top of the plants. Now children may choose between allowing them come into flower or pinching out the first buds. The first option will give them early flowers, but the second one will lead to bigger

Tagetes patula, French marigold

Tagetes patula 'Jolly Jester,' French marigold

Tagetes patula 'Pack Star Spry,' French marigold

278

plants that will bear many more flowers in the course of the summer. Let them pinch out the growing tips of some and leave the others, so that they can see the difference for themselves. The marigolds are taken out-of-doors after the last frost, regardless of whether they are in flower. Children can use the flowers for painting – just rub them vigorously across the paper. African marigolds will grow in any soil that is not saturated. They like sunlight. *Tagetes patula* and *Tagetes erecta* are a natural way of combating eelworms. Plants belonging to the nightshade genus, including tomatoes, aubergines, tobacco plants (*Nicotiana*), and petunias, benefit particularly from having African marigolds growing close to them. French marigolds are usually – but not always – smaller than *Tagetes erecta*: there are cultivars in the latter group which do not grow more than about 4 in high, whereas the "small African marigolds" can shoot up considerably. *Tagetes patula* 'Jolly Jester' is clear example of that. The plants ultimately grow to about 24 in high. They carry very striking striped flowers – golden yellow with a deep brownish red. In ex-

tremely wet or hot weather, or if the plants are kept too dry, new flowers will be entirely yellow. A plant which closely resembles them, but reaches only half their height (with flowers correspondingly reduced in size), is *Tagetes patula* 'Mr. Majestic.'

Tagetes patula 'Pack Star Spry' is a plant that might be called a typical French marigold. These bedding plants grow to a maximum height of 8 in. They flower for a long time, bearing charming little flowers – double, yellow, with brownish-red margins.

[2–4] 4-5   ▼

Tagetes patula 'Striped Marvel'

See *Tagetes patula* 'Jolly Jester.'

Tagetes pumila

See *Tagetes tenuifolia.*

Tagetes signata

See *Tagetes tenuifolia.*

Tagetes tenuifolia 'Carina,' star marigold

Tagetes tenuifolia 'Golden Gem,' star marigold

Tagetes tenuifolia

STAR MARIGOLD

The star marigold is quite different from the above species and cultivars. Even people who dislike marigolds will be pleased to put one of them in a pot or a large bowl to enjoy the flowers, which are about ³/₄ in wide and appear just above the finely divided foliage. They are all single, so they can rely on being visited by insects. The plant grows in a domed shape, 8–16 in high, and at least equally wide. In most instances, they will flower for a long time, and you will be unlikely to resist the temptation of collecting seeds for next year. For sowing and care, see *Tagetes patula*.

Tagetes tenuifolia 'Carina' has plain orange flowers.

Tagetes tenuifolia 'Golden Gem' belongs to the compact Gem Series. The small golden-yellow flowers often have orange blotches.

Tagetes tenuifolia 'Lemon Gem' has just as

Tagetes tenuifolia 'Lemon Gem,' star marigold

Tagetes tenuifolia 'Paprika,' star marigold

Tagetes tenuifolia 'Golden Gem,' star marigold

Tagetes tenuifolia 'Lemon Gem,' star marigold

Tagetes tenuifolia 'Paprika,' star marigold

Tanacetum parthenium, feverfew

compact a habit, although, in richer soil, it will certainly grow taller than the 8 in indicated to by the grower. The small flowers are a uniform lemon yellow.

Tagetes tenuifolia 'Paprika' is a plant for which I have a soft spot because of its warm color combination of orange and an intensely deep red. This variety does not flower for quite as long as the other star marigolds.

[3–4] 4–5   !

Tanacetum parthenium

FEVERFEW

Feverfew is a perennial from south-east Europe. It was brought to western Europe as a medicine and became naturalized there. The herb appeared to alleviate the one-time primary cause of female mortality – puerperal fever. It also speeded up the process of giving birth.

Nowadays the plant's main use is ornamental, and it is often grown as an annual. Professional growers sow the cultivated vari-

eties of the species as early as January to enable them to market flowering plants three to four months later. There is no need for you to bother any more after that. Feverfew self-seeds in open ground year after year. It likes sunlight and tolerates drought. The foliage smells of camomile. The plant, which grows to an average of 20 in in height, bears flowers throughout the summer. The ray flowers are white and the fertile tubular florets in the centers are yellow. Many of the commercially grown varieties lack ray flowers and are like spherical buttons.

Tanacetum parthenium 'Golden Ball,' feverfew

Tanacetum parthenium 'White Ball,' feverfew

Thelesperma burridgeanum 'Brunette'

Tanacetum parthenium 'Golden Ball' is extremely low-growing – its maximum height is 12 in. It has yellow flowers.
Tanacetum parthenium 'White Ball' is just as compact, but has white flowers.

[2–3] 4–5 € ✿ 🏺 ⚱

Temari

See *Verbena.*

Thelesperma burridgeanum

The flowers, 1½ in wide, of this annual species from Texas are balanced on thin stems about 20 in high. The plants make a very airy impression. It is best to sow them outdoors in loose and not unduly wet soil in a sunny position in April–May.
It is best to grow these plants on their own in a small field, or else in a mixture of annuals so that their lax stems are supported by other plants. *Thelesperma*, unfortunately, is not very good at standing on its own feet.

The few suppliers who may be able to help you to acquire the seed, usually stock that of the cultivar *Thelesperma burridgeanum* 'Brunete.' This jewel of a plant flowers from July until far into September, bearing golden-yellow blooms with mahogany-brown centers. Don't stint on your vases!

[3–4] 4–5 ✿ 🏺

Thunbergia alata 'Alba,' black-eyed Susan

Thunbergia alata

BLACK-EYED SUSAN

Press the large brown seeds into a pot early in March and you will be able to admire Susan's eyes for the first time six weeks later. It was the orange flowers with their black 'pupils' that gave the plant its name. It grows naturally as a climbing plant in tropical

Thunbergia alata 'Bakeri,' black-eyed Susan

Thunbergia alata, black-eyed Susan

Africa, but we can enjoy it throughout the summer.

Don't put Susan out-of-doors until night-time temperatures have ceased to fall below 50 °F, because she hates the cold. Give her a warm and sheltered position in moisture-retentive and nutritive soil and the results will amaze you. The winding stems will catch hold of a fence or any other support and climb unstoppably upwards, while new flowers continually appear a short distance below the growing tips. If the plant becomes bare at its base while the flowers disappear over the fence, cut back some of the stems to encourage them to produce new flowering shoots. This may continue until well into October. When the flowers are over, fruits are formed that vigorously eject the ripe seeds.

The species bears orange flowers with black throats. There are several other cultivars with flowers in different colors:

Thunbergia alata 'Alba' has white flowers with dark pupils.

Thunbergia alata, black-eyed Susan

Thymophylla tenuiloba 'Golden Dawn'

Thymophylla tenuiloba 'Sunshine'

Thunbergia alata 'Bakeri' has entirely white flowers.
Thunbergia alata 'Florist Mixture' provides a mixture of orange, yellow, and white flowers.

[2–3] 🌻 🌿 ▼ !

Thymophylla tenuiloba

This small plant, which grows 6–12 in high, flowers most profusely in warm summers. The broad tuft of finely divided foliage will then be entirely covered in small yellow flowers, over

Tolpis barbata 'Black Eyes'

$1/2$ in wide. Sow directly in the garden in very well-drained soil in May (or earlier under glass) and make sure it is a sunny position. The plant is ideal for a rockery or for adorning flower-beds and edges, but it is also excellent for growing in containers. The various suppliers have developed a whole raft of names for what are clearly divergent cultivars: *Thymophylla tenuiloba* 'Golden Dawn'; *Thymophylla tenuiloba* 'Golden Fleck'; *Thymophylla tenuiloba* 'Golden Fleece'; *Thymophylla tenuiloba* 'Gold Spot'; *Thymophylla tenuiloba* 'Sunshine'; and *Thymophylla tenuiloba* 'Yellow Carpet' are names of plants that I cannot distinguish from one another.

[3–4] 4 € 🌻 🌼 ▼ ⚱

Tolpis barbata

In the arid regions of southern Europe, *Tolpis barbata* grows amidst the scanty grasses. The size of both plants and flowers depends on where they are growing. In the poorest soils, the flowers will be no more than $1/2$ in wide. In

Tolpis barbata 'Black Eyes'

our fertile garden soil, their average width will be about 1¼ in. The plant itself, which grows to about 20 in in height, has a somewhat coarse, robust habit, and is most suited to a natural garden. Sow in situ from April, and thin the seedlings to a minimum distance of 8 in apart. They will flower from July until far into October.

The name of the cultivar *Tolpis barbata* 'Black Eyes' provides a precise description of the feature that the species itself also possesses – a dark "eye" in the center of an otherwise yellow flower.

4-5

Torenia fournieri

WISHBONE FLOWER

You are most likely to find these plants from south-east Asia in the indoor plant sections of garden centers and florists. They are grown from seed by professional nurserymen. The time for sowing them is March–April, at an ideal temperature of about 66 °F. The seedlings also like to grow on in warm conditions.

Torenia fournieri, wishbone flower

Still, they are also suitable for flower troughs, hanging baskets, and pots in the garden. Don't put them out until June, because *Torenia* has a definite aversion to the cold. They should also be protected from the fiercest sunlight in the hottest part of the day to prevent the delicate foliage from scorching.

It is also possible to sow indoors from the end of March onwards. Keep the seedlings under glass or plastic for a long time to enable them to grow on in a moist atmosphere. They eventually develop into compact little plants about 4 in high. After the main flowering pe-

Torenia fournieri, wishbone flower

Torenia fournieri 'Alba,' wishbone flower

Torenia fournieri 'Clown,' wishbone flower

Torenia 'Sunrenibu'

Tripleurospermum inodorum, scentless mayweed

riod, the number of flowers gradually decreases and then it will be time to throw the plants away.

The following cultivars are worth mentioning: *Tourenia fournieri* 'Alba' that, strangely enough, is not entirely white but has large mauve blotches; and the one most frequently on sale, *Torenia fournieri* 'Clown,' which comes in a mixture of colors.

[3–4]   ▼

Torenia 'Sunrenibu'

This hybrid is better known under its trade name *Torenia* 'Summer Wave Blue.' The plants belonging to the *Torenia* Wave Series have an even more compact habit than *Torenia fournieri*. Because of their spreading growth and wide ramification, they are particularly suitable for hanging baskets and containers. They are also more able to tolerate the outdoor climate of countries in the north-western regions of Europe. They are also better at withstanding cool temperatures and fierce sunlight.

 ▼

Trachymene caerulea

See *Didiscus caeruleus*.

Trifolium incarnatum

CRIMSON CLOVER

Crimson clover is a well-known fodder plant and is also used as a green fertilizer. The species originally came from more southerly parts of Europe. On its own, the plant grows

to about 8 in tall, rising up out of the surrounding vegetation to about 20 in. During the summer, it continually bears new flowers, usually red, sometimes rose red to white. Sow between March and May where it is to flower.

3–5

Trifolium incarnatum, crimson clover

286

Tripleurospermum inodorum

SCENTLESS MAYWEED

This close relative of *Tripleurospermum maritimum* lacks white ray flowers (the petals round the center) and merely forms tubular florets in its spherical head. These small flower heads resembling yellow buttons, are carried at the top of grey-leafed stems that may grow to 20 in high, an ideal height for cutting purposes, for which the plant is highly suited. It is also rewarding in grey borders, rockeries, and other places where a splash of bright color is required. Sow this annual indoors in April, or – even better – in a sunny spot outdoors, preferably in poor soil, from the end of April.

[4] 4-5 🏺

Trochocephalus stellatus

See *Scabiosa stellata*.

Tropaeolum majus, nasturtium, naturalized

Tropaeolum majus, nasturtium, archetype

Tropaeolum majus, nasturtium, bicolored flower

Tropaeolum canariense

See *Tropaeolum peregrinum*.

Tropaeolum majus

GARDEN NASTURTIUM, INDIAN CRESS

Classifying all the following cultivated varieties under *Tropaeolum majus* is a something of a white lie, though they are featured under that name in nearly all catalogues. In fact, we are dealing with the results of hybridizing various species, in which *Tropaeolum minus* and *Tropaeolum peltophorum* often played a part as well. These lower species ensured that there is a wide choice of low-growing cultivars today.

The archetypal form of *Tropaeolum majus*, a climber from Colombia and Peru, arrived in Europe as early as the 17th century. It bears orange flowers and uses stems and leaf stalks to grasp any available supports – threads or the thin twigs of shrubs and hedges. Over the years, nurserymen also developed plants with other colors, such as red and yellow. Still,

Tropaeolum majus, nasturtium

Tropaeolum majus, nasturtium, new varieties in trial fields

Tropaeolum majus, nasturtium

those tall varieties also had a disadvantage. The flowers were often hidden by the foliage when the plants were cultivated in particularly rich garden soil. In such circumstances, the leaf stalks become longer and the leaves larger. That is why it is still better to grow the climbing varieties in very poor, dry soil.

For the modern cultured varieties, however, this is no longer necessary. They have a compact, usually spreading, but no longer a climbing habit, and flowers are carried above the foliage from the end of June until far into autumn. To distinguish them from the taller varieties, they are sometimes referred to nowadays as *Tropaeolum majus nanum* or *Tropaeolum minus*, followed by the name of the cultivar.

As for cultivation, the modern cultivars are even less complicated than the old-fashioned kind. The seeds are enclosed in a fleshy covering, which need not be removed before sowing. The entire round seeds go straight into the soil and are then covered thoroughly

Tropaeolum majus 'Alaska,' nasturtium

288

Tropaeolum majus 'Cherry Rose,' nasturtium

Tropaeolum majus 'Fire and Ice,' nasturtium

with soil. When sowing indoors in pots or compressed soil blocks earlier in the year, it is sufficient to introduce two seeds in each one. After germination, just pull out the weaker seedling. You don't need many plants to cover a large area. If sowing climbing varieties, you should provide a support at the time of sowing or planting out to avoid the need to disturb the larger and more fragile plants later on. A wigwam of canes, mesh, threads, the uprights of a gate, or shrubs or hedges, all provide good support for climbers. Low-growing cultivars grow into luxuriant

Tropaeolum majus 'Mahogany Jewel,' garden nasturtium

Tropaeolum majus 'Empress of India,' nasturtium

tufts, or spread across the ground, covering it in a very short time. Fallen nasturtium seeds are likely to germinate spontaneously in the garden, especially in loose soil and after relatively dry winters.

The plants' young leaves are sometimes used in salads. They have a pungent taste with some resemblance to mustard-and-cress or water cress. Indian cress, in fact, contains *glucosinolates*, which otherwise occur only in plants belonging to the *Cruciferae* family, of which *Tropolaeolum* is not a member. The glucosinolates protect *Cruciferae* such as cabbage plants from being devoured by insects. Some of them, however, including the caterpillars of cabbage whites, are immune to these substances, and cabbages are their favorite food. For the same reason, caterpillars also eat nasturtiums sometimes. All parts of the flower may be eaten by humans: the flowers make an edible garnish to salads and may be preserved in vinegar; buds and young seeds are sometimes preserved as an alternative to capers.

Children can have a lot of fun with nasturtiums. The leaves are more or less round, with their veins meeting slightly off-center. Each leaf therefore forms a flat saucer. The surface of the leaf is provided with a layer of wax impenetrable to water, which rolls off it like a drop of mercury. Nocturnal dew in the form of a pearly droplet is often left in the slight hollow of the leaf, and children can try to roll it on to another leaf holding a drop. The two drops will merge into a larger one, after which the game may be continued, becoming increasingly difficult. At the slightest mistake, the fat drop will roll off the leaf on to the ground.

Usually, however, nasturtiums are cultivated for their decorative appearance. Many forms have been developed in the course of hundreds of years of cultivation. This process is currently gathering huge momentum and the number of new introductions is considerable. *Tropaeolum majus* 'Alaska' is cultivated for its foliage, which is covered in a fanciful pattern of green, greyish-green, and cream-colored blotches. The leaves of the older strains

Tropaeolum majus 'Whirlybird Golden Yellow,' nasturtium

of the 'Alaska Series' sometimes reverted to uniform green, but the problem has been solved in the newer strains, and the variegated foliage is retained even in the event of propagation by seed. The single flowers have very diverse colors – creamy white, yellow, orange, pink, red, and every imaginable shade in between. The plants do not climb and grow to about 10 in in height.

Tropaeolum majus 'Peach Melba,' nasturtium

Tropaeolum majus 'Tom Thumb,' nasturtium

Tropaeolum majus 'Tip Top Apricot', nasturtium

Tropaeolum majus 'Tip Top Gold,' nasturtium

Tropaeolum majus 'Tip Top Gold,' nasturtium

Tropaeolum majus 'Cherry Rose' bears double flowers in a washed-out shade of cherry red. This color goes well with many other shades, so 'Cherry Rose' is very suitable for various color combinations. The freely flowering plants grow 10–16 in high and have a considerable spread. There are also slightly different cultivars, referred to as *Tropaeolum majus* 'Cherry Rose Jewel' (a deeper cherry red) and *Tropaeolum majus* 'Whirlybird Cherry Rose' (bright cherry red).

Tropaeolum 'Empress of India' remains low-growing and has strikingly dark foliage. Above it, flowers bloom in a lovely toning shade of warm red.

Tropaeolum 'Fire and Ice' is a low-growing cultivar with variegated foliage and bright orange-red flowers.

Tropaeolum majus 'Mahogany Jewel' bears magnificent deep-red flowers that show up best in partial shade, looking mysterious at the foot of trees and shrubs. The plants tend to remain low-growing but are not determined to do so – as soon as they find a support, they will climb up it to about 20 in.

Tropaeolum majus 'Peach Melba' provides a showy display in large pots or tubs. The plants grow about 8–12 in high. They do not flower profusely, but the peach-colored blooms are magnificent.

Tropaeolum majus 'Tom Thumb' has been cultivated for over a century, but has remained low-growing (8–12 in). It does not produce long shoots, and is therefore very suitable for planting up flower-beds. The single flowers appear in all kinds of fresh colors.

Tropaeolum majus 'Tip Top Apricot.' 'Tip Top' is a mixture of all kinds of flower colors on low-growing plants 8–12 in, from which certain colors were isolated. Those of *Tropaeolum majus* 'Tip Top Apricot' look apricot-colored, but might just as well be soft yellow, salmon pink, or peach with blotches of warm, brownish red. It flowers more profusely than 'Peach Melba.'

Tropaeolum majus 'Tip Top Gold' is comparable to the above, but its flowers are deep golden yellow.

Tropaeolum majus 'Whirlybird Golden Yellow' belongs to the popular Whirlybird Series. It is particularly remarkable for the lack of the long honey spur at the back of the flower. The plants flower freely, remain low-

Tropaeolum peregrinum, canary creeper

growing (8–12 in), and do not produce excessively long shoots, which makes them very suitable for use as bedding plants. At one time, the series was marketed as a mixture of all kinds of colors and semi-double flowers, but the newer range contains varieties selected according to color, and includes single flowers.

[4] 4-5 🌿 ☀ ☙ ▼ ⚱ ⚘ ⚜

Tropaeolum peregrinum

CANARY CREEPER

The flowers of this annual climber from the Andes Mountains have a very remarkable shape. The three bottom petals have shrunk to crumpled threads, whereas the top two are spread out like the wings of a bird flying away. They are bright yellow. The light, greyish-green foliage is deeply lobed and resembles the miniature foliage of a fig. The entire plant works its way upwards with curving leaf stalks, attaching itself to every possible support. A canary creeper can climb as much as 6–12 ft in a single season.

This remarkable plant is very easy to grow from seed. It does best in moderately nutritive and moist soil, and in full sun.

[4] 4-5 ☙ 🌿 ⚜

Tweedia caerulea

The sky-blue flowers of this relative of silk weed will delight many spectators. The flowers are as radiant as forget-me-nots and quite a lot bigger ³/₄–1¹/₄ in wide. Even so, the plant

Tropaeolum peregrinum, canary creeper

Tweedia caerulea

is available only from patio plant specialists (sometimes under the name of *Oxypetalum caeruleum*).

The species needs at least three months to come into flower. Usually, it takes much longer, particularly if the tips are pinched out. The species is naturally inclined to grow tall and lanky and, if you want to avoid tying it up, you will have to remove the tips several times. Mind the plant's poisonous sap, which irritates the eyes and skin.

Tweedia is by nature a perennial from southern Brazil and Uruguay – in other words, from the warmer regions of South America. In western Europe, too, it has a great need for warmth, and is therefore often supplied as a hothouse plant. It is quite feasible, however, to grow the plant in a warm and sheltered position out-of-doors from June until early October.

You may, if you wish, cut back the plants in October, and overwinter them in light, airy, and moderately humid conditions at a minimum temperature of 41 °F.

[3–4] 4-5 🌿 ▼ ⚱

Vaccaria hispanica

Vaccaria hispanica is one of the easiest annuals to cultivate, and the results are sensational. After two months of growing from seed, the small clumps – height and spread both about 20 in – are entirely covered with pink flowers. The relatively short flowering period is the sole drawback. Even so, by sowing several times in the course of the season, you will be able to enjoy the plants throughout the summer. The flowers are carried at the top of thin, branching stems and are very suitable for cutting and subsequently drying. Sow the plants where they are to flower, because the taproots are difficult to transplant. The plant likes a sunny position in normal garden soil.

Vaccaria hispanica 'Florist Rose' bears very pale pink flowers; *Vaccaria hispanica* 'Florist Snow' has pure white ones; and those of *Vaccaria hispanica* 'Pink Beauty' are pink.

4–6

Verbascum blattaria

MOTH MULLEIN

Although mullein is by nature a native European biennial, it is cultivated as an annual by sowing it very early in spring. In the late sum-

Vaccaria hispanica 'Pink Beauty'

Verbascum blattaria 'Albiflorum,' moth mullein

mer of the same year, impressive and attractive flower stems will grow to 5ft tall, with yellow flowers unfurling from neatly folded buds.

The young plants form green rosettes, which are easily mistaken for those of dandelions. Put them in a sunny or partly shaded spot in moisture-retentive soil.

Verbascum blattaria 'Albiflorum' carries creamy white flowers and is regarded as one of the most rewarding plants for the natural garden. Their self-sown seeds come true to type.

[2–3] 3–5   !

Verbascum phoeniceum 'Southern Charm,' red mullein

Verbena bonariensis in the background

Verbascum phoeniceum

RED MULLEIN

This mullein closely resembles moth mullein, but it is shorter (maximum height 39 in), and its leaves are different, with a wrinkled surface similar to that of the common foxglove. The flowers of the species are purple, but plant breeders did not remain idle and added pink, salmon pink, white, red, and violet to

the options. Professional growers start sowing as early as February to enable them to market the first flowering plants in May–June. You can also sow the seed yourself. And should you be too late to have flowers in the first year, that is not a problem. *Verbascum phoeniceum* is a perennial which will survive our winters in a position that is not excessively wet.

Since 1998, there has been a hybrid on the market, which in many ways resembles *Verbascum phoeniceum*. Its name is *Verbascum* 'Southern Charm,' a plant with magnificently smoky, soft pink flowers. Obtaining seed from it for next year is impossible, as the plant is sterile. Plants and seed may be purchased. It takes three to four months to grow flowering plants from seed.

[3–4] 5–6   **!**

Verbena aubletia

See *Verbena canadensis.*

Verbena bonariensis

The stems of this South American verbena are almost bare stalks up to a height of 5 ft. Small lilac-blue flowers develop at the top and give this perennial a remarkable appearance. Unfortunately, it is not very easy to grow. The plants do not live long and are not quite hardy. They are therefore usually grown as annuals, but, in that case, they must be

Verbena canadensis

sown early if they are to flower the same year. If sown indoors in February–March, the species may come into flower by the end of June.

[2–4] 5

Verbena canadensis

The name suggests that this is a very hardy plant – unfortunately, this "Canadian" verbena will not tolerate temperatures below 5 °F. It is therefore advisable to grow it as an annual. Sow indoors early in the year and put the plants out-of-doors in April or May. They have a considerable spread, with the leaf buds taking root easily. This creates a green mat, about 8 in high, with purplish-pink flowers appearing above it until well into autumn.

[2–4] 5

Verbena × hortensis

See Verbena × hybrida.

Verbena × hybrida

GARDEN VERBENA

The ancestry of garden verbenas is so complicated that research scientists specializing in this area have lost their way. Many South American species played a part in the development, and scientists are still searching for new species in order to improve the charac-

Verbena 'Adonis Mango,' verbena

Verbena 'Artemis,' verbena

teristics of the plants. Ever since the mid-nineteenth century, species have been crossed, selected, and crossed again, and so on. The process has now gathered further momentum and many new varieties have been developed as a result. The older varieties had a spreading habit, which meant that, in open ground, they grew mainly as ground cover. In troughs and pots they struck out in all directions and eventually began to

Verbena 'Blue Knight,' verbena

trail over the rims and edges. Newer cultivars are compact – miniaturized to an alarming degree – or straggly and intended to adorn hanging baskets and balcony troughs.

The range of colors of garden verbenas is now very varied, whereas pink was formerly the most common color. White, all kinds of red shades, and many blues have now been added. Modern colors include peach, cherry red, and lavender. Quite often, each flower is bicolored. The individual flowers are not so big, $^1/_2$–$^3/_4$ in wide, but they are packed together in dense racemes, thus creating small false umbels full of color. In some varieties, the racemes are extended to form spikes and can then go on flowering for a long time. In other cultivars, the false umbels wither and should then be cut off, because they spoil the appearance of the plant. If you cut off the faded flower stem low down and include a piece of leafy stem, the plant will branch out there and sprout vigorously, producing new flowering shoots. It is not worthwhile collecting the seed yourself. Many modern verbenas do not produce seed or do not come true to type. Furthermore, seeds and plants are marketed in vast quantities.

For most people, buying plants is the obvious way to acquire them. Sowing only makes sense for experienced gardeners, because the seed often fails to germinate well. Underneath the seed covering, there is a waxy layer that prevents the penetration of water and subse-

Verbena 'Imagination,' verbena

Verbena 'Novalis White,' verbena

Verbena 'Peaches and Cream,' verbena

Verbena 'Pink Parfait,' verbena

Verbena 'Peaches and Cream,' verbena

quent germination. Some varieties germinate considerably better than others. Experienced sowers also have a few tricks up their sleeve to improve the seeds' capacity for germination. For example, soak the seed in tepid water for a day, or stand the covered propagator with the seed in damp soil in a cool, dark spot for a week, so that the seeds suck up moisture before warmth is added. Then allow the seed to germinate at about 64 °F, and grow the seedlings on in somewhat cooler conditions. Pinch out the growing tips several times to encourage bushy growth. They may be taken out-of-doors at the end of May, and planted in flower-beds, borders, and, above all, in flower troughs, pots, and hanging baskets. Provide nutritive soil, water regularly, and provide a sunny position for them. Wind is tolerated well, so garden verbenas will also flower beautifully on balconies.

Some varieties can be propagated only by cuttings. Professional growers take them in winter to enable them to market flowering plants in May.

Verbena 'Romeo Lavender,' verbena

Verbena 'Romeo Violet With Eye,' verbena

The following is a limited selection of the huge supply of cultivars:

Verbena 'Adonis Mango' was introduced in 1998. It was a brighter-colored counterpart of *Verbena* 'Romance Apricot,' which carries flowers in softer shades: cream and apricot. 'Adonis Mango' is propagated by seed. The plants branch out well, spread slightly, and grow up to 12 in in height. Personally, I still prefer 'Peaches and Cream' (see below).

Verbena 'Artemis' bears flowers in a modest shade of old rose which, unlike so many other shades of pink, goes well with other flower colors. Splendid for hanging baskets.

Verbena 'Blue Knight' is another treasure for hanging baskets. It forms sturdy tufts of foliage and, at a distance above them, flowers that are called lilac, but are more like pale pink – very lovely, though. This plant is propagated by cuttings.

Verbena 'Rood' serves as a model for innumerable garden verbenas with bright-red flowers, including *Verbena* 'Dema Rood' and *Verbena* 'Temari Scarlet' (official name *Verbena* 'Summarisu'), which is propagated by cuttings, as is the plant in the photograph.

Verbena 'Imagination,' with its loose, spreading habit, grows into an ideal plant for hanging baskets and balcony troughs, and is propagated by seed mainly for that purpose. The violet-purple flowers are carried in large quantities throughout the summer.

Verbena 'Novalis White' is an early-flowering, upright, and bushy plant that is propagated by seed. Its flowers are in peaches-and-cream shades.

Verbena 'Pink Parfait' has striking bicolored flowers in cherry red and creamy white. It develops into a plant about 12 in high, with long shoots that make it suitable for use as a trailing plant.

Verbena 'Quartz Burgundy' was awarded a gold medal in 1999 for achievements in professional cultivation. The plants grow to about 12 in high, have a good resistance to mildew, and bear deep-purple flowers in racemes $2^3/_4$ in wide. The plants are propagated by seed which appears to germinate well.

Verbena 'Romeo' consists of a series of very compact plants specially intended for cultivation in sets, which allows them to be sold in trays of four or six plants. They must be very compact for that purpose and, at a height of less than 8 in, this is certainly true of the Romeo series. Professional growers sow them from January onwards for selling after three to four months. The small plants are particularly suitable for growing in flower-beds, but are a little too "prim and proper" even for plant troughs. *Verbena* 'Romeo Lavender' has pale pink flowers with a touch of lavender and some yellow in their centers. The harsh colors of *Verbena* 'Romeo Violet with Eye' (violet with white centers) shriek for attention. *Verbena* 'Romeo White' is one of the better varieties because of its pleasant combination of white and pale green foliage.

Verbena 'Silver Anne,' verbena

Verbena 'Sissinghurst Pink,' verbena

Verbena 'Romeo White,' verbena

Verbena 'Quartz Burgundy,' verbena

Verbena 'Silver Anne' is a very old hybrid that does not produce any seed. The plants are propagated by cuttings and form handsome full tufts with bright-pink flowers, which grow paler in the course of flowering. They have a delightful fragrance.

Verbena 'Sissinghurst Pink' differs from the better-known *Verbena* 'Sissinghurst' in that its flowers are lighter in color. The plants form large tufts, which show up beautifully in pots and hanging baskets.

Verbena 'Tapien Pink' is presented as something different, or so the plant breeders would have us believe. For the sake of convenience, they conjured up a new generic name, and 'Tapien Pink' is what you will find on the la-

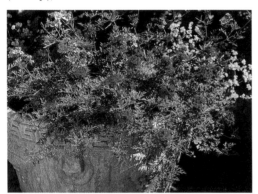

Verbena 'Tapien Pink' ('Sunver') and 'Tapien Violet' ('Sunvop'), verbena

Verbena 'Temari Scarlet' ('Sunmarisu'), verbena

Verbena 'Tapien Pearl' ('Sunvat'), verbena

Verbena 'Temari Pink' ('Sunmaripi'), verbena

Verbena 'Temari Violet' ('Sunmariba'), verbena

bels; the official name, though, is *Verbena* 'Sunver.' Tapien are, in fact, modern trailing verbenas propagated by cuttings. The plants are not affected by mildew, grow rapidly while producing a lot of deeply divided foliage, and flower freely. *Verbena* 'Tapien Violet' (official name *Verbena* 'Sunvop') has violet-blue flowers; *Verbena* 'Tapien Pearl' (officially *Verbena* 'Sunvat') has pearly-white flowers with a soft pink bloom.

The same plant breeder dreamed up another generic name – 'Temari.' These plants are also trailing verbenas, but this time the leaves are more egg-shaped. *Verbena* 'Temari Pink' is registered under the cultivar name *Verbena* 'Sunmaripi.' *Verbena* 'Temari Scarlet' is officially called *Verbena* 'Sunmarisu,' and the official name of *Verbena* 'Temari Violet' is *Verbena* 'Sunmariba.' The have the same resistance to mildew, grow vigorously, and bear a profusion of pink, red, and violet flowers respectively.

[1-3]   **!**

Verbena speciosa 'Imagination'

See *Verbena* × *hybrida.*

Verbena patagonica

See *Verbena binariensis.*

Verbena rigida

This perennial verbena is mainly cultivated as an annual. Professional nurserymen sow in January to enable them to supply flowering plants three months later. Amateur gardeners to sow later in order to enjoy the magenta-colored flowers from early July until the end of October. Initially, they develop as umbels, but more and more new flowers are formed at the top, thus creating a false spike. The plants themselves ultimately grow to a maximum height of 20 in. They produce seed, which may germinate spontaneously in the garden in spring. In autumn, you will find tubers in the soil, and these may be overwintered in the same way as dahlias (cool and slightly moist in peat dust). In spring, you can take cuttings of the basal shoots with a piece of tuber attached, and then get them to root. It may be more convenient to sow after all.

Verbena rigida 'Lilacina' is perhaps the most rewarding cultivar because of its blue flowers, which are so light that they appear to be al-

Verbena rigida

Verbena rigida 'Lilacina'

Verbena rigida 'Lilacina'

Viola Cornuta Group, horned violet

most white. Wonderful for combining with other colors.

Verbena rigida 'Polaris' closely resembles 'Lilacina' and some people equate it with that cultivar. Its flowers are light silvery blue.

[2–4] 5

Verbena rigida 'Lavenderwolke'

See *Verbena rigida* 'Lilacina.'

Verbena venosa

See *Verbena rigida.*

Vinca rosea

See *Catharanthus roseus.*

Viola Cornuta Group, horned violet

Viola Cornuta Group, horned violet

Viola 'Belmont Blue' (Cornuta Group), horned violet

Viola 'Belmont Blue' (Cornuta Group), horned violet

Viola 'Etain' (Cornuta Group), horned violet

Viola 'Irish Molly' (Cornuta Group), horned violet

Viola 'Jackanapes' (Cornuta Group), horned violet

Viola 'Rebecca' (Cornuta Group), horned violet

Viola Cornuta Group

HORNED VIOLET

The horned violet grows naturally in southwest Europe, but became naturalized in numerous other European countries, including The Netherlands. The Cornuta Group was named after one of the ancestors of the present cultivars. In fact, other species were also involved in the development of the group.

The result is a huge supply of cultivars. Basically, they are all perennials, but often live for only a short while, and are therefore frequently cultivated as biennials or annuals. Some cultivars need to be cultivated by cuttings to retain their typical characteristics. The others – by far the most, in fact – produce pure descendants from seed.

Although it is quite feasible for amateurs to sow the violets, most people buy them.

Viola 'Molly Sanderson' (Cornuta Group), horned violet

Viola 'Skippy Blue-Yellow Face' (Cornuta Group), horned violet

Viola 'Skippy Purple-Yellow Face' (Cornuta Group), horned violet

Names are rarely provided, since the consumer does not really need them – purchases are simply based on the appearance of the small plants. Professional nurserymen manage to grow flowering plants from seed in two to three months. They are mainly supplied as bedding and pot plants in spring and early summer. The choice is huge and sowing them oneself is hardly worth the effort. But anyone wanting to enjoy the flowers in the real viola season, the earliest part of spring, must sow them. They are then cultivated as biennials. Sow during the period between mid-June and the end of August. The seeds will germinate more easily at that time. Sprinkle them in a seed pan and cover lightly. They should be kept permanently moist during germination, so cover the seed pan with glass or plastic and keep it out of fierce sunlight. Put it under a table in a greenhouse or in the shade out-of-doors. As soon as the seedlings are manageable, you should transplant them into a larger container, but be careful – they are fragile. Continue to keep the soil thoroughly moist, but do not cover the tray, to prevent grey mould. In winter, place the tray placed indoors in a light and unheated room, or in a cold frame or, or an unheated greenhouse. The seedlings themselves tolerate a considerable amount of frost, but rarely survive winter out-of-doors.

Cultivars that can be propagated only by vegetative means are divided in late summer. Cuttings may also be taken at that time. The plants are treated in the same way as seedlings in winter.

It is best to cultivate violets in a partly shaded place, and in soil that is always kept moist. In the event of their drying out (which is most likely to happen in a pot or trough) then cut them back until stumps about 2 in long are all that is left. After a thorough watering, they will often recover and come into flower again.

Viola 'Belmont Blue' is usually called *Viola* 'Boughton Blue' in the trade. The cultivar is

Viola 'Skippy Yellow-Blue Top' (Cornuta Group), horned violet

Viola 'White Perfection' (Cornuta Group), horned violet

Viola 'Skippy Yellow-Purple Top' (Cornuta Group), horned violet

propagated by cuttings. The plant produces long shoots that become pendulous without support, making it very suitable for hanging baskets. Its modest shade of blue is easy to combine with other colors, and contributes to its popularity.

Viola 'Etain' is a very special violet, and you would be lucky to find one. It is not easy to cultivate cuttings, and 'Etain' is rather short-lived, but very beautiful, with small flowers in cream and yellow, surrounded by soft pur-plish-blue margins.

Viola 'Irish Molly' is to be seen rather more frequently nowadays, and rightly so. Its soft, warm shade of copper brown color is unsur-passed. The centers have yellow chocolate spots. 'Irish Molly' needs to be propagated regularly by cuttings, as the parent plants are short-lived.

Viola 'Jackanapes' is one of the most popu-lar violets in Britain. This is hardly surprising, since it forms handsome clumps of greenery,

with bicolored flowers above it. Their upper petals are chocolate brown and the lower ones a warm shade of yellow. The variety is clearly more difficult to cultivate in The Netherlands, and for that reason is available only from specialists there. It is propagated by cuttings and needs regular renewing.

The flowers of *Viola* 'Molly Sanderson' are relatively small but very distinctive in that they are an almost black shade of aubergine, with yellow centers. In view of the popular-ity of black flowers – goodness knows why, because they scarcely show up in a garden – 'Molly Sanderson' is much sought-after.

Viola 'Rebecca' is a very old cultivar as well as a special one. The petals are striped – pur-plish blue on creamy white.

Viola 'Skippy Blue–Yellow Face' is one of the color combinations in the Skippy Series, which came on to the market in 1998. The small plants remain low and flower freely. They are sold mainly as bedding plants grown from seed.

Viola hederacea, Australian violet

Viola tricolor 'Hortensis,' wild pansy, heartsease

Viola hederacea 'Blue Form,' Australian violet

Violas tolerate frost reasonably well and may therefore be planted out-of-doors as early as April–May. Other cultivars in the series include: *Viola* 'Skippy Purple–Yellow Face,' *Viola* 'Skippy Yellow–Blue Top,' and *Viola* 'Skippy Yellow–Purple Top.' The names give a good indication of the flower colors.

Viola 'White Perfection' is also best grown from seed. It has pure white flowers with small yellow centers.

6–8

mer. The centers are purple, the edges white. The Australian violet is a perennial that is propagated by division. It tolerates no more than a slight frost and must therefore be taken indoors in winter if it is to survive. Many people just buy new plants every spring.

Besides the species, there is a very rare and sought-after cultivar, *Viola hederacea* 'Blue Form' with entirely lilac-blue flowers. This cultivar may be cultivated in the same way.

Viola hederacea

AUTRALIAN VIOLET, IVY-LEAFED VIOLET

To find this violet, we must go to the other side of the world, to Australia, where it grows in damp soil. The plant forms a mat of creeping stems with finely divided foliage above it, which reminded those who named it of ivy. Small bicolored flowers with a somewhat rounded appearance as a result of the turned-back petals are carried throughout the sum-

Viola tricolor

WILD PANSY

Our native tricolored wild pansy self-seeds very easily. The small plants do not tolerate much competition from other plants, and therefore germinate and flower mainly in loose sand and in gravel. They usually come into flower in April or May. The species itself rarely grows in gardens. Plants that do so have usually been modified artificially in the past, al-

Viola × wittrockiana in flower-beds in March

though they are still quite clearly recognizable as tricolored violas. These are specimens of *Viola tricolor* 'Hortensis.' There are also quite a lot of named cultivars that often differ considerably from the species. *Viola tricolor* 'E.A. Bowles,' for instance, is sometimes called *Viola tricolor* 'Bowles Black' because of its blackish-purple appearance.

If you want to gather the seeds of wild pansies, you have to act very quickly. The fruits burst open when they are ripe and scatter the seeds around. Cut off the closed fruits as soon as they begin to turn straw-colored and put them in a tray, then cover it with a cloth to prevent the seeds jumping out.

[2-9]

Viola tricolor 'Jackanapes'

See *Viola* Cornuta Group.

Viola × wittrockiana

PANSY

Pansies were on sale in Greek markets four hundred years before the beginning of the Christian era. There has been so much hybridization with the wild species since then that it is no longer possible to trace their ancestry precisely.

Select the plants by color and, if you like, according to scent. They are on sale as bedding plants in spring and as so-called winter pansies in autumn. All pansies can flower for a long period if you provide moisture-reten-

tive soil that is never allowed to dry up, and also protect them from fierce sunlight. If the number of flowers is declining, you can try a little trick to revitalize them: cut them back to about 2 in above soil level and give them water and fertilizer. In most cases, they will start flowering again. In open ground and large containers, the plants will tolerate a fair amount of frost and may flower well into winter. You may still enjoy them in a cool position, under glass, in early spring.

For propagation by seed see *Viola* Cornuta Group.

6-8

Viscaria cardinalis

See *Silene coeli-rosa.*

Viscaria oculata

See *Silene coeli-rosa.*

Viola × wittrockiana, pansy

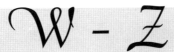

W – Z

Wangenheimia lima

This ornamental grass has been on the market under the name *Wangenheimia lima* 'Vulcan' since spring 2000. It grows to almost 20 in in height. The plant is primarily intended for cutting. If sown outdoors in situ in May, it may be harvested by the end of July. The feather-shaped spikes also look very decorative in a border for grasses, and it is to be hoped that seed merchants supplying private customers will also distribute the seed.

4–6 🌱 🏺 ⚜

Zaluzianskya capensis

NIGHT–BLOOMING PHLOX

In the daytime, *Zaluzianskya capensis* looks somewhat leggy, with stems about 12 in long, sticky foliage, and unsightly chocolate-brown buds. Nobody would choose a plant like that, and it is therefore not often available from nurseries. Customers, after all, shop in the

Zaluzianskya capensis, night-blooming phlox

daytime, and it is only on summer evenings that the miracle happens: the buds gradually open. The flowers are some $1\frac{1}{2}$ in long, but a mere $\frac{1}{2}$ in wide, and, being white, they are not very striking, except to moths, who gladly visit them. They are attracted to the flowers by their very sweet scent irresistibly reminiscent of marshmallows. Towards morning, the flowers close up again into small chocolate-colored balls, waiting to flower again in the evening.

Wangenheimia lima 'Vulcan'

Zinnia angustifolia, hairy zinnia

Zinnia angustifolia 'Crystal White,' hairy zinnia

Zinnia elegans, zinnia

Sow night-blooming phlox indoors in March, or outdoors from mid-April. Pinch out the growing tips to encourage bushier growth and do not put them out-of-doors until after the last night frost, as these annuals come from South Africa. Their flowering season is between July and September. It is easy to collect the seed yourself.

[3] 4–5 🌸 🌱 ▼ ⚜ 🦋 !

Zinnia angustifolia

HAIRY ZINNIA

Orange flowers about 1¼ in wide are carried in summer above a tuft of stems and oblong leaves about 12–16 in high. The hairy zinnia comes from Mexico and the south-east of the United States – in other words, from a warm and dry climate. Still, the plant does quite well in the climate of north-west Europe. Hairy zinnias are less susceptible to the fungous diseases that often affect the larger species. They should, however, be placed in a very sunny position in very well-drained soil, which may also be fertile. Hairy zinnias will flower all the more freely for that. They usually come into flower in July and continue to bloom until well into October. For sowing, see *Zinnia elegans.*
Zinnia angustifolia 'Crystal White' has been awarded several prizes for, inter alia, its compact growth, which makes it highly suitable for growing in pots, and also because it proved not to be susceptible to blight.
Zinnia angustifolia 'Mexican Orange' closely resembles the species. The orange

color of the flowers goes beautifully with its greyish foliage.

[3–4] 4–6 € 🌸 🌱 ▼ 🏺 ❀

Zinnia elegans

ZINNIA

The popularity of zinnias keeps pace with that of dahlias, and now that dahlias are becoming more fashionable again, a revival of interest in zinnias is unlikely to be far off, especially now that plant breeders are also marketing subtler shades. For a long time, zinnias were available only in glaring colors. They were developed mainly for cutting and providing colorful bouquets. Increasingly, the flowers became double, thereby aggravating the problems that already existed in the cultivation of zinnias: the species comes from the warm climate of Mexico and, in cool and damp conditions, is highly susceptible to all kinds of fungous diseases. The water left behind in the compact flowers after every shower then causes them to rot.

Zinnia elegans 'Envy,' zinnia

In general, zinnias are highly susceptible to all kinds of rot. This begins when they are still seedlings and prone to foot rot. In older plants, roots, stems, and flowers may be affected. It is therefore advisable to plant zinnias in the sunniest spot available, and in very well-drained soil which may also be nutritive (to encourage a greater profusion of flowers).

Sowing directly in the garden in April and May gives the best results, because the plants do not like having their root-balls disturbed. It is also quite feasible, however, to sow indoors in March–April. In this case, plant them out in a very early stage, or sow in compressed soil blocks, that may be planted out in their entirety at the end of May or in early June. For autumn flowering, sow directly in the garden in June.

The plants usually grow 20–39 in tall, bearing flowers that are on average 2 in wide, and flower in mid-summer. Zinnias are divided into groups according to the shape of the flowers. There are dahlia-flowered and cactus-flowered zinnias.

Zinnia elegans 'Envy' is an exception in every respect. The color of its flowers, pale green with delicate shading, is exceptional for zinnias. Furthermore, there is no need to expose this soft color to glaring sunlight. This plant, which grows to 24 in in height, will also thrive in partial shade, and may therefore be planted in a mixed border. This treasure is obviously also very suitable for sophisticated bouquets.

Zinnia elegans 'Isabellina' has soft creamy-yellow flowers and is therefore also very suit-

Zinnia elegans 'Isabellina,' zinnia

able for combining with other flowers in a bouquet. Its height is about 32 in.

Zinnia elegans 'Sprite Choice Mix' is a series in which *Zinnia acerosa* (syn. *Zinnia pumila*) also played a part. The flowers have a more vertical structure and, at a height of 18 in, the plants are considerably shorter. The mixture includes white, pink, and crimson flowers, each color coming in its softest form, so that it is quite possible to combine them with other colors.

[3–4] 4–6

Zinnia elegans 'Sprite Choice Mix,' zinnia

Zinnia peruviana 'Caramel,' zinnia

Zinnia peruviana 'Indian Red,' zinnia

Zinnia 'Profusion Cherry,' zinnia

Zinnia linearis

See *Zinnia angustifolia*.

Zinnia pauciflora

See *Zinnia peruviana*.

Zinnia peruviana

ZINNIA

Even on the sunniest days, the scarlet or yellow of this zinnia seems to catch the light. This makes the plant, which grows to 28 in in height, suitable for combining with other flowering plants. The flowers show up beautifully in bouquets and are also good for drying if cut at an early stage in their development and hung up to dry upsidedown. Its modest growth makes it feasible to grow *peruviana* in a pot or hanging basket. For sowing, see *Zinnia elegans*. The plants are rarely affected by disease or infestation.

Zinnia peruviana 'Caramel' carries flowers in such a soft and deep shade of yellow that its name is highly appropriate.

Zinnia peruviana 'Indian Red' has flowers in a warm shade of red.

[3–4 4–6]   ▼ 🏺 🌿 **!**

Zinnia '**Profusion Cherry**'

ZINNIA

It is no longer possible to trace the original species of some zinnias. They were developed from selections of hybrids, including 'Profusion Cherry,' which was awarded a prize in 1999. Its bright, cherry-colored flowers are carried from midsummer until well into autumn on plants are a mere 12 in high and have the same amount of spread. They branch out continually and do not suffer from mildew. Professional growers can market flowering plants two months after they were sown.

[3–4] 4–6 🌸 ▼ 🏺 🌿

Zinnia tenuifolia

See *Zinnia peruviana*.

311

Register

316

Acknowledgements

The author/photographer and publishers wish to express their thanks to the following people who contributed to this publication. Thanks to their knowledge of plant breeding and the information provided by them on the various species, the book has become a major compilation of knowledge relating to annuals and other bedding and patio plants.

Lieve Adriaensens of Silene, Bruggenhout (Belgium); Ans Advocaat of De Paardestal Peize; Frank Benders and Jan van Berkel of Novartis, Enkhuizen; Paulien Brummelaar and Geerle Wijma of Pastel, Sebaldeburen; Dick van der Burg of Cruydt-Hoeck, Groningen; Marijke Crãvecoeur of Stichting Smerper Tuin, Hippolytushoef; Laneke and Joost van Doorn, Putten; Jeroen Egtberts of Moerheim New Plant, Leimuiderbrug; Mrs G. Gerken of Fleuroselect, Noordwijk; Kees Helderman, 's-Gravenzande; Peter van der Heijden of Stekbedrijf G. van Aartsen, Harderwijk; Heikie Hoeksma, Harkema; Han Jansen of Gebr. Jansen, Dinxperlo; Joop Kooijman of Kieft Seeds Holland, Venhuizen; Feiko Lukkien of Botanische Tuinen Universiteit Utrecht; Mr Molenkamp of Kasteel Twickel, Ambt Delden; Wiert Nieumann of the Botanische Tuinen Universiteit Utrecht; Jan Willem Plankeel of J.W.P.'s Bloemzaden, Engwierum; Ruud Ruiter of Ernst Benary, Hannover Muenden (Germany); Frank Singer of Hem Zaden, Hem; Krijn Spaan of Kwekerij Krijn Spaan; Kortenhoef; Ab Stuurman of PanAmerican Seed Europe, Enkhuizen; Willem Jan Troost of Hamer Bloemzaden, H.J.Ambacht; P. van Wijk & family, Nuis; Hannie Wouda of Kwekerij De Egelantier, Paterswolde; Stekbedrijf Van Zanten & Co. B.V., Bovenkarspel; Fleur van Zonneveld of De Kleine Plantage, Eenrum.

Special thanks are due to the experts who cheerfully endured having their work interrupted by the author's countless visits, telephone calls, letters, and emails. They include Gerard Buurman of Kwekerij Overhagen, Velp; Koen Delaey of Kwekerij Sollya, Hertsberge (Belgium); Rob Leopold of Cruydt-Hoeck, Groningen; Rob van der Voort of Van Hemert & Co, Waddinxveen; and Ton Vreeken of Vreeken's Zaden, Dordrecht.